CRACKING THE SUCCESS CODE

Published by CelebrityPress™, Orlando, FL
A division of The Celebrity Branding Agency®

Celebrity Branding® is a registered trademark
Printed in the United States of America.

ISBN: 9780985364304
LCCN: 2012935436

This publication is designed to provide accurate and authoritative information with regard to the subject matter covered. It is sold with the understanding that the publisher is not engaged in rendering legal, accounting, or other professional advice. If legal advice or other expert assistance is required, the services of a competent professional should be sought. The opinions expressed by the authors in this book are not endorsed by CelebrityPress™ and are the sole responsibility of the author rendering the opinion.

Most CelebrityPress™ titles are available at special quantity discounts for bulk purchases for sales promotions, premiums, fundraising, and educational use. Special versions or book excerpts can also be created to fit specific needs.

For more information, please write:

CelebrityPress™
520 N. Orlando Ave, #2
Winter Park, FL 32789

or call 1.877.261.4930

Visit us online at www.CelebrityPressPublishing.com

CRACKING THE SUCCESS CODE

Contents

CHAPTER 1

Position Yourself for Success

By Brian Tracy

Welcome to the revolution. Throughout most of human history, we have been accustomed to evolution, or the gradual changing and progressing, and the moving forward of events in a straight line. Sometimes the process of change was faster, and sometimes it was slower, but it almost always seemed to be progressive, from one step to the other, allowing you opportunities for planning, predicting and changing.

Today, however, the rate of change is not only faster than ever before, but it is discontinuous. It is taking place in a variety of unconnected areas and affecting each of us in a variety of unexpected ways. Changes in information processing technologies are happening separately from changes in medicine that affect our life spans and lifestyles. Changes in transportation are taking place separately from changes in education, while changes in politics are taking place separately from changes in global competition.

Changes in family formation and relationships are happening separately from the rise and fall of new businesses and industries in different parts of the country. And if anything, this rate of accelerating, discontinuous change is increasing. As a result, most of us are already suffering from what Alvin Toffler called, "future shock."

You can't do very much about the enormity of these changes, but you can think seriously about yourself and provide for your basic needs for security and stability. In no area is this action more important than in the areas of job security and financial security. You must give special attention to your ability to make a good living and provide for yourself in the months and years ahead. You must think about your earning ability, how you earn a living today and how you might be earning a living tomorrow.

In effect, you must position yourself for tomorrow, even if it is increasingly unpredictable. You must think continuously and seriously about your work today, your earning ability, and the work that you will be doing one, three and five years from now. You must set goals and plan to achieve your own financial security, no matter what happens.

Lord Maynard Keynes once said that you should give a lot of thought to the future because that is where you are going to spend the rest of your life. One of the greatest mistakes that people make, and the one with the worst long-term consequences, is to think only about the present and give very little thought to what might happen in the months and years ahead.

In terms of your future happiness, security, joy, satisfaction and personal fulfillment, there is no area where thinking about the future is more important than in the area of how you will be earning a living in the medium and long-term future.

American corporations lay off hundreds of thousands of people every year. One large, well-known Fortune 100 Company recently laid off more than 100,000 professional employees. These were not hourly workers. These were men and women who had been selected from the best universities in America. To be considered for employment, they had to have a minimum grade point average of 3.9 out of 4.0. They were then trained from two to five years before they were put to work in their positions. When they were laid off, they had an average of 11 years of experience, on top of their education and training. And yet more than 100,000 of these extremely intelligent, highly skilled, well experienced men and women were laid off by one company alone.

These men and women could not go home and wait for the phone to ring for them to be called back to work. Their jobs were gone forever. Everything they had learned through education and experience was largely obsolete. It had little or no value in the workplace. Most of them had to start over in different jobs and different industries. And this trend toward job displacement is going to continue at an accelerating rate in the years to come.

When our grandfathers started working, it was quite common for them to get a basic education, go to work for a company and stay with that same company for the rest of their working lives. When our parents went to work, it was more common for them to change jobs three or four times during their lifetimes, although the changes were difficult and disruptive.

Members of the baby boom generation, joining the work force in the 1960s and 1970s, entered a new world of turbulence and change in the job market. They still looked for large companies and lifelong employment, but they were more likely to change jobs a half-dozen times during their work lives and maybe even start new careers in their 30s and 40s.

Today, with increased turbulence and change in the national and global economy, a person starting work can expect to have five full-time careers between the ages of 21 and 65, and 14 full-time jobs lasting two years or more. According to Fortune Magazine, fully 40 percent of American employees are "contingency" workers. This means that they will never work permanently for another company. They will continue to move from company to company, from job to job, as they are needed, being paid less than full-time employees and accruing very few, if any, benefits in terms of health care and pension plans. America has become a "free agent nation."

THE FOUR Rs

Fully 40 percent of Americans today have been at their current jobs for less than one year. We are going through a period of the "four Rs," which will continue throughout our working lifetimes. These four Rs are restructuring, reorganization, re-engineering and reinventing. To survive and thrive in the economy of tomorrow, you will have to memorize these words and fully understand their implications in everything you do.

All four words are responses to change and competition. **Restructuring** means reallocating the resources of a business so that more time and attention is spent producing the products and services that customers value most and cutting back in every other area.

Reorganization means changing an entire business to adjust to changes in knowledge, technology and competition that render many functions of the business unnecessary or obsolete.

Re-engineering refers to the process of analyzing every single job—and every step in every job—to eliminate redundant activities and make the entire process function more smoothly and efficiently.

Reinventing a business means having the courage to imagine that the company had burned to the ground and that key players were going to start all over again. What would they do more of and less of? What would they get into and what would they get out of? Would they continue in their current business, or would they get into a totally different business altogether?

There is a story about Ole and Sven immigrating to America on an old freighter going across the North Atlantic. The freighter gets into a huge storm and begins to break up. Ole runs up to Sven and says, "The ship is breaking up! It's going to sink!" Sven says, "What do we care? It's not our ship!"

Many people, when they read and hear about turbulence in the economy, make the mistake of thinking it has nothing to do with them. They, in effect say, "What do we care? It's not our problem." But we are all on the same economic ship, and anything that endangers the ship at any point has the potential of affecting us in some way. We are all in this together.

PLAYING DOWN THE BOARD

This widespread economic turbulence means you must also be restructuring your work and your activities so that you are contributing ever-greater value to your company and to your customers. You must be reorganizing yourself to allocate your scarce resources of time and attention more efficiently and effectively. You must be re-engineering your work each day to increase the speed at which you deliver higher qualities and quantities of work. Finally, you must be in a continuous process of reinventing yourself for the future.

Like a chess player, you must be playing down the board. You must be looking toward the horizon and thinking about the person you must become in order to preserve and enhance your earning ability in the years ahead.

Imagine what your job will look like five years from today. Because knowledge in your field is probably doubling every five years, fully 20 percent of your knowledge and your ability in your field is becoming obsolete each year. In five years, you will be doing a brand-new job with brand-new skills and abilities.

Ask yourself, "What parts of my knowledge, skills and work are becoming obsolete? What am I doing today that is different than what I was doing one year ago and two years ago?" What are you likely to be doing one year, two years, three years, four years and five years from today? What knowledge and skills will you need, and how will you acquire them? What is your plan for your economic and financial future?

Planning for your future job or jobs often requires a major shift in the way you think about work. Throughout most of human history, at least 95 percent of the population lived on the land, working in agriculture, and supporting the few who lived in cities. With the invention of the steam engine in 1776, low-paid and unproductive workers from the farms streamed into the cities to take industrial jobs where they could produce and earn far more, and enjoy consequently higher standards of living. At the end of World War II, we entered into the service age, where more people were working in the delivery of services than were working in manufacturing plants. In the 1960s we moved into the information age, where more people were working in the businesses of processing and delivering information of different kinds than were working in services or manufacturing.

As a result of all these changes, we are now in the knowledge age. Today, the chief factor of production is knowledge, and the ability to apply that knowledge to achieving results for other people. Your earning ability today is largely dependent upon your knowledge and skill and your ability to combine that knowledge and skill in such a way that you contribute value for which customers are going to pay.

The "Law of Three" says you must contribute three dollars of profit for every dollar you wish to earn in salary. It costs the company approximately double that person's salary to employ them, in terms of space, benefits, supervision and investment in furniture, fixtures and other resources. For a company to hire an employee, the company has to make a profit on what they pay that employee. Therefore, the employee must contribute value greatly in excess of the amount they earn in order to stay employed. To put it another way, your earning ability must be considerably greater than the amount you are receiving, or you will find yourself looking for another job.

Newspapers are full of stories of men and women who have been laid off from highly paid jobs and forced to take jobs paying considerably less. These are simply examples of people who were being paid above their earning abilities now being forced to find jobs more consistent with the value of their current contributions. This reduction in pay is not arbitrary, subjective or personal. It is merely a fact of life. It is the way our economy works. People are inevitably paid exactly what they are worth, no more and no less, based upon their earning ability.

THE TRIUMPH OF COMPETENCE

To position yourself for tomorrow, here is one of the most important rules you will ever learn: "The future belongs to the competent." The future belongs to those men and women who are very good at what they do. Pat Riley, who earned multiple championships as an NBA coach, wrote in his 1994 book *The Winner Within*, "If you are not committed to getting better at what you are doing, you are bound to get worse." To phrase it another way, anything less than a commitment to excellent performance on your part is an unconscious acceptance of *mediocrity*. At one time, you needed to be excellent to rise above the competition in your industry. Today, you must be excellent just to keep your job.

The marketplace is a stern taskmaster. Today, excellence, quality and value are absolutely essential elements of any product or service, and of the work of any person. Your earning ability is largely determined by the perception of excellence, quality and value that others have of you and what you do. The market only pays excellent rewards for excellent performance. It pays average rewards for average performance, and it pays below-average rewards or unemployment for below-average per-formance.

All the strikes, protests, marches and demonstrations cannot change the fact that customers today want the very most and the very best for the very least amount of money, and on the best terms. Only those indi-viduals and companies that provide absolutely excellent products and services at competitive prices will survive. It's not personal. It's just the way our economy works.

Perception Influences Reality

Many people seem to be promoted faster and paid more in their careers even though they don't seem to be as competent or as capable as others. This doesn't seem fair. Why should some people get ahead when others, who seem to be working far harder, get passed over for promotion and additional rewards?

The fact is, to be a great success, it is not only important that you are good at what you do, but it is also important that you are *perceived* to be good at what you do. Human beings are creatures of perception. It is not what they see, but what they think they see that determines how they think and act.

If your co-worker is perceived as being more promotable than you, for whatever reasons, then it is very likely and quite common that your co-worker will get additional responsibilities and higher pay, even though you think you could do a better job, if given the chance.

Fortunately, there are several things that you can do to increase your visibility and accelerate the speed at which you move ahead in your career.

The starting point of high visibility is *competence.* Determine what parts of your job are most important to your superior and to your company and then decide to become very good in those areas. Read, research, study, take additional courses, listen to audio programs and seek advice from others. Your key to the future is to be perceived as being very competent at what you do.

This perception alone will bring you to the attention of more people, faster than you can imagine. The perception of excellent performance will open up opportunities for greater responsibilities, higher pay, better positions and wider opportunities. Becoming good at what you do should be the foundation of your strategy for higher visibility and rapid advancement in your career.

Some years ago, when I was a consultant to the president of a large conglomerate, he was offered the distributorship of the Suzuki line of Japanese vehicles for Western Canada. Before he accepted, he assigned to me the responsibility of researching the market for these vehicles. He wanted to be thoroughly convinced of the market potential before he made a final decision and a commitment that would involve several million dollars.

For the next two months, I traveled, researched and worked busily to gather information on vehicle sales trends, servicing and warranty policies, sales, marketing and price strategies, importation and distribution complexities.

I kept the president informed as I went along, knowing full well that he was looking at hiring an executive with extensive experience in the importation and distribution of Japanese vehicles to head up the new company. At the end of two months, I put together a complete report and then sat down with the president to give him my findings and my recommendations.

The Japanese executives responsible were also present. They too were waiting for the results of my research and for a final decision. At the end of my report, based on all of my research, I told them the prices over the next three to five years.

The executives listened intently, then laughed and spoke together in Japanese. Finally, they told the president that they had privately commissioned a complete research study to investigate the market potential for their vehicles. They had paid $50,000 for this study, and it had reached identical conclusions to mine. The president was so impressed with how knowledgeable I had become on the importation of this particular line of vehicles that he offered to put me in charge of the entire division.

This breakthrough enabled me to leapfrog over at least a dozen other executives. In the next three years, I set up 65 dealerships and coordinated the delivery and sale of $25 million of Suzuki four-wheel drive vehicles in Western Canada. Suzuki Motor Corporation used my model to enter the U. S. market a few years later. My career path changed dramatically because I had paid the price to become extremely competent in this area.

Employers everywhere are looking for men and women of action. They are seeking people who will plunge in and get the job done well as soon as possible. When you develop a reputation for competence and speed, you will very quickly become visible to all the key people in your working environment. You will move onto the fast track in your career.

Image Influences Perception

Excellent performance at what you do is essential, but it's not enough. There are other elements that contribute to the perception other people have of you. One of the most important of these elements is your overall image, from head to toe.

A recent survey of personnel executives concluded that the decision to hire, or not to hire, was made in the first 30 seconds of the first meeting with the candidate. Some research suggests that the decision to accept or reject a candidate is actually made in the first *four* seconds. Many very capable men and women are disqualified from being hired or promoted simply because they do not look the part.

A young man with long hair and sloppy clothes came up to me at one of my seminars and demanded to know why other people paid so much attention to his external appearance. He insisted to me that people should judge him on his character and on his ability, not on the way that he looked on the outside.

I explained to him that what he was asking was simply inconsistent with human nature. It is a fact that each of us judges other people by the way they look on the outside. I told him that, just as he judges others by their appearance, they take the liberty of judging him by his appearance, as well.

But there is another issue with regard to image and appearance. There are many elements of your life over which you have no control and which you cannot choose. But the elements of your external dress and appearance are totally a matter of personal preference. Individuals deliberately choose their clothes, their grooming and their overall appearance in order to make a statement to the world about the kind of person they really are. The way you look on the outside is a representation of the way you see yourself on the inside. If you have a positive, professional self-image, you will take pains to make your external appearance reflect that image.

You should dress the way the senior people in your company dress. Dress for the job or a position two jobs above your own. Since people largely judge you by the way you look on the outside, if you look thoroughly professional and well turned out on the outside, the perception of the people who can help you in your career will be positive and supportive. They will open doors for you in ways you cannot now imagine.

THE IMPORTANCE OF VISIBILITY

Another great way to increase your visibility is to join one or two professional associations connected with your business or field. Join organizations that contain members who are the kind of people you would like to know and who are ahead of you in your career.

Before you join, you should attend meetings to carefully assess whether or not the organization can be of value to you. Then, if you decide that becoming known to the key people in this association could advance your career, take out a membership. Once you are a member, get involved.

Most people who join any club or association do very little more than attend the regular meetings. They usually feel they are too busy to assist with the various things that need to get done in any voluntary association. But this path is not for you. Your goal is to pick a key committee and volunteer for service on that committee. Find out which committee seems to be the most influential in the activities of that organization, and then step up to the plate. Volunteer your time, intelligence and energy, and get busy.

Attend every meeting. Take careful notes. Volunteer for assignments. Complete them on time and in an excellent fashion. In every activity of the association, you have an opportunity to perform before other key people in your profession in a nonthreatening environment. You give them a chance to see what you can do and what kind of a person you really are. You expand your range of valuable contacts in one of the most effective ways possible in America today. The people you get to know on these committees can eventually become extremely helpful to you in your work and in your career.

You might also join a well-known charitable organization, like the United Way, and become active by donating your time and your services to the annual fund-raising programs. You may not be wealthy to begin with, but you have time that you can invest in your future. Your willingness to give of yourself will soon be noticed by people who are higher up. Many men and women with limited contacts and limited resources have risen to positions of great prominence as the result of getting to know the key community leaders who participate in professional associations and charitable organizations.

Some years ago, I joined a statewide Chamber of Commerce and volunteered to work on the economic education committee. As usually happens, very few of the members contributed any time to the committee, and so there was always lots of work for those few people who were willing to put in the effort.

Within one year, I was chairing the national annual convention for this association. The audience was composed of some of the most influential business executives in the entire state. In the following year, I was invited to give a key briefing to the governor and his aides at the state capitol. I became so well known in the business community that within six months I was offered a position to run a new company at triple my former salary and with profit-sharing benefits. This was solely as a result of becoming active in the Chamber of Commerce and making myself known to key people.

About three years later, I volunteered to work with the United Way and had a very similar experience. I became deeply involved in helping that charitable organization in its annual fund-raising drive. I met several of the most prominent businesspeople in the city. Doors opened up for me in my business. In the following year, I generated more sales and profits than I had in the previous three years.

You will be amazed at how far and how fast you will move ahead when you begin contributing your time and energy to others on a volunteer basis. It is one of the fastest ways to move up the ladder of success in America.

THE IMPORTANCE OF PERSONALITY

You can do many other things to increase your visibility, things that don't occur to most people. For example, a recent study of 105 chief executive officers concluded that two qualities would most quickly put a person onto the career fast track. The first quality they named was the ability to set priorities—to separate the relevant from the irrelevant when facing the many tasks of the day. The second quality was a sense of urgency, the ability to get the job done fast.

Many managers have confirmed the truth of this study. They place an extraordinarily high value on a person who can set priorities and move quickly to get the job done. Speed and dependability in job completion is one of the most valued traits in the American work force. When your employer can hand you a job and then walk away and not worry about it again, you will have moved yourself onto the fast track. Your subsequent promotion and increased pay are virtually guaranteed.

Another way for you to become more visible is to develop a positive mental attitude. People like to be around and to promote employees they like. Everybody quickly notices a consistent, persistent attitude of cheerfulness and optimism. When you make an effort to cultivate an attitude of friendliness toward people, they will make extraordinary efforts to open doors for you.

You can also increase your visibility by continually upgrading your work-related skills and making sure that your superiors know about it.

Seek out additional courses you can take to improve yourself at your job and discuss these courses with your boss. Ask him or her to pay for the courses if you pass, but make it clear you're going to take them anyway.

A young woman who worked for me was able to double her salary in less than six months by aggressively learning the computer, bookkeeping and accounting skills we needed as our company grew. And she was worth every penny.

Ask your boss what books and audio programs you should read and listen to. Whatever he or she recommends, take his or her advice immediately. Then report back and ask for more. You will be amazed at how quickly this strategy brings you to the attention of the person who can most help you at each stage of your career.

Bosses are very impressed with people who are constantly striving to learn more in order to increase their value to their companies. Upgrading your knowledge and skills as a part of your life can really accelerate your career.

Probably 85 percent of your success in the world of work will come from your personality and your ability to communicate effectively with others. It will be determined by how much people like you and respect you. You can greatly improve how other people perceive you by continually looking for ways to boost their self-esteem throughout the workday.

As Ken Blanchard says in the *One Minute Manager,* "catch people doing something right." A little genuine praise and appreciation, on a regular basis, will cause people to like you and want to help you. They will even overlook the fact that occasionally you make mistakes in your work. A likeable person is often perceived as being better at what they do than a person with a negative personality.

When you are with your superiors, make it a practice to listen with respect, attentiveness and interest. The more you honestly and sincerely listen to another person, the more that other person will like and trust you and want to give you additional help and responsibilities.

All leaders are excellent listeners. It is a key method of influence. If you want to get people on your side, practice asking interested questions and then listening intently to the answers.

THE FIVE KEYS

Let us summarize the key ideas of this chapter. Here are the five keys to increasing your visibility so that you can be more successful, faster in your career.

1. Become excellent at the important things you have been hired to do. Excellence in your chosen occupation is the first stepping stone to getting paid more and promoted faster.

2. Look, act and dress the part. Become knowledgeable about styles, colors and fabrics. Dress the way senior people in your company dress. Never take anything for granted. Remember, in the area of image, "casualness brings casualties."

3. Develop your contacts, both inside and outside the company. Use one of the most powerful laws of all, the "Law of Reciprocity." Always be looking for ways to give of your time and effort to others, as an investment, so that others will be willing to give of their time and effort to help you sometime in the future. The most successful men and women in any community are those who know and are known by the greatest number of other successful people. Begin with a professional association or club. Join a local charity that you care about and which also has a prestigious board of directors.

4. Take additional courses to upgrade your skills and make sure everyone knows about it. Ask your boss for book and audio program recommendations, then read and listen and go back to your boss for more, with your comments. Often, when your

boss feels that you are eager to learn and grow, he or she will become a mentor to you and will help you climb more rapidly up the ladder of success. This process has been instrumental to the careers of many successful executives in America.

5. Be positive, cheerful and helpful. Be the kind of person that other people want to see get ahead. Treat other people with friendliness and kindness, and always have a good word to say to the people you work with.

In the final analysis, taking the time to become an excellent human being will do more to raise your visibility, enhance the quality of your life, and improve your chances for promotion than anything else you can do. And you can do it if you really want to.

About Brian

Brian Tracy is chairman and CEO of Brian Tracy International, a company specializing in the training and development of individuals and organizations. Brian's goal is to help people achieve their personal and business goals faster and easier than they ever imagined.

Brian Tracy has consulted for more than 1,000 companies and addressed more than 5,000,000 people in 5,000 talks and seminars throughout the U.S., Canada and 55 other countries worldwide. As a keynote speaker and seminar leader, he addresses more than 250,000 people each year.

For more information on Brian Tracy programs, go to: www.briantracy.com.

CHAPTER 2

The Inner Game of Success

By Eric Amidi

*Some people make things happen, some watch things happen,
while others wonder what happened* ~ Anonymous

Tom stared out the window of the coffee shop, gazing far into the distance while focusing on nothing. Tossing a curled-up magazine on the table, he slouched back into his chair with a blank expression on his face. After a few moments of what seemed like his usual tour through parallel universes, he looked up at me, pursed his lips with frustration and shook his head in disgust. Had I not known him for more than 10 years, that look would have surprised me.

He then reached for the folded-open magazine and while tapping his index finger on an article, he complained, "This is the exact same idea that I told you about two years ago, right here, in this coffee shop."

He was right. He had mentioned the same idea two years earlier. In fact, I remember the many other great ideas he has shared with me over the years, and almost all of them were now multimillion-dollar businesses. I made no mention of that.

Tom is one of those people you might call "An Idea Man." Being highly educated and skilled, he can slice and dice any problem from every conceivable angle and come up with a solution. Tom sees details and possibilities that most people miss completely.

When it comes to new ideas and tracking social and economic trends, Tom is always right on the money. Despite all that, he is not what people consider successful.

He will get all excited about new ideas or investment opportunities, but by the time he has decided to move on them, the idea is no longer new. He seems to be always out of sync with opportunities. He will identify opportunities sooner than others but consistently misses his moment. Tom is both ahead of his time and always too late.

It all seems like a cruel joke to him, and it has happened far too often to be mere coincidence, or so he believes. It happens so often that he has grown used to the familiar cycle of excitement, delay and regret.

John, on the other hand, is hardly interested in detecting patterns or predicting the future. You won't catch John talking about great opportunities or new ideas, and yet he has been incredibly successful in many businesses he has started. He seems completely in tune with trends and opportunities. His investments are always timely and rewarding.

What is most interesting about John is that he was never a great student. He was average at best, yet always ready to jump into any assignment or task with enthusiasm and confidence.

Because I have known Tom and John for a long time, I can list their habits—the behaviors that separate extremely successful people from the rest. Even though habits alone cannot make you successful, they give you a clear view of the successful mind: how it is organized, what makes it work, the core mindset that cultivates successful behaviors. Once that core mindset is changed for the better, successful habits manifest naturally.

In this chapter, I will reveal some of the habits of successful people and dig below the surface to uncover the underlying mindset that drives behaviors in the direction of success.

In many cases where the habits of highly successful people have been examined, mere mimicking of those habits and behaviors has brought little success. However, once you know what core qualities cause these habits and learn how to attain that core quality reliably and repeatedly, the habits of successful people will be of second nature to you.

HABITS TO HARNESS

One of the habits of successful people that stands out more than any other concerns how they make decisions. Successful people make decisions quickly, and once they have made their decision, they don't change their mind easily. On the other hand, those who miss great opportunities tend to delay decisions, and once they have made a decision they easily alter that decision or simply give up. Too often, this delay or indecision results in them looking for another opportunity; and once they have found it, they will follow the same route to inaction and failure.

To act like successful individuals, some people try to adopt the habit of fast decision-making without acquiring the core quality that is the true source of this habit. Such mimicking often results in emotional decision-making—a method that may be fast but is often based on hope, false optimism and unrealistic expectations instead of sound judgment. The fast decision-making of successful people is never at the expense of proper analysis of the opportunity, and mere emotion is suppressed from the final decision.

Those who delay decision-making usually try to justify their delay with more analysis. However in reality, once information gathering is complete, delay in decision-making is more a sign of hindering emotions than extra analysis. Oftentimes, that extra analysis is only a cozy and comfortable sanctuary from the fear of taking action. Analytical individuals usually feel comfortable with more analysis because that is safer terrain than the uncharted territory of new opportunities. Nevertheless, analysis without action leads to nothing.

Another quality that separates highly successful people from others is their level and type of belief in their ability. I rank these levels from one to three:

1. The lowest level belongs to those who don't believe they have the ability to succeed in an undertaking. Obviously, no one can be successful in a task with this level of belief.

2. The second level belongs to those who believe they have the ability to succeed in a task. This leads to occasional success if it turns out opportunities out there match the abilities and qualifications of this person. Most people with specialized skills fall into this category. If the trends and opportunities match their

skill set and abilities, they can be successful, absent a paralyzing emotion such as fear.

3. The third level is the level of highly successful people. Highly successful people believe they can "acquire" the ability to succeed in any undertaking. Extremely successful people tend to embrace and succeed with regard to most any opportunity. These highly successful individuals tend to invest and succeed in various business opportunities in different industries. Due to this level of belief, they are not tied down to a set of skills and abilities, but they are fueled by the belief that they can obtain the tools required to successfully complete a task.

After going through some of the habits of highly successful people, you begin to see more clearly the core quality needed for success.

THE CORE QUALITY FOR SUCCESS

Attempts to imitate habits of successful people will only result in short-term and sporadic success. To unleash the consistent power of a successful mindset, you need to adopt a manner of thinking that goes deeper than the habits and behaviors we observe at the surface. When change occurs at the deepest level, habits on the surface will manifest in a positive way.

So what is the deepest core quality from which all habits of highly successful people naturally flow?

I have studied many successful people, including many that I have been able to interact with closely. The core quality that makes them successful is deeply rooted in their belief system—a belief system that defines their world and reality.

Highly successful people live in a reality that is fundamentally different from the reality of others.

Every one of us believes that to some extent what happens in the external world affects us and that to some extent we can control and affect the circumstances in our lives.

However, highly successful people live in a reality based on the belief that they, more than external happenings, have the most influence over the outcome of any undertaking.

The level of success you can achieve in your life is directly proportional to how much you believe you are in control of the events in your life, as opposed to being a slave to circumstances.

For successful people, this belief is ingrained in their core reality, as if for them that's how the world is. They are the ones who can change and steer events to their benefit, regardless of situations.

Once this belief becomes your reality, you become unstoppable.

Looking back at the habits of successful people you can see that these intrinsic mindset habits are natural manifestations of their core beliefs.

For instance, core beliefs of successful people directly explain why they make decisions quickly and with determination, while others delay the decision, ponder it too long and ultimately do not act on it. Since they believe they are in control of the outcome, successful people may not spend a lot of time looking for the best opportunities and ideas, nor do they engage in excessive analysis. They are doers who know that the most important ingredient to success is the confidence and determination they bring to any enterprise. They know that they—not circumstances or external factors—contribute the most to the success of the idea.

Those whose reality assumes that external factors contribute the most to the success of a venture keep looking for that great opportunity, great idea or the best way to approach and finally take action. Those people end up like Tom—just staring out the window, wondering why they can't get a lucky break.

Knowing as John does, that he is the source of his success—not luck or circumstances—enables him to seize an opportunity, move on it quickly, and believe that no matter what crops up he can meet all variables and do so to his advantage. That's why successful people like John hardly engage in predictions, analysis or speculations; rather they focus more on action and outcome.

Due to this core belief, successful people tend to exude energy. They are the source of and in control of their own energy. They don't seek energy and motivation from external sources.

You hardly ever find a highly successful person in a state of despair or depression. After all, depression most often occurs when you believe that you are not in control and are the victim of circumstances.

Failures rarely disappoint successful people because failure is viewed as a learning experience and the source of greater opportunities.

Believing the locus of control is within themselves, they don't spend a lot of time searching for great ideas or regretting missed opportunities; instead, they are busy creating projects, acknowledging and accepting opportunities, and bringing them to fruition. Successful people don't ask, "Why can't I get a lucky break?" That is not part of their mindset or mode of operation.

Signs of this core belief are more apparent in people who operate on the third level of success, mentioned earlier, where successful people believe that they can "acquire" the ability to bring any opportunity to fruition. Successful people are natural managers who reach out to and rely on those who have the knowledge, skills and experience to get the job done.

So, the habits leading to great success are all results of the core beliefs you construct to create opportunities and drive them to completion.

Core beliefs define reality for us. Through creating mental filters and inner dialogues, they create self-affirming realities. Those who believe external situations are the most important factors in determining success succumb to the faulty thinking that luck, circumstances, "getting a break," "being in the right place at the right time" and knowing "the right people" are what it takes to be successful. Worse than that, they believe that the absence of tangible success is the equivalent of absolute failure. That, my friend is a recipe for misery!

On the other hand, those who believe they are responsible for making their own good fortune as a result of habitual behavioral patterns that are fully integrated into their lives understand that luck, planetary alignments, serendipity, angels, etc. have little to do with achievement, success and prosperity. Such individuals believe that setbacks are temporary retreats on the way to finding a better route to the finish line, and that the success mindset and motivator of action leads to triumph and reward.

Keep this in mind. Any reality tends to reaffirm itself. That is the very essence of our personal belief systems. Believe as your friends, teachers, classmates and others may have told you that you are nothing special, capable of very little, destined to accomplish nothing of significance, and you will likely create that reality for yourself. Break free of those bonds and DO instead of PONDER, and all shackles and impediments will fall away, leaving only the sky as your limit.

About Eric

Eric Amidi is a self-improvement and productivity expert. His concise and direct, to-the-point advice has helped a network of more than half a million people around the world. Eric Amidi holds a Ph.D. in particle physics, and, along with a group of physicists at Fermi National Laboratory, he discovered the top quark on March 2, 1995.

While using Artificial Neural Networks, which simulate the human brain, in his research, Eric's interest in the potentials and the power of human mind deepened.

Eric Amidi now writes and provides advice in the areas of productivity, self-improvement and peak performance. His advice and methods are best known for their clarity, simplicity and effectiveness.

To learn more about Dr. Eric Amidi and obtain free material on self-improvement and productivity, visit: www.WinnersRoadMap.com.

CHAPTER 3

10 Steps to Overcoming the Insecurities that Hold You Back

By Genny Williams

The reminders on my phone telling me that Katie would soon be arriving for her coaching appointment had just been deleted. It was now time for her personal appointment to work on her business. I always get excited about meeting with Katie Barber because she is a sweet spirit who is full of life and always smiling, unless, of course, she is sad. Katie gets down and depressed regularly. It must have been one of Katie's down days because she was late, and it didn't look like she was going to show for her appointment. Because she had also missed our last few sessions, I felt I had to reach out to her immediately to let her know how important she was.

As I dialed her number, I was praying she'd answer my call. Thankfully, she did. "Katie, it's Genny. I'm so glad you answered. Are you in a corner right now feeling sorry for yourself? Katie, there are people out there that need you!" Shocked by what I had said, Katie asked, "Am I that obvious? How did you know?" Delicately, I began, " You haven't been to coaching in a while, and it seems like you are slipping away. Tell me what's going on with you."

She started crying as she began telling me how she just felt like she wasn't good enough to help anyone. "People need an agent that is smarter than I am. I just can't seem to stop screwing up everybody's deals and I continually have to give up part of my commission to pay for my mistakes! I'm thinking I might need to quit," she explained.

This is when I had to really go to work. I knew that if I said the wrong thing, Katie could be lost forever to her feelings of overwhelming insecurity. But, if I could convince her how special she truly is, then she'd start believing in herself again, although ultimately the decision would be hers no matter what I said or did. I told her to get up, brush herself off and think of all the clients she had helped in the past, how happy they had been to work with her and how appreciative they had been of her service. I reminded her that even the best agents overlook items within the process. After we talked for a while, I encouraged her to make a commitment to the program so that she could discover how good she really was. She agreed to fully commit to the program, and she kept her word.

At the time we made this break-through, Katie had just joined. Having closed only four transactions the previous year, she felt extremely inadequate. After making the commitment to the program, she closed an amazing 17 transactions, quadrupling her income in 12 short months. She finally realized she IS good enough to help people. By overcoming one of her insecurities, she made a huge positive difference in her life. She is now well on her way to doubling her income again this year.

HELPING CLIENTS DEAL WITH INSECURITIES

As a business coach, I work on the issue of insecurities more than anything else. This surprises most people who think I'd be working on scripts, marketing strategies and goals. Truthfully, we can't get to systems and strategies until we deal with insecurities. When people don't complete their action items in order to grow their businesses the way they SAY they WANT to grow them, I have to get to the real root of the problem. It's not normally time management, procrastination or laziness. It's always a deep-rooted insecurity that holds them back from achieving their dreams and accomplishing their goals.

When my clients overcome insecurities, their lives change for the better. We are all insecure about something. It's completely normal and definitely not a character flaw. But our insecurities can cause so much damage in our lives. When we feel insecure or threatened, we tend to lash out at other people, blame others for what we don't like in our lives and create highly destructive situations that only make things worse.

One of the most common forms of insecurity I see is "call reluctance." Most people experience this at some level. They are literally afraid to call people. You can give them perfect scripts, practice with them and prepare them for the worst that can happen, but they will still be afraid to do it. Something else is going on that we have to address and adjust. For many people, they feel they might not be worthy enough or good enough to call a prospect in a certain price range or in a certain neighborhood. That attitude is what must be overcome; it's the real issue. If agents can't overcome it, their businesses will never grow to a satisfactory level.

Through the years, I've witnessed people feeling like they don't fit in or believing that others may not like them for whatever reason. This insecurity is tough to overcome. It really means you don't like yourself and don't feel as if you're worthy to be a part of a certain group. By far, this one insecurity can create the most destruction in your life. When people are constantly trying to get validation from other people in order to feel like they fit in, every action is judged and overanalyzed through their highly sensitive filter. Most people try to match actions to their already pre-conceived ideas or thoughts. For instance, if people feel like they don't fit in, they will constantly test others to validate that feeling. It's a LOSE for all parties.

I've witnessed lots of drama from these situations. Insecure people don't even realize they are "testing" a group when they do it. But, their insecurity often drives them to come on way too strong, be too familiar too quickly and cross boundaries they aren't even aware exist. When they receive negative feedback, they blame the group or a person they may feel is the group leader for not being inclusive, for being rude, for being racist, or thinking the group is "too good" for them. No matter how much you give to people who experience this insecurity, it is never enough. They are rarely ever thankful for how much you do give them because all they see is what they don't get. It's sad really because the one thing that these people need is to feel accepted, yet they will push everyone away. In fact, the agents who I've seen suffer with this insecurity often fire their clients or have dramatic confrontations with them about how they will not tolerate the way they are being treated.

Insecurities are those invisible issues that cause income loss, stale businesses, damaged relationships and ruined lives. But you don't have to be a victim to your insecurities.

10 STEPS TO OVERCOMING INSECURITIES

By following these 10 steps, you will discover a happier life full of freedom. Of course, you must first DECIDE that you're ready to be free, that you no longer want to cling to all the little things that hold you back. It can be scary to work on yourself, but with your decision made and your commitment strong, let's get started conquering your insecurities.

1. Make a List of Everything You Like about Yourself

Start with the positive. Write down everything that makes you proud to be who you are—your talents, your gifts, your looks, your personality. All of it. Get it laminated and keep this list with you everywhere!

Now, make a list of everything you *don't* like about yourself, then change it. Wow. That sounds way too simple for such a complex issue. But, now you have to have a place to start. You have to LIKE yourself to conquer your insecurities. We all have things about ourselves that make us self-conscious. When we know and understand what those things are, we can begin to make a difference.

Many of the things we don't like, we *can* change. If you feel like you need to lose weight, do it. Follow an easy plan, so you will be successful. If you hate your hair color or style, change it. If you're not confident wearing the wardrobe you have, start building a new one. You don't have to spend a lot of money on anything. In fact, that could be another issue. If you have zero in your bank account, start by saving a few hundred dollars. You can have a yard sale or sell some of the things you don't like anymore or can't use within your home. Use this money to start your security stash. Many people I coach feel better about themselves when they have a little money set aside. It takes away the disparity.

You don't have to do everything at once. Simply becoming aware of what you don't like will initiate the momentum you need so that you can actually make these changes.

2. *Take Ownership of Your Flaws and Use Them To Grow*

The blame game will get you nowhere in life. In order for you to grow and become the person you really want to share with the world, you must take responsibility for your own actions. You could have been a victim of many terrible things, such as a violent father, a hate crime, a near-fatal car accident or a cheating spouse, but that misfortune doesn't have to make you WHO you are the rest of your life. When you live as a victim, you give all of your power to something or someone else. Your special gifts will never be seen and appreciated by the world. Personal accountability will help you enjoy these special gifts. In fact, when you take responsibility for what you CAN do and do it, you become a strong, powerful person who is capable of doing anything!

3. *Speak Positive Words to Yourself*

Isn't it funny that you can continually hear numerous people tell you how wonderful and talented you are but still not believe them? Beloved celebrities are the greatest example of this. Your own words are more powerful than any others you'll hear. So, be careful how you speak to yourself. Start each morning listening to yourself saying wonderful things to yourself. If you can't hear the words from your own mouth telling you what a special, unique gift you are to the world, how will you ever believe anyone else giving you praise? This action item alone is the most powerful. That's why you've read it and heard it so many times. It works.

4. *Listen to Powerful, Positive Messages Every Morning*

Fill your iPod, laptop, or car stereo with motivational CDs from your favorite leaders. Brian Tracy's *The Psychology of Achievement* is a great choice. Avoid watching or listening to the news in the mornings and listen to encouraging and inspirational messages instead. You have to counteract all the negative messages you'll receive during the day. So, start your fresh mind correctly.

5. *Do Three Things per Day That Make You Proud of Yourself*

When you use your talents or keep promises to yourself, you will develop a sense of accomplishment and pride in yourself.

It can be something as easy as exercising for 30 minutes, eating a specific diet plan, writing in your journal or randomly doing something nice for someone else.

6. *Make a Contribution Every Day*

Many people suffer from insecurities and even depression because they feel as if they don't matter. To matter, a person must make a contribution to something or someone. Every contribution matters. Contributing doesn't have to cost you a lot of money or even a huge effort, but it can make an impact to someone's life. Cook someone a meal, send a handwritten note of praise, or paint a picture for somebody. Use your talents to benefit others!

7. *Become an Expert*

One of the greatest ways to overcome any kind of insecurity is to become proficient on a topic, a hobby or something within your business. This is extremely important. When you know you have the ultimate solution to help yourself or someone else, your insecurities will fade because your confidence will rise. When you have complete confidence in yourself, you will eliminate self-sabotage and start creating more opportunities for yourself. So, how do you become an expert? Create two "top-five lists"—one list should be the top five topics you'd love to know about and the other should list your top five talents and interests. These lists will guide you toward developing your personal expertise. Once you discover your focus, learn everything you can through courses, experiences and books.

My mom is a great example of someone who found her expert niche. She set out to learn everything she could about a type of accounting software; she took courses and practiced with the software until she became extremely proficient. Now, she has job security. She finds joy in helping other people get set up with the software because she knows it can transform a small business for the best. Because she's now an expert and has become so efficient in this area, she has been able to cut back her work hours to part time—allowing her to pursue her new passion of painting. Her once deep-rooted insecurities have faded, and her confidence has soared! She is highly unlikely to cause herself any struggles or obstacles in her own life.

8. Forgive Yourself Quickly

We all make stupid mistakes, say things we shouldn't, or exude some sort of strange behavior at times. The people who can forgive themselves quickly and forget it are the ones who tend to accomplish more and are happier people. When you focus on your mistakes by reliving them over and over in your head, it is impossible to overcome your insecurities.

9. Find Someone Who REALLY Believes in You

You have to have someone on your side who feeds you positive messages constantly. A spouse that supports you is nice, but not quite the person who can help you overcome your insecurities. Please understand, you cannot put the responsibility of your insecurities on someone else. Ideally, a mentor or a coach who knows YOU—the good, the bad and mostly the possible—and sees all the potential and possibilities, is the support you need. Don't put this kind of pressure on a friend. It's too much to ask of him or her. Search the internet or ask a friend for a referral to find the right coach who can help you make a significant difference.

10. Don't Compare Yourself to Anyone Else!

You are special with your own unique gifts and talents. No one else has your experiences or back ground. Your perspective, your personality, and your thought process is different from anyone else's. How can you compare anything about yourself to anyone else? Not to mention, we all have our different thresholds of tolerance and work on our own personalized time lines. So, please don't trap yourself into the unhealthy act of comparing yourself to anyone else.

Now, that you know how to conquer your insecurities, get started sharing your gifts. Don't let these issues ever hold you back again!

About Genny

The 6-Figure Coach, Genny Williams is a real estate business coach and CEO of Get a Real Estate Life, LLC. Growing up in the real estate industry, Genny became very familiar with the nature of the business while watching her father serve as a broker, home builder and investor. She reluctantly joined the family business and quickly became a top producing agent, consistently closing more than 60 transactions per year. For the past 15 years, Genny has been involved in many aspects of the industry as a team leader, an owner, a managing broker, a trainer and a recruiter. Through this experience, she found her true passion: business coaching.

The blood, sweat and tears earned while exploring these various capacities enabled her to develop a 6-Figure Income System, which she uses to coach the multitude of real estate agents and loan officers within her program. Now Genny focuses on her passion—increasing the incomes of real estate agents and mortgage professionals by sharing what she has learned through the many mistakes she has made, obstacles she has faced—and even sometimes created. Her proven system puts agents on the path to earn a 6-(often Plus) Figure Income in any market and any economy.

Catering to mostly prospering pre-recession agents, Genny has mastered the art of pinpointing insecurities, obstacles, personal learning responses and individual motivators in order to accurately customize her methods for each client. Providing "a different perspective" to business obstacles, Genny offers a unique but personal sounding board for leading agents to develop a tailor-made plan reflecting their personalities and core values. Offering top industry resources and detailed support, Genny's team eliminates distractions, allowing each agent to focus on their distinctive talents and exceed their income goals.

To learn more about Genny Williams, The 6-Figure Coach, the Get A Real Estate Life Team and how you can receive a free copy of "Secrets to 6 Figures with Home Buyers Preview Call," visit www.GetARealEstateLife.com or call 205-223-1044.

CHAPTER 4

The Big Fat Zero

By Jennifer Hilburn

Recently, a guy—let's call him Rich, cuz he wishes he was—came to see me after hearing me speak about the importance of reputation management for local solopreneurs. Rich has a 15-year career in construction, but when the economy tanked, construction jobs did too, so after a year of being mostly out of work Rich had decided to start a lawn maintenance company. He maxed out his credit cards on print ads in the local paper, a Yellow Pages ad, and inserts in the local Valpak coupon mailer. His first year in business, he had made just enough money to cover his minimum credit card payment and to afford rent after taking in a roommate.

I asked him if he knew who his biggest competition was, and he said he knew a couple of guys who had an "in" with some of the homeowners associations of the wealthier subdivisions, but his biggest competition in general were guys who didn't advertise at all. They didn't need to because if you Googled "lawn maintenance" or "lawn care" or "lawn mowing" in his city, these two guys were the first two listings under Google Places, where they each had several reviews for an average 5-star rating. They also showed up right under or over Google Places because they also had reviews on a local social media platform that usually comes up in local searches.

So here is the initial momentum-gathering strategy we used: we found the top five search-keyword phrases for lawn care and the top five for snow removal (because there's a good chance that if you won't shovel your snow, you won't mow your lawn either). We used his keywords to optimize a three-page website, his profiles on the local social media platform, Facebook, Twitter and a Google profile.

Rich asked his clients to leave reviews on the local social media site and on Google, using one of those five keyword phrases if appropriate. (We have plans to expand to several other review/citation sites as his business grows.) After a customer writes a review, Rich sends a thank-you card and then calls and asks for referrals. Any time a referral signs on, Rich mows the referrer's lawn for free.

Rich isn't rich, but he now makes a good living and plans to expand his business, offer more services and hire specialty crews. For a local service business, social proof is everything. For the expansion, he'll scale his reputation management efforts and implement lead capture strategies as well.

That's fine for Rich, you say, but I'm in the B2B (business to business) arena; things just aren't that simple. You're probably right, but just to be sure, let's look at a couple of diagrams and use some acronyms.

In the old days, say 10 years ago, the sales cycle was simple. And by sales, I mean everything from selling your widget or service to getting hired. Anyhoo, there were basically 3 main events in the sales cycle that looked like this.

It went like this: Something sparks an interest in a person, product or service (interest driver). The deep fryer has begun to sputter out at Joe's Grease Pit, and Joe gets a postcard announcing the newest model of his fryer is available, and if he orders now he'll save 10 percent and avoid losses of hundreds of dollars per day if he's without a fryer. The IT department at XYZ Company is expanding rapidly and on the day she gets budget approval for a new systems analyst, Kristen receives an impressive resume from Susan. Sean's R&D company needs a thermonucleardiscombobulator (TMDR), and he finds an article about just such a device in a trade journal.

Ten years ago, the combination of interest driver (postcard, resume, article) and current circumstance would likely have been enough persuasion to get Joe to order the new fryer, Kristen to call Susan and Sean to call in ACME's TMDR rep. Such experiences are labeled the First Moment of Truth or FMOT. (The terms First Moment of Truth and Second Moment of Truth were coined by Procter & Gamble in the mid-2000s in an article in the *Wall Street Journal*.)

A consumer's experiences of products, services, and customer service would determine their word-of-mouth praise or discouragement to their peers, which was labeled the Second Moment of Truth or SMOT. Their SMOT would directly impact someone else's FMOT and the bottom lines of the fryer manufacturer and ACME's TMDR division. But that was 10 years ago. How retro.

Now, there's a fourth event that occurs for more than 95 percent of consumers, employment recruiters, and B2B decision makers. That moment is ... drumroll, please ... The Zero Moment of Truth or ZMOT. (The term Zero Moment of Truth was coined by Jim Lecinski of Google in his book by the same name.)

In today's world, we arm ourselves with smartphones and other not-dumb devices to avail ourselves of the myriad online resources that will help us make smart decisions. Not even a word-of-mouth recommendation from a friend or trusted colleague or awe-inspiring celebrity (except for Brian Tracy, of course) is enough to make us pull the trigger on that fryer, job candidate, dog groomer or thermonucleardiscombobulator. We make a pit stop at Amazon to check the number of gold stars on the fryer; we go to LinkedIn to see if that systems analyst has recommendations from previous employers and colleagues; we cruise over to Facebook to make sure a job candidate isn't gloating about winning lawsuits against her last two employers; we drop by Yelp to make sure that groomer didn't shave the leg off a Shih Tzu (or, if she did, that there was a really good reason for it).

Reputation will be critical for the TMDR manufacturer, but when every sale is worth millions, ACME needs to expand Zero Moment. They'll need to be all over the place "framing the problem" for their target market. With today's Internet, we begin to solve problems by researching our symptoms. That research helps us understand the underlying problem and gives us language to use for further research into a solution. Now, here's the amazing statistic: If the business that supplies the solution product or service is the business that framed the problem for us, they are 80 percent more likely to get our business than their competition. Eighty percent!

So, there's Sean and his R&D company, looking for a missing link. He knows exactly which atomic activity he needs to document, but he doesn't know how to create it and record it. Along comes the online trade journal article about ACME's thermonucleardiscombobulator. Sean seeks social proof via Google and LinkedIn, finds it, and calls a sales rep. For B2B, Zero Moment has to be about framing the problem as well as reputation management.

From $10 to $10 million, we as consumers require social proof. Then, and only then, will we decide to buy, hire or invite that B2B provider in to make a sales presentation. And when that B2B rep shows up, we know exactly what questions to ask. In fact, if a job candidate or business is on top of their ZMOT and SMOT, we establish a level of confidence and trust during our Zero Moment that likely predisposes us to spending or offering more money during our First Moment (sales presentation and closing, job offer).

If we take delivery of the goods and everything/everyone works the way they're supposed to, we crow about it to our friends and colleagues online and off; we leave reviews; we give testimonials. Our SMOT triggers ZMOT in others, and the next thing you know, ACME's TMDR Division single-handedly reverses the U.S. trade deficit.

Now, you're smart (you have a smartphone), so you know where I'm going with this. FMOT, the decision to fork over the big bucks doesn't happen without ZMOT. So here's the dealio, Emilio. You have to show up for ZMOT, and you have to show up with bells on.

SIX-STEP BLUEPRINT FOR CREATING
A WINNING DIGITAL FOOTPRINT

1. Strategy—Don't Leave Home Without It

Digital marketing is part of an overall marketing plan. I think because it's new, people tend to think of it as a different beast. Just as you will include offline marketing strategies and tactics, you'll include digital. (A caveat: If you decide to hire a digital marketer to help create your strategy and tactics, be sure to hire an Internet/digital *marketer*, not an Internet technician. There are a lot of people calling themselves Internet marketers when, really, they know only how to implement really well. Internet technicians are great after you've got your strategies and tactics outlined and integrated with your overall marketing plan.)

If you do just one thing online, it should be to establish and maintain your reputation. Remember, one person's Second Moment of Truth is the next person's Zero Moment. Run a Google search on your top keyword phrases and see which review sites and directories show up for your competition and how they look. Visit LinkedIn and search using your keywords. Check out your competition to see what you need to beat. You need to show up before them and look better.

When you hire a digital marketing consultant to help develop a strategy for your business, you should walk away with a blueprint of actionable steps that you can begin working immediately. The blueprint should also contain actions to pursue later, as many businesses and individuals don't have the resources (time, money, staff) to simultaneously implement all strategies.

If you have multiple people engaged in marketing and sales, your consultant should spend time on cross-channel alignment of strategy, tactics and communication flow.

If you are a professional, your blueprint may consist simply of blogging on a regular basis and putting yourself all over LinkedIn. These two activities produce the most opportunities for most professionals on a corporate career path.

Stick to the blueprint. Don't be distracted by every shiny digital object. If some new digital platform seems pressing, ask your digital marketing consultant whether it should pre-empt some part of your blueprint. Technology and the way we use it changes swiftly, but you need to focus your resources on the activities that bring the highest return on investment.

2. Keyword Research

Ideally, everything that you or other people post (like testimonials) online will include a keyword phrase for which you want to rank on page one of the search engines or social media platforms. When you post a video on YouTube, put keywords in the description along with a link to your website. When you create your LinkedIn profile, place your keywords. When you create a blog post, use keywords.

Keywords are vital. You can do some keyword research yourself (I offer some resources for you on my site), or you might consider investing in someone to research them for your business. It's like building the foundation of a house. Whoever does it had better get it right.

3. Valuable Content

Nothing establishes credibility faster than providing quality content that your prospects (or potential employers) can use. I highly recommend creating a stockpile of content that you can use for blog posts, forum comments, Q&A on LinkedIn, short videos, Chamber of Commerce presentations, etc. The same content can be delivered in a variety of ways. Want a fast way to get started?

Make a list of the 10 questions you are asked most frequently and your answers to those questions. Write as much as you can; you can edit down as needed later. Then, make a list of the top 10 things people don't ask but you think they should. These are typically your best points of persuasion because people are unaware of the issues, but when you bring them up, you help the prospect recognize a problem, and there you are—the solution!

B2B companies will generate the best leads by framing the problem with white papers, case studies, webinars and the like.

4. Social Proof

Create a process in which you collect positive feedback from your clients, customers, employers, colleagues, and key influencers in your community or industry. Get most of it in written format and some in video. Video testimonials and case studies are very powerful ZMOT drivers.

Written testimonials will, ideally, be left on a review or citation site (LinkedIn, Google Places, Yelp, directories). Then, you can compile the best of those and place them on your website and printed material, including cover letters and resumes.

A very elegant way to get testimonials is to give them. Very often when you give someone a testimonial, they'll reciprocate without any prompting.

5. Social Profiles

You should determine, perhaps with the help of a digital marketing consultant or career coach, which social media platforms are most likely to generate the most and best-quality leads or opportunities. Your profiles should be branded with your photo or logo, include a link to your website, and use at least one of your top keyword phrases.

If you'll be doing all of the social media engagement yourself, I recommend starting with just one platform and working it regularly. Once you have that one platform going, you'll probably find that it's fairly easy to add another. There are efficiency tools for streamlining your blogging and social media activities.

When you connect with people offline, immediately find them online. For most of us, that means finding them on LinkedIn and Twitter. But Facebook may be very appropriate, especially if you are a business to consumer (B2C) provider. Following up with a handwritten note is also a great way to be remembered because nobody does this anymore.

6. Authenticity

The single most-important thing about social media is to be authentic. People do business with those they know, like and trust. Just let your passion and personality come through (unless you're a psycho-killer-stalker—that requires a completely different strategy).

THE TRUTH ABOUT THE ZERO MOMENT OF TRUTH

The new sales/hiring cycle is real. Businesses and professionals who fail to create a winning Zero Moment of Truth are losing money, opportunity—and perhaps even their business or career elevation.

About Jennifer

Jennifer Hilburn conducts strategy workshops for successful businesses to develop and refine online lead generation, cross-channel marketing, and reputation management tactics that escalate sales revenues. She also speaks and trains for corporations, associations and conferences. Current and past clients include AT&T, Hewlett-Packard, Sprint, Rocky Mountain Chocolate Factory, Mercury Payment Systems, Burlington Northern Railroad, Agilent Technologies, Seagate, University of Nebraska, State of Colorado, State of Nebraska, Internal Revenue Service and many more.

Jennifer is also the founder of the U.S. Vetpreneur Marketing Challenge, a program designed to help U.S. veterans successfully market their new businesses online and offline.

Reach Jennifer at Six Degrees Digital Marketing, http://get-clicked.com; jen@get-clicked.com or 970-799-4941.

CHAPTER 5

"I'll Take Care of That" Are You a Problem Solver or a Peddler?

By Jim Collyer

Time and again I run into people who are looking for success or are just plain waiting for success to find them. They dream of stratospheric success, but they just don't know how to get started. It's like the *"big idea"* is just out of their reach. They are waiting for a niche, a break-through, a new and unique product idea or an invention that will revolutionize the world. They have the misconception that if they can just hang in there long enough success will find them. Sadly, it rarely works this way. The truth is, waiting for success to find you is like waiting to be struck by lightning. Odds are it won't happen.

Let's face it, 99.9 percent of all sales worldwide are "me-too" products and services and not unique. In fact, people are much more willing to buy improvements on existing products than they are to purchase completely new, innovative and untried products or services. Your clients aren't looking for new products; they are looking for adaptations of existing products that better fill their needs. I personally don't know of any revolutionary niches for revolutionary products in the marketplace. If I did, I'd be trying to fill them.

Our problem is our potential clients or customers are already getting everything they need. They're just buying them from someone else. Our goal is to create a product or service that is just a little better than what is currently out there. While this may sound easy, it's going to take more effort than simply saying, "I can do that."

You'll need a proven success system to achieve your goals. If you are not manufacturing a product, then you'll have to figure out how to improve and authenticate your service.

By far, the vast majority of the successful business people I know had no idea that they would wind up in their current line of business when they started out. They simply found a niche and filled it.

There are plenty of niches out there ready to be filled with existing products right now. So, quit waiting for lightning to strike.

HOW TO FIND A NICHE

"So ... where are all of these niches?" you might ask.

They exist everywhere. There are niches in every business, in every location and every product line. Niches are created for ordinary and mundane products and services as well as for exotic ones. Simply put, niches are products and services that can meet a client's expanding needs or wants. If you can *"take care"* of a client's problems, issues or wants, then you can find and fill that niche.

People want their problems to be taken care of for them.

I'll take care of that is one of the oldest and greatest success strategies in history.

I'll take care of that is more than a phrase—it's an attitude.

Taking care of that is an attitude that means we are willing to tailor our services and products to meet our client's specific needs. Filling niches properly will create a better and more rewarding future for both you and the client. The attitude says, "we don't want to sell a product to the client, we want to provide the client with the exact product he needs."

Far too often, salespeople resort to the old hard sell when it comes to products and services. We spend all of our time talking. We try to convince the customer that the unique benefits and features of our product or service will fulfill their every need. I was guilty of this mistake myself early on in my sales career. But we can't dictate to the market, we must let the market tell us what it wants to do. A good way to keep our minds on track is to continually ask ourselves this question: "Are we problem solvers or merely peddlers?"

Imagine going into a shoe store and seeing a pair of shoes you really like, but the store doesn't have them in your size. The shoe salesman talks you into buying the display pair anyway, telling you that he thinks they will stretch a little after you wear them. The next day, you have sore toes and a blister on your heel. You'll buy more shoes but probably not from that store. The salesman made a sale but lost a customer. Selling what's in your wagon without finding the right fit is bad business in today's market.

One product- or service-fits-all may have worked 40 years ago, but it doesn't work in today's economy. The roles in the market have reversed. Back then we could develop an organization or product and find a market to support it. In today's economy, we have to find a market and then adjust our organization or product to support that market. The market no longer supports a product; the product must support the specific market.

LISTEN UP: A SKILL NEEDED TO SUCCEED

A common mistake in both sales and the corporate world is that we tend to think of what we are going to say even before the other person has finished speaking. We pay more attention to what we are going to say than to what our client or boss is saying. If we try to provide a solution without listening, we are only showing our ignorance, and we lose. We would be far more successful if we would spend more time listening to the needs and wants of our customers or bosses and less time talking.

The one skill all top executives and salespeople share is the ability to listen and to listen intently.

Listening is a skill, and it must be learned if we ever hope to achieve success. First of all, everyone likes to be listened to. Secondly, listening shows we care.

Caring is the basis of relationship building, and people are much more willing to do business with friends than with someone they don't know. Caring also equates to quality in our products and services. You can't *take care* of an issue without providing quality products or services.

Now we just need to have someone who will let us *take care* of a niche for them.

THREE STEPS NECESSARY TO ACHIEVE
NICHE-FILLING SUCCESS

1. Learn what your client really wants. (Listen)

2. Discover how you can support the client.

3. Communicate to the client about what you can do.

All three steps need to be aligned for this system to work. Each step is dependent on the preceding step for successful execution of the entire process.

The foundation to all success is listening. I mean to listen with everything you've got and to resist the temptation to be thinking of answers while the other person is talking. Take notes if you have to, but don't let your note-taking interfere with your listening. Eye-to-eye contact is important. It shows that you are listening. Don't just talk about business either; remember we are building relationships here, and ask about your client's family, golf game or hobbies.

When you do talk business, do it in the form of questions. Offer no solutions at this time. This is question-and-answer time. You ask the questions, and the client supplies the answers. Don't be afraid to ask questions, even dumb questions. It is vital you have a clear and complete picture of exactly what the client wants and expects at this time.

Step 1 can rarely be accomplished in one meeting; more than likely it will take several meetings over several weeks to gather all of the information you will require in order to assess the problem accurately.

Next we need to step back, evaluate what we have heard and determine what we can do to support the customer's need. We might need to make several phone calls. We might need to build a team and discuss possible solutions within that team. Remember, having several people involved helps to ensure the best solution to any problem, so, don't hesitate to include and ask for input from others. Surround yourself with good, intelligent people; be part of a team and don't try to fly solo. And always, always have a plan B, just in case your original idea doesn't pan out.

Taking care of it isn't a shotgun approach aimed at a large target. It's a calculated risk aimed at one specific client. The rule of thumb for calculating risk is to double your expected costs and to divide your projected income in half. After this is done, if it still looks like you can make a profit, then the project is a go.

The final step is to talk to your client about your proposal. If you have done the work properly in the first two steps, this will be the easiest step. You approach your client in this final step much the same way as you did in the first step: questions and answers.

Ask the client if she remembers your discussion on the problem. Ask her to look at your proposal. Ask for her input on your proposal. Ask her what she likes about the proposal. Ask her what he dislikes about it. Ask how she thinks you can improve it.

You get the picture—ask, ask, ask. Don't force it. Be patient. Patience isn't just needed at this point; it's vital. In the end, it is our customer, not the product or service, which determines our success.

If he likes the proposal, ask for the sale, but don't forget that it is your relationship with the client and the quality of your service that made the sale. If you nurture the relationship and service, you'll have a good customer for life. If you ignore the customer and the quality of your service, you are opening the door for someone else to take your hard-earned business away from you.

If the client doesn't like your proposal, let him know that *you'll take care of the problems* and ask to schedule a meeting to talk again. Begin the three-step process all over again.

PERSISTENCE AND PATIENCE ARE REQUIRED

Be persistent; finding success is a lot like fishing. If the hook isn't in front of the fish's face, it will never bite.

Ideas, unfortunately, have no monetary value; only results pay. It is important to move as quickly as possible since time has a way of diminishing ideas. If the client is looking for a niche to be filled and you are too slow, someone else will come along and fill it for you. Don't be afraid of making mistakes. If you're not making any mistakes, you're probably moving too slow. Mistakes are inevitable. It is always possible to correct small mistakes as we proceed.

This entire system is designed to build a trusting relationship between you and the client. If you don't have a previous track record of success or a good and trusting relationship with the client, when you ask for the sale you will be told "no." Who's going to trust the success of a multimillion dollar business with someone they don't know? That's right, no one would. You must build those relationships and learn to handle rejection—its part of the game. Don't expect instant success; it rarely happens. A business idea is just a business idea, it's not personal. I've had my hand cut off more than once, and I survived. Keep in mind, the client is rejecting the idea not you.

People appreciate a person who shows care. Don't be surprised, even if the answer is no, to be offered another niche to fill. It happens all the time and is a primary reason why there are so many successful people who end up in lines of work they never dreamt of.

Taking care of a client's needs is as old as business itself, but it's funny how few people really understand the principle. Today, people want instant gratification, the quick profit. The *I'll take care of that* method is based on long-term relationships and a high quality of service.

The world is obdurate. People avoid change. Business avoids change. In order to acquire success, we must become change advocates. If we apply our skills and carefully present proposals, we'll find our niche and our opportunity to say, *I'll take care of that.*

About Jim

Jim Collyer is a writer, lecturer and sales professional living in Idaho. Jim's lectures take him throughout the western United States where he has trained more than 2,000 people in the past five years. A 1977 graduate of the University of Idaho, Jim's focus is on success training. Specializing in sales, Jim can help you and your team get trained, motivated and on your way toward meeting your sales goals.

Even during this recessed economy, Jim's company has enjoyed an annual 20 percent increase in sales. For information about having Jim speak at your event, please contact Jim at collyerjc13@hotmail.com or call 775-397-0761.

CHAPTER 6

Cracking the Success Code with Branded Films™

By JW Dicks, Esq., Nick Nanton, Esq., Lindsay Dicks and Greg Rollett

Nobody will hear you until they know you.
~ Jonathan Sprinkles, motivational speaker

All of us at the Celebrity Branding Agency have seen, used and even created a lot of powerful celebrity branding tools that enable our clients to become recognized as leaders in their areas. But, in our more than 50 years of combined experience in celebrity branding, we've never seen a more powerful tool than a properly-produced *branded film.*

An effective branded film has the potential to really break you through to a whole new level of success—and maybe even allow you to skip a few other levels that you'll never have to spend time in!

Here's just one example of how a branded film changed somebody's life in an incredibly dramatic fashion.

CASE STUDY: THE STRUGGLING STUDENT

What hope was there for a 5'6" kid with bad grades who dreamt not only of being admitted into one of America's most famous colleges, but also of playing on its legendary football team?

Not much—but he didn't give up on either count. He battled severe dyslexia to finally gain admission to the college for his final two undergraduate years—and he demonstrated such an incredible level of motivation and dedication to the football coach that, during his senior year, he was put on the field for the final minutes of the last home game. The crowd loved him—and showed that affection by making him the first player to ever be carried off the field by the school's fans.

Of course the attention couldn't last. College ended; his brief moment of glory was gone; and he was left to toil anonymously for an insurance company.

That was when he came up with another, even bigger, crazy dream—to get a big Hollywood movie made about his life.

After 10 years of struggles, legal battles and frustrations, the movie actually got made—and became a film ESPN ranks as one of the 25 greatest sports movies ever made. "Rudy," the against-the-odds story of Daniel "Rudy" Ruettiger's triumph at Notre Dame University, was released in 1993—the same year that Daniel got a call from a motivational speaking bureau and launched a whole new career based on his new-found celebrity. Today, his fee for a speaking engagement is $17,500, and he has authored several best-selling inspirational books.

All because of the power of branded film.

BRANDED FILM: THE ULTIMATE GAME CHANGER

As you probably already know, there are many ways to develop a personal brand—through books, personal appearances, newsletters, newspaper articles and so forth. But these methods can take a great deal of time—and also require a constant and consistent effort just to begin to raise awareness of who you are and what you're all about.

However, if you're looking for an immediate and impactful way to supercharge your personal brand, the *branded film* contains a unique power that is impossible to duplicate elsewhere—as you can see from "Rudy" Ruettiger's story. When that power is properly put to work for the purposes of personal branding, it can immediately raise an individual's profile in many beneficial and enduring ways.

Proof of a film's power is demonstrated by the fact that professional filmmakers make films of themselves to raise *their* profiles as well as that of their projects. Take Michael Moore—here was a guy who dropped out of college during his freshman year. He then got fired from his first big job—wrongfully, he thought, so he sued and settled for a $58,000 pay-off. But he didn't stash that money in the bank to live on—no, instead, he put that money into producing a documentary, into which he repeatedly inserted himself, even though the movie-going public had no idea who this fat guy with the glasses was. That film was the controversial documentary, "Roger and Me," which was as much a branded film as a corporate exposé, and which allowed Moore to turn that $58,000 into millions by establishing his brand and providing the springboard for other movies and TV shows.

Morgan Spurlock is another documentary filmmaker who makes sure to insert himself into his movies, such as "Supersize Me" and "The Greatest Movie Ever Sold" (which was, ironically, a movie about product placement). This method has made him into a celebrity just as it did for Moore—he's now hosted his own TV shows and is more easily able to obtain financing for other projects.

Hollywood even produces branded films for its own projects. When you see one of those "First Look" featurettes on HBO about an upcoming release, you're looking at a branded film *about* a film. These documentary-style shorts are designed to make you want to run to a theater to see the featured movie—but they're anything but real documentaries. They're actually advertisements produced to *look* like the real story behind the movie—but, of course, you'll never see any material that might be interpreted as being negative.

Film has many unique qualities that make it ideal for personal branding. Here are a few of them.

FILMS MAKE STARS

In the early days of Hollywood, there was no "star system." Actors were not credited, and no one thought twice about what actor to put in a film. It was the audience that created movie stars—by demanding more movies featuring certain performers.

In a branded film, you are the "star": you are the central figure in your own story and are presented as a likeable and magnetic individual. The audience responds to you on a gut level that just can't happen with the printed word.

FILMS TELL STORIES

People love stories—and all of us have a story that separates us from everyone else. The fact is, film is the best medium to tell that story. Using a branded film to build your narrative in a visually compelling way allows people to identify with your struggles, as well as cheer for your successes. In any action movie, Western, romantic comedy or other popular film genre, various time-tested devices are used to make sure audiences like and root for the main "star."

A branded film uses those same Hollywood elements to present your story in the best way possible—through the words of real people and the visuals of real locations—giving it a genuine power that a Hollywood film can't match. That power is accentuated when you go beyond your basic business to tell your human story. Whether it's chronicling your early struggles, your family life, or those you've helped along the way, a branded film can spotlight the areas of your life that will truly resonate with your audience and bond them to you.

FILMS CONTROL THE MESSAGE

The long-running CBS news show "60 Minutes" built its reputation initially through "ambush" interviews. The reporter would show up, without warning, at the office of the person they were investigating and ask very confrontational questions. That person had no control of the message. If he answered honestly, he might incriminate himself. If he didn't answer at all, he risked looking incredibly guilty.

A branded film aims for the exact opposite product that you can get from this nightmarish scenario. Interviews and location shooting are highly planned and scheduled; the questions are designed to shape a narrative that will convey the exact story that the subject of the film wants to tell. Elements such as music, lighting and camera angles are all utilized in the service of the branding.

FILMS ALLOW PEOPLE TO KNOW WHO YOU ARE

In a book, you can read that a person is attractive. In a film, you can *see* that a person is attractive. The difference is crucial—in the first instance, someone is telling you something that you have to accept as being true; in the second instance, *you see it for yourself.*

Books are great at conveying ideas and demonstrating your expertise on a subject; they are essential to personal branding. Films do something else entirely—they allow your audience to experience *who you are*—how you walk, talk and look—and respond to you in a *personal* way. As brand strategist Scott Talgo says, "A brand that captures your mind gains behavior. A brand that captures your heart gains *commitment*."

Film gives your brand the best opportunity to gain that commitment.

BRANDED FILMS: WHY IT'S THE RIGHT TIME

A branded film is a relatively new arrow in the marketing quiver of entrepreneurs and business owners for two key reasons, both having to do with technological advances.

Reason number one: Creating and editing high-quality films has become much more *affordable* in recent years. You no longer need millions of dollars to create a professional Hollywood-level production. Equipment is much cheaper, more people have access to train on that equipment, and post production can be accomplished on computers not that much more powerful (or expensive) than your average home or office PC.

Reason number two: Video has exploded on the Internet, becoming much more prevalent and powerful. That means a branded film can be shared not only through YouTube.com, but also through popular social media sites such as Facebook and LinkedIn. Best of all, Google *likes* video. Video results show up much higher in Google search results than text pages do, according to SEO expert Bruce Clay: "The biggest element of video is that it's high-engagement. And as an engagement element, that's kind of an object or something that Google's going to look for."

Of course, for personal branding to really be effective, it has to stand out from the herd. Branded films do. That's because, even though an incredible amount of videos and films are being posted to the Internet, most of the ones that attempt branding do it in the most basic way possible: the subject merely speaks to the camera and explains who they are or what they do. This is effective as a quick introduction to a website, or explaining a specific product or service, but, as far as establishing and building a brand goes, this kind of film can do only so much.

A successful branded film, in contrast, boasts high-production values and an impactful emotional story. It raises the bar for the entrepreneur who really wants to present the most polished and professional brand possible, while, at the same time, makes the strongest possible emotional connection to both customers and non-customers.

This is just the route the Justin Bieber management team took to boost their client's already red-hot profile when they released the Bieber documentary, "Never Say Never," to theaters in 2011. This was the ultimate branded film event—and a giant financial success as well, grossing over $70 million in the U.S. alone. As *Forbes* put it in an article published in the Feb. 25, 2011 issue, "The Secret Behind Justin Bieber's Success," "Never Say Never" was a brilliant way for the Bieber brand team to tell its story and, just as brilliantly, get it out there when the media wind was at its back. When you're on a roll, do what you can to keep the momentum going.

LEVERAGING YOUR BRANDED FILM

A branded film shouldn't be dumped on the Internet as an afterthought. Instead, it should be utilized in an exciting "premiere" event that fully exploits its marketing power and takes advantage of its top-level production values. Again, the branded film is still a unique commodity in marketing circles—and publicizing it allows you to strongly differentiate yourself from the competition in the public's mind.

For example, when Barack Obama was about to face down John McCain on election day in 2008, he used a branded film event to push him over the top. A week before the election, his campaign team bought a half-hour of time on three major networks—Fox, CBS and NBC—as well as four smaller channels—all at the same time. Suddenly, a half-hour infomercial was perceived as a multi-channel event, and ended up with a total viewership of more than 25 million people. In contrast, only 19.8 million viewers had watched the final game of the World Series that year.

Few have the resources of a well-financed national political campaign to pull off that kind of media stunt. However, there are still a myriad of effective ways you can put your branded film to work for you, including the following.

THE RED CARPET PREMIERE

Many successful professionals hold events for their customers, clients

CRACKING THE SUCCESS CODE WITH BRANDED FILMS™

and/or patients. Financial advisers will often hold a steak dinner; dentists might host a "Patient Appreciation Day," and so forth. A red carpet premiere of a branded film can be a different kind of breakthrough event that not only allows you to get your new movie the best possible exposure, but also gives your current and potential customers a fun night out. You can actually rent out a local theater for a very reasonable amount, have a red carpet in place outside for the evening of your premiere, have search lights illuminating the skies and offer free popcorn and drinks to your movie audience.

DVD RELEASE

What comes after the theatrical release of a film? The DVD release, of course. Create your own custom DVD case and disc, and include DVD "extras" as well — perhaps some outtakes from interviews done for the movie that were not used in the original version. The DVD can be sent out to your current client list as well as to new customers and leads interested in possibly working with you. If you send a prospect your branded film along with a bag of microwave popcorn, what do you think they are going to do? Right, they're going to check it out ... then they're going to hire you.

ONLINE EVENT

You can also premiere your branded film online, as long as you do it with an appropriate splash. Featuring a prominent online "countdown" to the movie's unveiling on your website and your social media sites can build anticipation. You can also allow potential viewers to officially register for the premiere and be given a special password to gain access.

PUBLICITY

Just as Hollywood movies have stories that are publicized, so does your branded film. Work on providing local media (radio, newspaper, local news websites) with interviews about your film and about the personal story it tells. Feature these stories on your own site to further publicize your branded film.

In the 21st century, the branded film will become the ultimate personal marketing tool. By presenting your story through a compelling, high-quality presentation, you become a flesh-and-blood person your audience can bond with—not just another businessperson trying to make a sale. You also create more personality-driven opportunities for yourself.

The power of film is undeniable. Putting that power to work for you is just good business!

About JW

JW Dicks, Esq., is America's foremost authority on using personal branding for business development. He has created some of the most successful brand and marketing campaigns for business and professional clients to make them the Credible Celebrity Expert in their field and build multi-million dollar businesses using their recognized status.

JW Dicks has started, bought, built, and sold a large number of businesses over his 39-year career and developed a loyal international following as a business attorney, author, speaker, consultant, and business expert's coach. He not only practices what he preaches by using his strategies to build his own businesses, he also applies those same concepts to help clients grow their business or professional practice the ways he does.

JW has been extensively quoted in such national media as *USA Today, The Wall Street Journal, Newsweek, Inc. Magazine*, Forbes.com, CNBC.Com, and Fortune Small business. His television appearances include ABC, NBC, CBS and FOX affiliate stations around the country. He is the resident branding expert for Fast Company's internationally syndicated blog and is the publisher of Celebrity Expert Insider, a monthly newsletter targeting business and brand building strategies.

JW has written over 22 books, including numerous best sellers, and has been inducted into the National Academy of Best Selling Authors. JW is married to Linda, his wife of 39 years, and they have two daughters, two granddaughters and two Yorkies. JW is a 6th generation Floridian and splits time between his home in Orlando and beach house on the Florida west coast.

About Nick

An Emmy Award Winning Director and Producer, Nick Nanton, Esq., is known as the Top Agent to Celebrity Experts around the world for his role in developing and marketing business and professional experts, through personal branding, media, marketing and PR to help them gain credibility and recognition for their accomplishments. Nick is recognized as the nation's leading expert on personal branding as Fast Company Magazine's Expert Blogger on the subject and lectures regularly on the topic at at major universities around the world. His book *Celebrity Branding You®* has also been used as the textbook on personal branding for University student.

The CEO of The Dicks + Nanton Celebrity Branding Agency, an international agency with more than 1000 clients in 26 countries, Nick is an award winning director, producer and songwriter who has worked on everything from large scale events to television shows with the likes of Bill Cosby, President George H.W. Bush, Brian Tracy, Michael Gerber and many more.

Nick is recognized as one of the top thought-leaders in the business world and has co-authored 16 best-selling books alongside Brian Tracy, Jack Canfield (creator of the *Chicken Soup for the Soul* Series), Dan Kennedy, Robert Allen, Dr. Ivan Misner (Founder of BNI), Jay Conrad Levinson (Author of the *Guerilla Marketing* Series), Leigh Steinberg and many others, including the breakthrough hit *Celebrity Branding You!®*.

Nick has published books by Brian Tracy, Mari Smith, Jack Canfield, Dan Kennedy and many other celebrity experts and Nick has led the marketing and PR campaigns that have driven more than 600 authors to Best-Seller status. Nick has been seen in US*A Today*, The *Wall St. Journal*, *Newsweek*, Inc. Magazine, *The New York Times, Entrepreneur®* Magazine, FastCompany.com. and has appeared on ABC, NBC, CBS, and FOX television affiliates around the country, as well as CNN, FOX News, CNBC, and MSNBC from coast to coast speaking on subjects ranging from branding, marketing and law, to American Idol.

Nick is a member of the Florida Bar, holds a JD from the University of Florida Levin College of Law, as well as a BSBA in Finance from the University of Florida's Warrington College of Business. Nick is a voting member of The National Academy of Recording Arts & Sciences (NARAS, Home to The GRAMMYs), a member of The National Academy of Television Arts & Sciences (Home to the Emmy Awards) co-founder of the National Academy of Best-Selling Authors, an 11-time Telly Award winner, and spends his spare time working with Young Life and Downtown Credo Orlando and rooting for the Florida Gators with his wife Kristina and their three children, Brock, Bowen and Addison.

About Lindsay

Lindsay Dicks helps her clients tell their stories in the online world. Being brought up around a family of marketers, but a product of Generation Y, Lindsay naturally gravitated to the new world of online marketing. Lindsay began freelance writing in 2000 and soon after launched her own PR firm that thrived by offering an in-your-face "Guaranteed PR" that was one of the first of its type in the nation.

Lindsay's new media career is centered on her philosophy that "people buy people." Her goal is to help her clients build a relationship with their prospects and customers. Once that relationship is built and they learn to trust them as the expert in their field, then they will do business with them. Lindsay also built a patent-pending process that utilizes social media marketing, content marketing and search engine optimization to create online "buzz" for her clients that helps them to convey their business and personal story. Lindsay's clientele span the entire business map and range from doctors and small business owners to Inc 500 CEOs.

Lindsay is a graduate of the University of Florida. She is the CEO of CelebritySites™, an online marketing company specializing in social media and online personal branding. Lindsay is also a multi-best-selling author including the best-selling book "*Power Principles for Success*" which she co-authored with Brian Tracy. She was also selected as one of America's PremierExperts™ and has been quoted in *Newsweek*, the *Wall Street Journal, USA Today, Inc Magazine* as well as featured on NBC, ABC, and CBS television affiliates speaking on social media, search engine optimization and making more money online. Lindsay was also recently brought on FOX 35 News as their Online Marketing Expert.

Lindsay, a national speaker, has shared the stage with some of the top speakers in the world such as Brian Tracy, Lee Milteer, Ron LeGrand, Arielle Ford, David Bullock, Brian Horn, Peter Shankman and many others. Lindsay was also a Producer on the Emmy-nominated film Jacob's Turn.

You can connect with Lindsay at:
Lindsay@CelebritySites.com
www.twitter.com/LindsayMDicks
www.facebook.com/LindsayDicks

About Greg

Greg Rollett, the ProductPro, is a best-selling author and online marketing expert who works with authors, experts, entertainers, entrepreneurs and business owners all over the world to help them share their knowledge and change the lives and businesses of others. After creating a successful string of his own educational products, Greg began helping others in the production and marketing of their own products.

Greg is a front-runner in utilizing the power of social media, direct response marketing and customer education to drive new leads and convert those leads into long-standing customers and advocates.

Previous clients include Coca-Cola, Miller Lite, Warner Bros and Cash Money Records, as well as hundreds of entrepreneurs and small-business owners. Greg's work has been featured on FOX News, ABC, and the Daily Buzz. Greg has written for Mashable, the Huffington Post, AOL, AMEX's Open Forum and more.

Greg loves to challenge the current business environments that constrain people to working 12-hour days during the best portions of their lives. By teaching them to leverage technology and the power of information, Greg loves helping others create freedom businesses that allow them to generate income, make the world a better place and live a radically ambitious lifestyle in the process.

A former touring musician, Greg is highly sought after as a speaker, having appeared on stages with former Florida Gov. Charlie Crist, best-selling authors Chris Brogan and Nick Nanton, as well as at events such as Affiliate Summit.

If you would like to learn more about Greg and how he can help your business, please contact him directly at greg@productprosystems.com or by calling his office at 877.897.4611.

You can also download a free report on how to create your own educational products at www.productprosystems.com.

CHAPTER 7

Your Network Is Your Net Worth!
7 Keys to Building and Leveraging Your Network

By Ginger Bell

A network behaves in such a way that the more you add to the network the more valuable the whole thing becomes for everyone.

You may have heard the saying "It's not *what* you know, but *who* you know" that counts. While this idea may hold merit, it really is more than just *who* you know, but *how* you can leverage that connection to help both of you in business.

I took the position as a Training Consultant for Dale Carnegie Training because I loved their programs and knew I would learn and grow in the position. I also knew that the Dale Carnegie name alone would allow me to expand my professional network. However, the reality was that I had convinced the regional manager for Dale Carnegie Training that I could quickly expand its market share into the high-tech arena, an area where it did not hold a strong presence. When I took the position, I was provided no book of existing business and no names of companies in the area. I was literally starting from scratch.

Typically, most sales people in this position would consider getting a list of businesses in that market, determine the key decision makers for those companies and start making cold calls to introduce their products and services. However, I did not have a lot of time to find out who those key decision makers were, so I developed a strategy to build a network that could help me connect with key decision makers quicker and more efficiently. It's not that I mind doing cold calling, but I have done that before (and maybe you have too), and it is not fun! This time I was going to cast a bigger net with the help of others who already had a good sense of who the decision makers were. I immediately set out to build my network. First, I had to determine my value proposition in order to provide my "expertise" to the network I was going to create.

BUILD VALUE FOR YOUR NETWORK

One of the most important keys to building an effective network is to provide value for all those involved. It is also critical for you to set yourself apart in the marketplace by establishing your expertise and leveraging that expertise with others.

I knew that working for Dale Carnegie Training provided me with a very valuable benefit to help me build my network. Deciding on my value proposition was easy. What is the number one fear for most people? Public speaking, of course! It ranks higher than death, which means that most people would rather die than give a speech. Amazing for sure! So, my value proposition would be a workshop on "Overcoming the Fear of Public Speaking."

With my value proposition in place, I set out to develop my network. First, I had to determine what I needed to make my workshop a success and who I could add to my network who not only would help me get connected with the key decision makers in the area, but who would also benefit from being a partner in the network. It is important to always make sure that everyone in your network is able to gain value by participating. That value may come from new customers, positive alignment or increased exposure.

DEVELOP A STRONG NETWORK

Now that I had my value proposition, I needed to build my network. I began by developing a short list of people or businesses that could potentially help me and would also benefit by what I was doing. For this workshop, I would need a location, someone with a strong database and influence with professionals in the area and a secondary marketing partner to establish further credibility and market reach.

MAKE IT EASY FOR YOUR NETWORK TO SAY YES!

It is important to make what I call smart and easy requests. These are requests that are simple for people to understand and easy to say "yes" to. Make smart requests in your network members' "sweet spots," which means that it is easy for them to help you and are consistent with what will most likely benefit them.

To start, I went to the best hotel in the area where a lot of high-tech companies would send their customers and employees. I met with the manager and shared what I was doing with the workshop. I explained how the hotel would benefit by having professionals in the area attend an event in their hotel. I told the manager we would list the hotel as a partner in all marketing and provide them time at the end of the workshop to promote the hotel. We would also give them a list of attendees who were interested in more information about the hotel and allow their sales professionals to attend the workshop and learn about developing effective public speaking skills. In return, the hotel would provide the room for the workshop, coffee and tea and a very light continental breakfast. The hotel officials were delighted to help! We decided on a date for the event, and off I went. I wrote up a marketing piece for the workshop, which included what attendees would learn and who should attend. Next, I set out to find a partner who could help me market the event.

I contacted the director for the local Chamber of Commerce and said I was with Dale Carnegie Training and was going to be conducting a complimentary breakfast workshop on "Overcoming the Fear of Public Speaking." I offered to add the Chamber as a partner for the workshop if they would send out the marketing piece to their database. I also shared the same opportunities I had offered to the hotel. In return, we only asked that they market the workshop to their database. They agreed and thought the event would be a great benefit to their members and nonmembers alike.

When meeting with potential partners you want to add to your network, always be sure to introduce yourself and be clear about what you are doing. Tell them the benefits as well as what you will do and what you want them to do. Be very clear and specific.

Next I needed to add someone to my network who could build credibility and help market the event. I contacted the local newspaper and radio stations. I shared with them what I was doing to help professionals become better public speakers. I told them about our current partners and the benefits they would have getting on board. I asked them to promote the event through their marketing channels. I also offered to write an article and participate in a few radio interviews to share tools and tips to help their readers and listeners. I shared how they could benefit by having one of their sales representatives speak at the workshop about their products and services. They were delighted to be able to be a partner in the event and the network we had created. We developed a series of print ads for the newspaper and an article on "Creating a Winning Presentation." The radio stations helped to develop radio spots to market the event, and I did a radio program for listeners to call in and ask questions about how to overcome the fear of public speaking.

PLAN FOR FOLLOW UP

The goal of creating a network is to help build business connections for all those involved. It is important to provide a viable means to collect information from those you are marketing to so that everyone can make best use of their efforts.

We collected information from those in attendance by giving away several books during the workshop. People could enter the drawing by dropping their business cards in a basket when they signed in. We also collected their email addresses, phone numbers, company names and titles when they signed in. At the end of the workshop, each of our sponsoring partners gave a 30-second pitch on the benefits of their product or service. Because the workshop was a means to quickly identify those in the area who would benefit from courses offered by Dale Carnegie Training or services from one of our partners, it was critical to have a plan in place for effective follow-up.

RECOGNIZE YOUR NETWORK

Dale Carnegie wrote in his book, *How to Win Friends and Influence People* that everyone's favorite word is their own name. This holds true for both people and businesses. The key to successfully building a network includes giving credit and recognition to those involved.

The day came for the workshop, and the room was packed! Standing room only! We had professionals from throughout the area who were eager to hear about how to overcome their fear of public speaking. I was delighted to also have in attendance the president of one of the graduate schools in the area. He was going to give a presentation before the state legislature in a few weeks and was looking for some pointers on how to successfully communicate his plan. The workshop had been a huge success! I wanted to be sure to recognize my network that had helped to make the event a success and be sure to build value to the products and services they provide. I introduced each of them at the beginning of the workshop and strategically promoted them throughout the meeting. Each partner had 30 seconds to talk about their businesses, and I then thanked each of them at the end of the workshop. We also provided a survey at the end of the session and had a box next to each sponsor's name so participants could check if they would like to be contacted by that company. We shared the requests with our network. Everyone was happy to receive several leads from professionals in the area who were interested in finding out more about their products or services.

CREATE ADDITIONAL OPPORTUNITIES
FOR YOUR NETWORK

The key to building a successful network you can work with long term is to create additional opportunities for you to work together on in the future. Look for events and opportunities to leverage your expertise and provide additional ways for you to work together or refer business to each other.

My workshop was a huge success, and all of those in our network were delighted to be a part of the event. In fact, it was such a hit that we went on to develop a series of monthly workshops all marketed in the same manner with the same original network, plus a few more who were eager to be a part of our group. We created an elite attendee list from that first event so that each of them could receive advance notice for all future events we did.

BE A GOOD FARMER FOR YOUR NETWORK

You've heard the saying "one and done." This is not how you want to be known within your network. It is important to stay connected. Find out what new products or services they offer and look to your own database for opportunities to return the favor and refer business. Make sure you keep your network informed of your new products and services, too. In addition, be sure to constantly look for new experts to add to your network from those you have worked with, been referred to or have developed.

From this one workshop, I was able to develop several in-house training classes for three high-tech companies who had never used Dale Carnegie in their training programs. The president of the graduate school went on to take the "High Impact Presentation Class" offered by Dale Carnegie Training and successfully orchestrated a merger between the graduate school and the health and science university, which created one of the most successful biotech schools in the country. I was also able to use the influence of this individual to connect me with other presidents of high-tech companies in the area who would benefit from our training. Within six short months I had created one of the most successful territories within the region—all by leveraging my expertise with others to build a very strong expert network. Since my tenure at Dale Carnegie I have gone on to create several expert networks of professionals and trainers who are very successful in working together to leverage their expertise.

Bill Gates has spoken of a "trilogy of trust—the trust that one person has in another, that is then passed on to the third party." (In W. Gates, "Be a Referral Giver," in I. R. Misner & D. Morgan (eds.), *Masters of Networking*, Bard Press, 2000.)

Always make sure to connect with those who hold the highest standards and can deliver value in their products and services to all those in the network.

You too can create and leverage a powerful network by developing the following strategies.

- **Build value for your network.** Set yourself apart in the market-place by establishing your expertise and leveraging that expertise with others.

- **Develop a strong network.** Build a short list of people or businesses that could potentially help you and would benefit by what you are doing.

- **Make it easy for your network to say YES!** Make smart and easy requests. These are requests that are in the "sweet spot" of those in your network. This makes it easy for your contacts to help you because the requests are consistent with what will most likely benefit them.

- **Plan for follow-up.** Provide a viable means to collect information from those who you are marketing to so that everyone can make the best use of their networking efforts.

- **Recognize your network**. Give credit and recognition to your network for their work and expertise.

- **Create additional opportunities for your network.** Look for events and opportunities to create ways for you to work together or refer business to each other and leverage your expertise. Write blogs for each other and share reports to help each other in your businesses.

- **Be a good farmer for your network.** Stay connected! Find out what new products or services they offer and keep them informed of yours. Be sure to look for new experts to add to your network from those you have worked with, been referred to or met along the way.

Happy Networking!

About Ginger

Ginger Bell is the networking queen! She is an experienced trainer, course developer, business owner, software developer and chief executive officer of Go2Training Consultants. Ginger has consulted for many companies, including Dale Carnegie Training, Mentor Graphics, IBM, Nike, Mortgage Success Source, The Todd Duncan Group, the State of Oregon Mortgage Lending Education Board, Plaza Home Mortgage and OnlineEd. She has more than 25 years of experience leading workshops in public speaking, leadership, customer service, sales and mortgage and regulatory compliance. She specializes in working with industry professionals to develop, write and obtain state and national approval for continuing education courses and has developed software for organizations to track and manage their training and education requirements. Her focus is always leveraging her expertise with others to develop strong networks focused on growth.

Ginger has more than 15 years of experience in the real estate, mortgage and banking industry. She is an approved course developer and instructor for the National Mortgage Licensing System (NMLS) and National Association of Mortgage Brokers (NAMB) and serves on the Oregon Association of Mortgage Professionals Board of Directors. In 2011 Ginger was awarded the "Professional Woman of the Year" award by the National Association of Professional Women for her commitment to training and education.

In addition to Go2Training Consultants, Ginger is a principal of Go2Comply and managing partner for Rehab Loan Network. Go2Comply is a compliance training and consulting firm offering the tools, training and compliance advice necessary in today's regulatory environment. Rehab Loan Network is dedicated to education and resources for renovation loans made available to borrowers wishing to take advantage of today's short sales and foreclosures market.

Ginger specializes in building networks with trainers and subject-matter experts for the development and implementation of sales, compliance and operation training programs.

To learn more about Ginger Bell and receive your complimentary report, "Networking Your Way to Success," visit www.go2trainingconsultants.com.

CHAPTER 8

Africa—The Next Frontier!

By Harry 'Tomi Davies

Over the past few years, the global economic landscape has been in turmoil as the U.S. economic crisis, Arab Spring uprising and European debt crisis have plunged the world into an economic downturn. One of the consequences of these events is that Africa—with its increasing prosperity—is fast becoming an investment target with growing interest from the U.S. and Europe in the West even as China and the Asian Tigers of the East start to consolidate their recent investments on the continent.

With regional markets expanding and the continent's vast diasporas being harnessed as sources of technical expertise and business networks, the African Development Bank (ADB) has projected a 5.8 percent economic growth rate for 2012 on the continent. Nigeria, the continent's most populous country, has been enjoying steady economic growth since 2005 with recent figures putting growth as high as 7.5 percent even with its unreliable infrastructure and security concerns.

These huge opportunities have their challenges, with the World Bank's global report on the "Ease of Doing Business Index" listing most African markets at the bottom. The 2011 report ranked Nigeria 133, Egypt 110, Kenya 109, Ghana 63 and South Africa 35 out of 183 countries with issues such as infrastructural deficiencies, corruption, currency fluctuations, inadequate human capital and political uncertainty making doing business in Africa a challenge.

While these challenges to doing business in Africa can be daunting, they are not insurmountable as the success of companies such as Google, Infosys, Caterpillar, WiPro, Airtel, IBM, Huawei, MTN, ZTE, Microsoft and a host of other global brands show. Beyond these large companies are thriving multibillion dollar industries in markets from Johannesburg to Cairo and Nairobi to Lagos. They abound in novel ventures that are frontiers of economic innovation providing companies with revenue streams derived from competitive advantages created in these emerging markets.

International companies experience difficulty operating in African markets mostly because they use inappropriate business models imported from other markets. Although they lower prices; sell smaller sizes; use low-cost labor, materials or other resources; and even manufacture products locally, their fundamental profit formulas and operating models remain unchanged. These companies end up with mediocre profits or no gains at all because the business model—ideal in the original market for which it was designed—does not take into account the peculiarities of the African market in which it is now being used.

An African saying, "Go the way that many people go for if you go alone, you will have reason to lament," speaks to the fact that most Africans believe their personal value as human beings is dependent on being known by, identified with and accepted in their extended families and native communities. This fact accounts for why individualism, a critical component of Western marketing philosophy, is an anathema to most people in Africa, which leads to failed commercial campaigns. Families and communities are a significant—if not the most important—aspect of African life, and businesses that have ignored this fact on the continent have done so to their peril.

Everything from processes to technology, organizations to institutions revolves around people. Nowhere else is the saying, "Our people are our greatest assets," more true. An embrace of human capital management as a core process driving operations opens a clear route to organizational success in Africa's markets.

CREATING ECONOMIC VALUE

Using nearly three decades of experience working with startup, growth and mature businesses in the U.S., Europe and Africa, I have developed a three-step approach that virtually guarantees success in creating economic business value in African markets.

>**Step 1: *Think Big!*** Conceive the business in a continent-wide or global context ensuring the business model is in line with the realities of the markets being targeted to generate revenues required to sustain growth.

>**Step 2: *Start Small!*** Begin operations with a limited-risk exposure strategy that tests all critical components of the business model to ensure profitability while allowing for continuous growth.

>**Step 3: *Scale Fast!*** Expand quickly to take market share by rapidly developing relationships which create opportunities that drive business operations, adjusting as you learn.

THINK BIG!

The first step to starting a business in Africa, as in any other market, is to ask critically, "In what market are we intending to play?" The answer to this question will essentially identify the industry and define the product or service the business aims to provide to its target set of customers across Africa, or within a specific country, state or county as applicable. This business-planning activity must focus on the universal or unique need potential customers have for such a product or service and should ideally be unmet or poorly so by existing competition—leaving a space in the market that can be filled for profit.

Conduct desk and market research into "who else?" to find out which competition is already doing this form of business in the target markets and what suppliers, customer segments (demo- and psycho-graphically speaking), potential new entrants, regulations and human capital exist. In addition, research each target country's legal and political systems, investment regulations and incentives, macro and micro-economic indicators and forecasted outlook.

The resulting business plan must paint a clear picture of what the business will look like when operational, including answering critical questions such as "What are the investor rules of engagement? What will the approach to corruption be? How will talent be identified and employed? What is the risk profile and how will it be managed?" While business planning is important in starting any business, it is critical when starting a business in Africa to ensure there is agreement between business sponsors and investors on expected market size and share. Finally, an innovative strategy for market entry and penetration must be developed.

One of my companies offers brand-product protection services for emerging markets. We started with an analysis of global counterfeiting and discovered that most of the top branded products in the world were being faked and sold in emerging market economies. To make matters worse, most of the governments in these markets had laws in place to fight counterfeiting but lacked the power to enforce them. In addition, counterfeiters were usually in collusion with corrupt government officials, leaving brand owners without recourse. With this knowledge, we designed a system that uses pervasively available SMS technology, cloud computing and cryptography to provide a solution that is challenging counterfeiters.

By empowering consumers to use mobile phones to establish the genuineness of a drug through free text messages, our system has no doubt saved lives. It is now protecting brands for local, national, multinational and global drug manufacturers and is earning the company decent revenues. This innovative business model based on the simple act of text messaging at no cost to the consumer found life in the Nigerian pharmaceutical industry where counterfeiting has been a perennial challenge and has led to significant market share in West and East Africa and recently India with potential for application in other industries.

START SMALL!

Thinking big is a must for capturing value in African markets, especially with a billion potential customers to cater to. However, starting big can be overwhelming and intimidating, leaving you less likely to take action even on a compelling business plan. The trick is to start small with the most basic components of the business required to make it meaningful enough to attract, service and retain customers. Do this with an unyielding focus on growth, remembering that affordability and access are the keys to successful customer value propositions in African markets. In starting small, there are three cardinal principles to keep in mind.

ONE GOAL AT A TIME!

Big Hairy Audacious Goals (BHAGs) from a vision such as "putting a man on the moon and bringing him back safely within 10 years" are accomplished only when they are broken down into smaller goals that are achieved one at a time. Start by taking small but assured steps towards your goal, making sure each step is specific, measurable, achievable and most importantly time-bound. If you can make $1,000 from a county in a week, you can most likely make one million dollars from that state in a quarter. Be sure that as you achieve success in each step you congratulate and celebrate to keep your team motivated.

EACH GOAL LEADS TO THE NEXT!

This is a simple and powerful way to overcome procrastination, maintain clarity of purpose and ensure accountability continuously. When progress is extremely slow, or extremely quick without a subsequent goal, a potentially infinite gap between current reality and the ultimate goal will set in with its attendant loss of motivation. Success and failure are both transient events on the lifetime journey of any business, and both imposters must be met with the same candor. Seeing the next goal from a distance brings the achievement of the one at hand a little closer, so keep your eye on both.

NEVER, EVER QUIT!

Keep the faith regardless of the situation. Adjust plans to reflect reality, change your approach to remove uncertainty, but the goal once set must be achieved! To borrow from a poem by an unknown author: "When things go wrong as they sometimes will, when the road you're trudging seems all up hill. When funds are low and the debts are high. Don't give up though the pace seems slow. You may succeed with another blow. And you never can tell how close you are. It may be near when it seems so far. So stick to the fight when you're hardest hit. It's when things seem worst that you must not quit."

Another of my companies started life as the first "in-story" branded comic publisher on the African continent using digital desktop publishing tools in production for a market where only foreign comics had the quality to command a premium. We started in the front room of my partner in South Africa going quite literally from door to door in search of sponsors who would buy into the idea of having their brands included as part of the storyline of our comic. Although we had mapped out the first 20 or so issues, publication each month was a ritual that involved sketching the story, inking it, including brands from whichever sponsors we managed to get an agreement from, printing (sometimes on credit) and finally distributing through an array of channels. More than once we ran out of cash and then went cap in hand to relatives and friends who grudgingly lent or gave on trust. Over the years, we went from South Africa to other African countries, South America and even Scandinavia.

SCALE FAST!

Once you have successfully started business operations and have a relatively stable revenue stream, it's time to expand! In my experience, scaling a business is usually most successful when relationship led and opportunity driven, even when you have to proactively develop both. Undoubtedly one of the brightest fronts where Africa has made tremendous progress recently and which presents a rich field of opportunity is information and communications technologies. As recently as 2008, there was only one fiber-optic cable operating at 5 percent capacity utilization that linked West Africa to the rest of the world with negligible economic impact. Today, no fewer than four multi-terabyte submarine cables link West Africans to the world and Northern, Eastern and Southern Africa are no less connected. Add to this the fact that more than 70 percent of adults in Nigeria, South Africa and Egypt and half the population in Ghana, Kenya and other African countries have become mobile phone owners within the last decade and the scale of the continent's opportunity for technology-enabled business—especially those using mobile telephones as a platform—starts to become clearer.

Growing revenues and associated profit in any business usually involves recruiting talent, building brands, instituting corporate governance and increasing investment commitments. In addition to these steps, scaling fast may include partnerships, mergers, acquisitions and even competition. In some emerging markets, a strategy that has worked well is "buy and build" where acquiring, and then growing strong local brands and businesses enables accelerated expansion. It is worth noting that as you scale, quality standards must remain a crucial consideration and be used as the key driver for success—even above competitive pricing and brand appeal—if the growth is to be sustained.

The comic company I mentioned earlier now has a footprint in more than 20 countries worldwide producing over a million copies of our comic monthly and broadcasting its animated series in more than 15 countries all within a decade. Our anti-counterfeit technology company I described started with one local contract drug manufacturer and scaled to four global, 10 multinational and 15 national pharmaceutical companies in five countries servicing more than a million users in just two years. This kind of growth was made possible because we were thinking big from the beginning.

Though I have focused on companies launching and growing in African markets, the issues addressed apply to anyone investing in most emerging markets. The challenges to succeeding in these markets could be huge, but the opportunities they present make them invaluable springboards for global success. By using the strategies and models highlighted in this chapter, businesses stand a greater chance of succeeding in them. Good luck!

About TD

Harry 'Tomi Davies (TD) is the CEO of TVC Lab, an African incubator of technology-enabled businesses. He sits on the boards of Sproxil, TechnoVision Communications, Strika Entertainment, PeoplePrime and SMS. He is a senior ICT Executive from a background of FTSE 100 level companies in the U.K., U.S. and Africa. He mentors individuals and advises organizations globally, blogs and maintains a significant network of connections, friends and followers on all major social media platforms. TD is a captivating public speaker whose personal goal is to "maximize the creation of social and economic value using digital technologies."

As Head of IT Research, he developed the first ever Marks & Spencer website. As executive consultant in the eCommerce Practice at Ernst & Young he helped AB&B HQ Zurich, Switzerland, develop and implement a 106 country e-business strategy. As strategy director at Sapient, he helped reorganize Siemens HQ Munich, Germany's wireless engineering division for UMTS and developed the U.K. government's award-winning DirectGov website for HMG Cabinet Office. As chief operating officer for Al-teq.ict, he was project director for the World Bank's integrated payroll and personnel information system six-Ministry pilot project for the federal government of Nigeria. As chief operating officer of Mobitel, he helped deploy the first 4G mobile broadband network based on Wimax 16e in Lagos, Nigeria.

A systems analysis graduate from the University of Miami, TD has numerous published articles on various topics and vast project & operations management experience; he belongs to various organizations including the Institute of Directors, the Genesis Project, One Laptop Per Child and the Project Management Institute.

CHAPTER 9

The Sales Success Code:
Three Proven Strategies for Growing Sales and Profits

By Ian Platt

How do you grow a business and its profits? How do you embrace success and empower it to flourish?

You likely want the answers to these questions—otherwise you wouldn't be reading this book. Well, in this chapter, you'll find street-smart, proven success principles for rapidly growing any venture from Solopreneur to Fortune 500.

Over the past 15 years, I've consulted, mentored, trained and coached more than 10,000 business leaders, sales VPs, sales managers and salespeople in more than 20 countries. I've also worked with such blue chip companies as Oracle, Philips Medical Systems and Shell Oil. I've run the gamut of business challenges developing proven approaches for sales growth. One of my CEO clients recently wrote a testimonial stating, "Ian's understanding of sales and marketing techniques, coupled with his keen insight and ability to quickly understand his clients' needs make him a perfect coach." Always nice to know you are helping lead positive change.

The big lesson? Growing sales and profits is definitely an art—but just as a painter needs a canvas, an easel and a brush to bring a vision to life, we all need to have on hand our own personal tools to enable success to happen. I'm going to help you develop those tools in a few pages by providing you with three proven strategic areas to focus on that are as simple as ABC (literally!).

First, let's talk a little about the mindset required for sales and business success. It takes a certain attitude to break through stagnant business systems and bring to the party the kind of out-of-the-box thinking that creates significant change and, more importantly, significant profits. It's not about propping up the "same old same-old"—it's about spurring true innovation that leads to true growth.

It doesn't matter what's been done before ... if it's not working *now*.

A UNIQUE SALES EDUCATION

I was lucky enough to be born with the kind of curious attitude that allowed me to learn early on how to "think differently" when it came to business. I was raised by a single, working-class mother near Liverpool, England, the birthplace of the Beatles. There have been many times in my sales career where the line "It's been a hard day's night, and I've been working like a dog" seemed appropriate. Money was tight for my mother—which is why I was so intent on making some. That led me to create my own business innovations and also led me to discover three important realizations about sales.

My first venture came to fruition when I was seven and brought me to Realization #1: *Focus on an activity that gets a result*. Being a little cheeky, I "borrowed" some flowers from my neighbor's garden and sold them all—and achieved my first paid sales position.

A little later, Realization #2 came to me: *Having a strong belief in a goal will help you reach it*. I wanted a bike, and my mother couldn't afford to buy me a new one. I knew, however, that many of my older neighbors had a lot of abandoned bicycles on their hands. I decided if I sincerely believed those neighbors would want to help a wide-eyed boy that they would give me their bikes for free. I approached them with that attitude—and I ended up with a lot of old bikes!

Which brought me to Realization #3: *Your skills can bring you profits*. I managed to get so many old bikes that I had many more than I needed to build my own. What to do with the extras? Well, that's where I discovered my inherent mechanical skills could create a whole new business for me. I stripped the bikes and put together "new" fully functioning two-wheelers, then spray-painted them with cool colors and added funky cow horn handlebars. Suddenly, I was the kid who was selling the coolest bikes in the neighborhood—allowing me to make enough money to move up from two wheels to four when I bought myself a car when I turned 17.

These early sales "lessons" were the start, but certainly not the finish, of what was needed for a proper sales education. I had to make sure to develop my personal potential to the maximum to really "graduate" to a sales and business growth professional helping some of the world's most successful companies realize their true sales potential. Luckily, each of those three realizations contained a vital key to that process. How? Read on...

GROWING YOUR BUSINESS BY DESIGN

My realizations contain three strategic areas we all need to focus on to improve both our personal performances and our sales results. These areas are illustrated in the diagram below.

The ABC Sale Growth Model ™

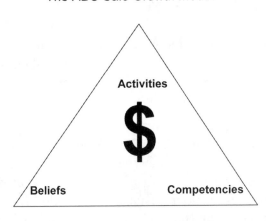

As you can see in the diagram above, these areas are activities, beliefs and competencies (competencies can be broken down into knowledge, skills and behaviors). Now, any *one* of these three strategic areas has the power to boost your team's performance when addressed correctly with the right tactics. However, you can *guarantee* yourself huge opportunities for sales growth when you systematically and consistently address *all three*.

Which is why that huge dollar sign sits in the *center* of the triangle.

ACTIVITIES

I place activities at the top of the triangle because they lead and decide all business results. Every day, no matter what your position, you engage in various business activities. The question is how meaningful and directed are those activities. Most salespeople are working *in* selling—not *on* selling. By that, I mean they're running around trying to close individual deals instead of looking at their overall approach. It's as if a chef were clutching at random ingredients, attempting to cook a dinner without actually having a recipe in hand or head. Yes, they can create a meal ... but is anyone going to actually *eat* it?

It's important to develop your own recipe for sales success—and that involves having in place meaningful activities that advance your potential for closing and giving the best value to your prospects. You can take three Action Steps to make this happen.

Action Step One: Don't rely on the leads you already have. Find a good source of qualified prospects and find a way to make contact and get on the calendar. Grow your list, and grow your profits.

Action Step Two: Make the necessary follow-up contacts with these prospects and other leads. Pursue additional calls and visits, remembering that most sales are made not on the initial contact, but during effective follow-ups.

Action Step Three: Create a system which allows you to up-sell and cross-sell to your current accounts as much as possible. One of the most powerful questions you can ask a client, if they're not buying everything they can from you, is "What do I have to do to get the rest of your business?" What do I have to do to become your "one-stop shop?"

Finally, it's fantastic to implement a concrete real-world way to push you forward. One of my clients, for example, is a former tech guy who's become the head of business development for a $20 million dollar company. And every morning, he puts 10 marbles in his pocket. Every time he undertakes a proactive sales activity, he removes one of the marbles - with the final goal in mind to have all of the marbles out of his pocket at the end of the business day. If you are going to lose your marbles at the office, this is certainly the best way to do it.

BELIEFS

The power of beliefs is phenomenal. If I were to tell you right now, that, for the next three seconds, *you must not think about a blue tree...* Well, you're almost certainly already dead in the water because you're probably thinking about *nothing* but blue trees.

What you carry forward in your mind, you also carry forward in your business. So ... what do you accept as true about your organization, its market potential, products and services, and, most importantly, your role in all this? Some beliefs will lead you forward (empowering beliefs) and some will hold you back (limiting beliefs).

Let's list some limiting beliefs:

- Our prices are too high.
- Our market is saturated.
- The competition can't be beat.
- We should play it safe and stay where we are.

Now, some empowering ones:

- There are definite areas for growth.
- There are ways to make customers more willing to buy.
- We're better at this than anyone else.
- Our pricing structure offers tremendous value for the market.

You may think that such statements aren't beliefs, but facts. However, it's not unusual to encounter someone who believes a product is too expensive—and another person at the same company who believes it has successful premium pricing, as it delivers outstanding value. Same product, same service, same pricing—and two *completely* different sets of beliefs.

I have seen it time and time again—when limiting beliefs are replaced with empowering beliefs, *growth becomes possible and achievements happen.*

That's because our mindset allows us to either maximize potential or block it.

COMPETENCIES

Competencies are the knowledge, skill and behaviors of company personnel in all positions. Traditional training usually focuses on developing people's skills, especially in the sales realm, and I highly endorse this kind of action. The higher the level of competencies, the higher the capability of your people and the more that can be accomplished. You can be pursuing the absolute right activities on a day-to-day basis—you can be going out there with the best of beliefs—but if you don't have the core skills necessary to pull all this off, you almost certainly will fail.

With that in mind, it's essential to keep developing your competencies. How do you do that? Well, when I work with clients, I ask them to pick three competencies they feel they need to work on. From there, we create a 90-day plan to develop those specific competencies. Then we review how that plan is progressing every *30* days to make sure it's yielding the desired results.

For example, let's say you want to work on your questioning skills with customers. The objective is to get them to talk more, get a better dialogue in motion and get them to reveal more about what they're looking for from someone who provides great solutions. As Stephen R. Covey wrote in his mammoth best-seller, *7 Habits of Highly Effective People*, "Seek first to understand, then to be understood."

To accomplish that understanding, you might write down, for every upcoming sales interaction, three great open questions that you will ask during your scheduled session`. These could be questions such as:

What do you look for in your ideal supplier?

If there was something you would like to change with your current supplier, what would that be?

What are some of the biggest challenges you currently face in the market?

THE BIG LESSON

I'd like to conclude by discussing something that's been a big topic of concern in the past few years—how to consistently grow sales and profits while serving our clients to the best of our abilities. Most would agree the recession has caused significant challenges for many organizations—and, unfortunately, also severely impacted their visions and strategies. Many want to know how to achieve again but can't quite get out of their old habits. They fear taking necessary new steps but also know that they have to break out of their old molds.

Well, as Albert Einstein reportedly said, "The definition of insanity is doing the same thing over and over again and expecting different results." Einstein had it right. If you bang your head against the wall and end up with a headache, you don't keep banging your head against the wall to get rid of the headache. Similarly, if you want higher growth, if you want different business results, *changes must be made*—the right changes, of course, that will make a huge positive difference to the bottom line.

So how do you get the results you want? You begin by observing The Big Lesson—You cannot do a result! Neither can anyone else who works with you or for you. The only thing you can do is concentrate on the activities that bring about those results—and redirect and coach your personnel so you bring up the level of beliefs and competencies brought to bear in the activities.

Now, let's talk about those activities. What are CEOs and board of directors asking for all the time? Results, results, results. "We're coming to the end of the quarter, we've got to report our numbers, we have to report to the owner, it's all about results," is the common refrain.

Let's remember The Big Lesson—you cannot do results. Results are all in the past— what you're focusing on is what has already happened. That means most executives are focusing the business *on things that are in the past*. You can't lead a business by concentrating on *effects*— you've got to concentrate on the *causes* of those effects.

A quick analogy. Imagine you're given a 5 Series BMW— capable of going 150 mph, in first gear, you're limited to around 40 mph. You get in this car and find that the windshield has been blacked out. You can't see ahead—all you can do is drive based on looking at the rear-view mirror. You start driving in first gear. You haven't hit anything yet. So you move up to second gear and floor it, still looking in the rear-view mirror. And you still haven't hit anything. How far can you go before there's a major disaster?

If you're only able to see in the rear-view mirror, it's only a matter of time before you wipe out—and it will be a long time before you hit your 150 "potential" on the speedometer. And that's because you're only looking at where you've been, not where you're going.

This is what most executives and sales people do, unfortunately—they get caught up in reacting to what's happened, rather than looking ahead to what's *going* to happen. You can put everything into a trend, but, by the time you do, the trend's probably already over. That's why being proactive is all important—and why the big question I ask in my sales training is, "Are sales results driving your sales strategies, or are sales strategies driving your sales results?"

The former gets you nowhere; the latter leads to growth and improvement.

So, look forward, not backward. And change things up when necessary. You're probably aware that Einstein was a pretty bright guy, even though he didn't have a lot of good hair days. So let's listen to Albert. As he also noted, "It's all relative"... so let's go ahead and make it relatively *profitable*.

About Ian

Ian Platt is a seasoned business growth specialist helping organizations rapidly increase sales and profitability. In the past 15 years, Ian has consulted, mentored, trained and coached over 10,000 business leaders, sales vice presidents, sales managers and salespeople in more than 20 countries for substantially improved business results. Following a successful sales career in the telecommunications industry from rookie salesperson to sales vice president, Ian founded a water and air treatment company that had operations in the U.K., Netherlands, France and Italy.

After selling this business, he joined Mercuri International, the world's largest sales development consultancy, where he worked internationally as a management consultant for five years. This role involved working with large, blue-chip organizations such as Oracle and Philips Medical Systems at country CEO level developing and implementing business growth solutions largely focused on guiding sales strategy and developing the sales division for increased sales and profitability.

He specializes in developing practical, usable strategies and tactics to improve business results quickly. One of his favorite questions to business leaders being, "Is your sales strategy leading and deciding your sales results, or are your sales results deciding your strategy?" Ian develops solutions for those who want strategy to lead sales and grow profitability.

Ian is an avid student of human potential, having studied with Dr. Richard Bandler, Dr. Tad James and Dr. Paul McKenna. He is a licensed master practitioner of neuro-linguistic programming by The Society of Neuro-Linguistic Programming. and certified trainer of neuro linguistics from the American Board of Neuro-Linguistic Programming and an instructor of hypnotherapy, certified and approved by the American Board of Hypnotherapy.

Ian has designed and implemented sales competency frameworks and balanced score card methodologies for companies such as Shell Oil and Philips Medical systems globally. He is a recognized expert in the successful implementation of these tools. Ian sits on advisory panels for the American Society for Training & Development (sales competency advisory panel) and the Sales and Marketing Trainers Association-SMT (sales leadership expert).

As part of consulting projects, Ian enjoys facilitating leadership and sales workshops. He is well-known for his innovative accelerated learning techniques, involving all participants in an active and fun way. He excels in taking academic ideas and transforming them into practical examples and explaining complex ideas in a straightforward way so all participants understand. Ian's consulting clients include Philips Medical Systems, Shell Oil, TACA Airlines, Mercedes, Nokia, Oracle, Hempel Paints, Standard Chartered Bank, Carrier Air Conditioning, Abn-Amro Bank and Zurich Life.

For additional tips on growing sales and profits, as well as developing sales teams to their maximum potential, visit Ian's website at www.ianplatt.com.

CHAPTER 10

The Missing Key to Success: Mental Time Travel

By Anthony Hamilton

One of the most profound ideas that has come to light recently is the notion that the mind operates as a kind of time machine. Information from both the past and the future has an impact on our present. Although a relatively new idea in the field of psychology, many people in the past have made references to this idea. Einstein has been quoted as saying, "The distinction between past, present, and future is only a stubbornly persistent illusion."[1] Philosopher Friedrich Nietzsche has said, "The future influences the present just as much as the past."[2]

I personally stumbled onto this "time travel" aspect of consciousness in my youth, when an especially vivid dream revealed parts of my future to me. When this dream turned out to be true, I began investigating how this could happen. This research eventually led me to write *Mind, Time and Power!—How to Use the Hidden Power of Your Mind to Heal Your Past, Transform Your Present and Create Your Future*." Eventually, I came to believe that our ability to receive information from the future is one of the greatest keys to success and that successful people in all walks of life have intuitively used this ability to create more successful lives. In my opinion, understanding and developing some skill in using mental time travel to visit different areas of the past and the future might just be the "missing link" people are seeking in trying to crack the success code.

Psychologist Dr. Endel Tulving, who coined the term "mental time travel," has shown that very similar processes are at work whether we are thinking of the past or the future. The term really means we have a kind of "future memory" which gives us information from the future similar to the way memory gives us information from the past. Dr. Tulving asks, "What if we have been looking at only half the picture?" "What if the thing we call "memory" works both ways, helping us both recall the past and imagine the future?"[3]

Harvard psychologist Dr. Daniel Gilbert echoes this sentiment. He asks, "What are you doing when you are doing nothing at all? The answer, it seems, is time travel." Through functional magnetic resonance imaging (fMRI), which provides the ability to look inside the brain as we are thinking scientists have learned that when we daydream, a part of our mind is actually moving about in various regions of the past or the future. He writes, "The mind can move through time in any direction and at any speed it chooses." In fact, he continues, "time travel ... is the brain's default mode."[4]

Just as pilots and astronauts learn their skills by practicing flying in flight simulators, all of us practice living in "life simulators," Dr. Gilbert writes. This time traveling ability has a valuable payoff, he says, because "Our ability to simulate future courses of action ... enables us to learn from mistakes without making them." He jokes that we don't have to actually bake a liver cake to realize it would be a mistake.[5]

Jessica Marshall writes, "There is evidence that mental time travel is such an important part of our inner lives that our brain will engage in it whenever it gets the chance."[6]

As we pay more attention to our thinking, we quickly realize Dr. Gilbert's point; much of our waking time is spent either reliving the past or sampling possible futures. We frequently are either reliving our past positive experiences or regretting in the negative experiences. Mental time travel allows us to explore in advance a seemingly infinite number of future possibilities in the hope of making better choices in the future.

Dr. Gilbert is not the only prominent scientist to write about the mind's time-traveling ability. Physicist Dr. Fred Alan Wolf has written extensively about the possibility of time travel, recently devoting an entire book to the subject. He says, "When I write, I realize that I am really time traveling, that the words I write down are not just popping into my mind, but are actually already written down in my mind, and that my mind is really a time machine just going ahead into time, bringing the words from the future, and copying them down." He continues, "Time traveling is not a fantasy of science fiction but a matter of scientific fact, and as such it has the potential for improving everyone's life. As we become more aware of just what time travel really is, the question of how and why time travel improves our lives will become more and more evident."[7]

Until we know what we are looking for, instances of mental time travel are remarkably subtle, but once we recognize them, we see how common they are. Dr. Gilbert says, "Every time you say, 'I think I'll go have lunch,' you've just thought about the future. That is just one small example of a general tendency to project ourselves forwards in time."[8]

If we want to become more successful, we must learn to recognize and make use of these subtle instances of mental time travel.

If you want to be successful, it's widely recognized that you need to set goals concerning what you wish to create, attract or achieve in order to be successful. This goal is really like a future destination you are trying to reach, and it is vital to have a clear idea or a mental picture of what you want to achieve.

As Dr. Gilbert might say, each time we think of that goal, we are mentally time traveling, and working toward the goal is where our ability to mentally time travel really enters the picture. Our ability to travel into the future to pre-experience our goal is an essential skill allowing us to better deal with difficulties and make better choices.

Just as memories can pop into our awareness at unexpected times, information from a possible future can unexpectedly pop into our conscious awareness too. Successful entrepreneurs have learned to expect these random gifts from the future and make use of them, often speaking of an idea that "just popped into my head from out of nowhere."

If our future memory is so similar to normal memory, techniques for enhancing memory of past events should be useful for enhancing our future memory as well. Indeed, we quickly discover that this is the case.

A key question to ask yourself: "Once I recognize the reality of mental time travel, how can I use this skill to increase my chances of achieving my goals?" Just as memory can be enhanced and strengthened by keeping a written record of our activities, having a journal containing a series of written goals increases our ability to recognize, organize and utilize this previously unseen information from the future.

Realizing that our future memory can be improved and understanding the need for a journal to keep track of our good ideas, the question becomes, "What exactly should I write in my 'success journal'?"

Having used such a journal for several decades and having taught many others to do the same, I believe we need to begin recording several categories of ideas. Here's a plan of action you can follow to develop your "mental time machine" muscles.

MENTAL MUSCLE BUILDING

Step 1: Write a List of "Past Successes"
Examples of past successful events might include graduating from high school or college; asking your partner to marry you and receiving a positive response; winning a contest; reaching a desired goal; learning to swim; getting rid of some unwanted habit; learning a foreign language. The size of the success is not as important as that you *feel successful* when thinking about it.

Step 2: Read Your "Past Successes List" Once Each Day
As you read, notice that the feeling of success instantly returns to your body as positive energy from the past floods into the present and reminds you how successful you already are. This exercise has an immediate, positive impact on your self-image and your self esteem. It is a great key to confidence and personal power. It helps build a success mindset, one of the most important attitudes you can develop.

Step 3: Write a "Benefits List" for Your Goal
In addition to a written description of your goal, your success journal should also include a "Benefits List," which details all the positive things you anticipate enjoying when you reach your goal. How will reaching this goal benefit you in each area of your life? How will it improve your life financially, socially, and spiritually? What will it mean to your ability to support your family, your community and your friends? How

will it add to your relationships? How will achieving this goal stretch you to use all of your mental, emotional and educational resources, so you become the best person you are capable of becoming? Just as your "Past Successes List" enables you to use the past as a source of positive energy and emotion, this "Benefits List" gives you a tool for bringing the positive energy of the future into your present.

Step 4: Hold the Success Feelings in Your Body
As You Imagine Reaching Your Goal
Learning to combine success feelings from the past with the positive energy from anticipated benefits of your goal builds a feeling of positive expectation and motivation, key ingredients in reaching your goal.

This practice is very powerful. Your past successes list and your benefits list are extremely valuable tools and should be an integral part of your success journal. Reading these two lists on a daily basis will increase your ability to use both your past memory and your future memory to enhance your present and move you into the future you desire.

VISUALIZATION EXERCISE

As our "Past Successes" list allows us to pull success energy from the past, our "Benefits List" enables us to use our future memory to bring in valuable, motivating information from the future. As Fred Alan Wolf might say, this is using our ability to mentally time travel in a very practical and powerful way to improve our lives now. It is almost a cliché to say that once we have a goal we need to imagine we are already enjoying its benefits in order for the goal to have any real power to motivate us.

One tangible benefit of making and reading these lists is that it enables us to exercise our visual imagination in a practical way. Visualization, which many have written about at length, can be enhanced to an almost unbelievable degree when we exercise it regularly. Having lists of goals, past successes, and the benefits of reaching our goals will give us a whole series of possible future events and powerful past events we can explore using this aspect of our imaginations.

Combining our visual imaginations with our ability to mentally time travel creates a powerful combination of skills that empowers us to make great progress in our quest to crack the success code.

NOTES

1. "Collected Quotes from Albert Einstein," accessed at http://rescomp.stanford. edu/~cheshire/EinsteinQuotes.html/.

2. *Brainy Quote* website, "Future Quotes," accessed at http://www.brainyquote.com/ quotes/keywords/future_2.html#ixzz1jxbOvzZl/.

3. George Musser, "Time on the Brain: How You Are Always Living in the Past and Other Quirks of Perception," Scientific American, Sept. 15, 2011.

4. Daniel Gilbert, "Time Travel in the Brain," Time Magazine, Jan. 29, 2007.

5. Gilbert, "Time Travel."

6. Jessica Marshall, "Future Recall: Your Mind Can Slip Through Time," New Scientist, issue 2596, March 24, 2007, accessed from http://www.newscientist.com/ article/mg19325961.400-future-recall-your-mind-can-slip-through-time.html/.

7. Fred Wolf,; quote from interview concerning article, "The Yoga of Time Travel," accessed from http://www.aum.ro/articole/articole/the-yoga-of-time-travel-how-the-mind-can-defeat-time.html/.

8. Marshall, "Future Recall."

About Anthony

Anthony Hamilton is a former professor of communication at Cap-ilano University in North Vancouver, Canada, and a best-selling author. His book, *Mind, Time and Power!—Using the Hidden Power of Your Mind to Heal Your Past, Transform Your Present and Create Your Future,* has transformed lives in several countries.

Hamilton has been called a "master of visualization" for his ability to lead people through simple exercises in "mental time travel," which can create radical shifts in how they perceive their pasts and futures. A certified Law of Attraction trainer, Hamilton is a business training consultant and popular speaker. His program, "The Inner Game of Success" has been used by some of the largest and most successful companies in Canada and the U. S.

To learn more about Anthony Hamilton and receive a free 10-part e-course, "Master the Law of Attraction," visit his website: www.anthonyhamilton.org.

CHAPTER 11

How Entrepreneurs Can Legally "Print Money"

By Carol Parks

Recently, the owner of an online business contracted with me to transform its core product's underperforming promo into one that would go gangbusters for them.

It wasn't hard to see why the business wasn't generating millions. So I applied the following principles and dramatically altered the course of that business.

What if *you* could add a zero to last year's profits without working any harder?

Imagine …

You send out 10 letters and get three recipients to buy your product or service. What happens if you send out 100? Or 1,000, or 10,000?

Unlike sales calls and "door knocking," your letter suffers from no time constraints, personal fatigue or gasoline prices.

Whenever I see these kinds of response rates, I ask myself, *"What if I could add a zero to it?"*

Without advertising copy—whether that copy is in print, on the Internet, displayed through social media marketing, or other methods—your prospect may not even know your product or service exists. What it can do for her. How it will make his life easier. Yet most entrepreneurs and business owners make this common costly advertising mistake.

DO *YOU* MAKE THIS EXPENSIVE ADVERTISING BLUNDER?

Have you heard the story about the New York retailer who once said that 50 percent of his advertising worked? Trouble was … he had no idea *which* 50 percent worked.

Do you make that mistake?

If you stick to what's known as direct-response advertising, you need never repeat his wasteful mistake, because direct-response advertising leaves a trail.

You see, *the sole purpose of direct-response advertising is to prompt your prospect to take some kind of specific action NOW*—buy something, request information, or take some other action.

Done the right way, direct-response advertising is *completely* measurable, so you always know how well your ad worked. You can even test one variation against another to see which performed better. And the concept can apply to many types of media.

Institutional advertising, also called image advertising, leaves you guessing. Its purpose is to build the company's image and entertain, but it is not accountable or measurable. There's no way to tell how well it's working.

Unfortunately, very few advertising agencies specialize in direct response copywriting; they typically seek creative awards, not responses. The only award you should give a hoot about is your customers handing you cold, hard cash. Obviously I recommend you steer clear of the typical agencies.

Too many entrepreneurs throw their precious money down a rat hole trying to imitate large corporations that can "afford" to throw money around. Don't fall into that trap—unless you don't care about your profits or return on investment.

HOW TO SELL ANYTHING—TO REAL PEOPLE

Before you write your first ad, you need to understand *why* people buy.

You'll be hard pressed to find *anyone* who wants to be "sold." People buy things for their own reasons … emotional reasons, not rational ones. Their heart leads their head. They only become rational when trying to justify their emotional decisions later. This is also true in business-to-business selling.

Buying makes a person *feel in control*. Being sold never does!

When you write copy, your goal is to help your prospect solve a problem or achieve a goal. To do that, utilize the following tips.

Use Emotions that Prompt Buying Decisions

Fear and greed are the most-cited buying emotions, but you'll need to appeal to other feelings as well in order to write copy that sells. Here are seven very common emotions:

- Fear
- Greed
- Pride
- Lust
- Envy
- Laziness
- Vanity

Go to my website, www.YourSalesGenerator.com for a list of *48* buying emotions to consider.

If You Don't Know Who Your Prospect Is, You Won't Know What to Say

To write sales copy that sells, you **must** know your audience. After all, if you write a personal letter with no intended recipient, how can you possibly know what to say? You should know these six things about your prospects before you begin writing.

- Age, gender, income: Where do they live—city/suburb, house/apartment, price?
- Hobbies, interests: What keeps them up at night?

- Core beliefs: What are their desires, dreams, feelings?
- Fears: What scares them?
- Passions: Who are they mad at? What do they secretly desire?
- Decision-making trends: Is there a bias to how they make decisions?

Make It Personal

Always visualize ONE person in your mind ... and tape a picture of that person to your computer. Write to that person, as if you're writing to your Uncle Ed. Your prospects will only respond to something that comes across as if it was written *just for them.*

Tell your prospects what your product or service will do for them. Make a promise. Help the prospects "see" themselves experiencing the benefits of your product.

Are you selling a weight-loss product? Help your prospect see himself as slim and trim, with six-pack abs and ladies to match. Lead him with ideas and images. Show him how your product will remove his fear or fulfill his desires.

Make It Conversational

Good copywriting is not the kind of writing your high school or college English teacher taught you. It's not formal or "proper."

Make your copywriting as close to **spoken** English as possible. Of course you lack physical intimacy with your prospects, but you should write like you're sitting at the kitchen table talking with them over coffee.

When you want to emphasize a point, you can use *italics*, <u>underlining</u>, **bold,** or CAPS.

You can pause ...

But always, your copy needs a conversational tone, with a certain exuberance and energy. The best way to convey energy is to personally get excited about your product's great qualities—as uncovered during your research.

If you're writing copy for your own business, you must decide which voice to use—serious, light, dramatic, hyperbolic, or whatever. Your natural voice is your best choice. When you hire a professional copy-writer, you'll want them to write in *your* voice, just as if it's you speaking.

THE MOST IMPORTANT FIVE TO 17 WORDS IN YOUR COPY

You have *five seconds or less* to grab a prospect's attention and sweep her into your copy...

These five to 17 words will make or break your sales letter, ad or email. (Email subject lines use the same principles.)

Many writers spend as much time creating a single headline as they do writing the entire rest of the sales package.

Why the effort? Simple ... *an unread ad is a failed one.*

The legendary David Ogilvy dubbed the headline *the most important part of the sales letter.*

Five times as many people read your headline as read the body copy. So you'd be justified spending 80 percent of your time on the headline. Your headline needs to answer the following:

- Who cares ...?
- So what ...?
- What's in it for me? (WIIFM—everyone's favorite radio station).
- Why are you bothering me?

A tall order, for sure.

Incidentally, *never ever* use your business name as a headline. *Never* violate this rule. And never mislead or trick your prospect. It will cost you their trust forever.

Seven of the most effective headlines in the history of advertising:

- **They laughed when I sat down at the piano—but when I started to play ...!**
- **Do you make these mistakes in English?**
- **Can you spot these 10 decorating sins?**
- **The Lazy Man's Way to Riches**

- **When Doctors "Feel Rotten" This is What They Do**
- **What Never ... Ever to Eat on an Airplane**
- **Bills It's Okay to Pay Late**

For a list of the *one hundred* best advertising headlines of all time, visit my website at www.YourSalesGenerator.com.

Now, for the next step ...

"HOOK" YOUR PROSPECT

Once you have your prospect's attention, keep it! Maintain his interest, so he keeps reading.

Deliver the big promise and the big idea of your promo *now*.

Show her how your product or service will make her richer, smarter, sexier, thinner, more powerful. ...

The "lead" immediately follows the headline and should compel the prospect to keep turning pages or scrolling down. ... What *BIG* benefit is different from all other promises?

For example, what's the big promise of exercise equipment? To be viewed as an attractive powerful person—a person of influence.

Your big promise must tap his deepest psychological nerve. Scratch below the surface to get to his core feelings, beliefs and desires.

"Lead" into your promise by:
- Painting a picture in her mind
- Debunking a popular myth
- Spouting off facts or figures
- Naming a common enemy

But never forget ...

Your prospect isn't buying the "thing"—he's buying the PROMISE ... whether it's power, privileged knowledge or whatever. Be sure your big promise connects with her core beliefs, feelings and desires (however complex they are).

By the time your prospects finish reading your lead, they should be mentally engaged in your copy. Even intellectually curious.

THEN DO THE "HARD SELLING"

Now you've got to make your case for your product or service ... prove it can do what you say it will. Demonstrate the many ways it can improve your prospect's life in this "proof" part of your letter.

Establish credibility using articles, reliable research and testimonials. Prove you can back up what you say... keeping with your big promise and your prospect's core beliefs, feelings and desires, of course.

So you've captured their attention, led them into your copy, written the body (proof)... and then they order, right?

Not quite.

YOU MUST FIRST SOLIDIFY THEIR BUYING DECISION

You need the written equivalent of looking your prospect straight in the eye and asking for money!

This isn't a place to be clever or cute. These four steps will lead him to open his wallet.

1. Remind him of all the wonderful benefits you've already discussed. Or throw in extras to sweeten the deal.

2. Make her an offer. Tell her what she's getting, plain and clear. If it's a kettlebell for $19.95, say it's a kettlebell for $19.95.

3. Once you reveal the price, prove to your prospects that he has nothing to lose by trying your product or service—and that his money will be refunded if he is displeased. This is your 100 percent, money-back guarantee, a critical risk reversal strategy.

4. Toss in a strong P. S. to throw your prospect over the top. Introduce a surprise benefit, show urgency, offer a special bonus he can keep even if he cancels. The P.S. is one of the most-read parts of promotions ... often read just after the headline but before the rest of the letter—when the reader turns the letter over to see who it's from.

Then finally, we get to the actual device that turns your prospect into a *buyer.*

WHAT YOUR ORDER DEVICE ABSOLUTELY *MUST* DO

To turn your prospects into actual buyers, you need to *remind* them of the big promise, re-stimulate their original desires … and keep them from that age-old malady—buyer's remorse.

Your order device should therefore restate the benefits, money-back guarantee and special bonus (if applicable).

It should also provide a place for all information relevant to selecting options, providing contact info, and making a payment.

THIS IS A SUBHEAD … SPRINKLE MANY OF THEM THROUGHOUT YOUR COPY

"Dust" your copy with these mini-headlines.

They break large chunks of copy into smaller segments, make it easier to read, and appeal to skimmers.

A serious prospect will read your letter from start to finish, even if it's 15 pages long. A skimmer will start by reading the subheads, and may then read the whole thing. Some people will order after reading just the high points.

Subheads should connect to the main benefit of your package. They may even power your copy enough to do the hard selling for you.

Headline ideas that were good but not quite strong enough to open your ad can be useful subheads.

YOUR AD AS A ROMANCING DEVICE

In a very real sense, your sales letter must woo your prospect. You can "stalk" for awhile, but there's an appropriate time to step back in order to rebuild interest.

Your prospect may become defensive once he senses you're about to ask for money. Now you surprise him by doing the unexpected… retreat a few steps, by using these types of phrases:

- By the way, there's one thing I almost forgot to tell you …
- Oh wait! I almost forgot …
- Before we finish, let me say this …

This is an advanced copywriting technique that may take some practice to do well, but is worth implementing because it lowers your prospect's sales resistance just when they think you're about to ask for money. After this "false close," you move to your real close.

OK, TIME TO IMPLEMENT

Now that you know *how* to write your sales promotions, it's time to do it. Put these strategies into practice in your business.

Oh, one more thing …

Typically a prospect who's never heard of you or your business needs multiple "touches" before they'll part with their hard-earned money.

Always plan an entire campaign with multiple "touches." Some sequences are as long as nine to 13 different pieces. Each touch should earn you higher sales and bigger paychecks. A combination of mailed letters, postcards, email, "lumpy" mail, and other strategies produces the best results.

This allows your prospects to get to know you. Always use a list with proven responsiveness for your type of product or service, too.

Once you have a proven winner (called a "control"): Rinse, repeat and prosper.

About Carol

Carol Parks, known as "The Sales Generator,"™ is an expert direct-response copywriter and marketing strategist. She is a sought-after ally to business owners and marketers who want to explode their sales through smart marketing strategies and extraordinary word-crafting—letting you legally reach into the wallets of your clients.

Carol has written extensively for some of the Internet's largest Business to Consumer consumer (B2C) marketers in alternative and natural health products, the fitness industry, and tennis, plus various business to business (B2B) services.

She advocates what some call *outrageous advertising*—lumpy mailing tactics that are impossible to ignore, ensuring a mailed promo gets opened. Carol is also available to speak on a variety of marketing, copywriting and social media topics to groups or associations, and her vast teaching expertise makes her a superb coach, trainer and mentor for up-and-coming copywriters and groups of in-house copywriters.

Carol brings a breadth of life experiences and deep understanding of human psychology (buying triggers) to her business. She has been married to her husband, Mark, for 35 years, and ushered her five children through 28 years of home education, all the while selling insurance, real estate, and educational services in the trenches, eyeball-to-eyeball.

To learn more about Carol Parks, "The Sales Generator™" and how you can receive her FREE Special Reports, visit her website at www.YourSalesGenerator.com or www.CarolParksCopywriting.com.

She may be contacted through her website, or at 248-219-0992.

CHAPTER 12

Personal Growth and Cracking the Success Code

By Sahar Aref

Always bear in mind that your own resolution to succeed
is more important than any other one thing.
~ Abraham Lincoln

After many years of being just a mother and a housewife, I decided to take the challenge of creating a career for myself and to resume my old track toward success. To accomplish that goal, I had to deal with different social challenges, but most of all, I had to deal with my personal points of weakness. For me, cracking the success code has been like solving a big puzzle; it takes time but if you are persistent you can fix all the pieces and create something beautiful. All you need is to make the decision to start.

The first social challenge I had to meet was to squeeze the time I was giving to my husband and my children after they had been accustomed to getting all my attention. My children had, indirectly, given me the alarm that I had gone too far in neglecting my own wishes. They slapped my dormant passion for success by starting to take me for granted and developing some selfish attitudes.

I also felt pressured when people said to me words like, "Today, you can be highly esteemed if you draw from your husband's success and status; after all, your assistance has brought him such success and status. But to seek, after all these years, your personal success through a career means you will be demoted to start-point." This true statement was not only difficult for me to hear but also to feel and to live.

A third challenge was related to the many contradictions present in Egyptian society. Actually, one of those contradictions is the reason I had become a housewife in first place: Many young Egyptian middle-class mothers have to accept being housewives because they would have to pay much more than they earned working outside the home to provide quality care for their families. Although the society admires and praises working women, it doesn't offer true solutions for working mothers. Consequently, committed housewives cannot find good part-time jobs or take-home tasks to help them start careers in the fields they prefer. In that respect, they are totally on their own: They have to create their careers by themselves.

An ordeal and additional social responsibility happened to me during my journey toward success: my younger sister passed away in a car accident. She and our mother had been living together and were very close. Since my sister's death, my responsibility toward my mother has grown. Being her only daughter now, I have to support her spiritually, emotionally and in many other ways so she can survive the trauma. I assisted her until she started a small charity organization in the name of my sister. Today, I still assist her but to a lesser point: She has found hope and energy in working for the sake of my sister.

However, the greatest challenge I faced was to start from where I was—at a point of uncertainty and lack of knowledge—to follow the path of personal growth till I reached a real point of success. My fears, worries and doubts left me with little power to step outside my comfort zone. My perfectionist attitudes had caused procrastination to get hold of me. My self-confidence had reached its lowest, so, I dared not dream big dreams. I had no concrete goals, no planning habits, not even a clear vision about the career that would suit me best. As a child, I always had a future-self-image of an important, confident and successful person. Even that once bright self-image had grown dim.

I decided to start with anything available for me, so I started by studying free Arabic/English translation courses. I studied translation for two years during which I did jobs for friends of friends. My self-confidence started to increase, and small successes aroused my appetite for bigger ones. Translating the writings and the talks of important people made me yearn to be among those important people; so, I decided to go back to graduate school.

I had been studying for my Master's degree when I gave birth to my second child. Unfortunately, I had to drop my studies. But because graduate studies promised more knowledge, status and better opportunities I became motivated to return. I tried to resume in the same college where I had dropped but failed to do so. I made other attempts to be admitted to other community universities and failed there too. Community universities that charge smaller fees were becoming very crowded, competitive, and a bit unfriendly to older graduates. I decided to go to an international university and to work hard in order to get a fellowship and a fee waiver.

Fellowships are awarded to high-caliber students who are usually young, active, fresh graduates with an international educational background. I am not any of that; yet I decided to go for it. I ended up winning but not before applying and failing three times. Studying for my master's degree in an international university has been the key for unending opportunities. I came across a treasure of books written by personal growth and success experts of today.

I decided to follow the advice I found in such valuable books. So, I refreshed my childhood self-image; I reviewed harmful beliefs or attitudes to get rid of them; and I began to define my goals and the plans that would enable me to reach there and started implementing different strategies. I foung my edge in a strategy similar to that of decision-making, namely, the use of intention.

The first time I try to use intention was in my final M.A. semester. Before that, two semesters had gone by with me finding excuses such as writing the first part of the thesis, preparing for the fieldwork, etc. It was the first time for me to tackle a large amount of first-hand data gathering; I felt uneasy and scared because of the amount of work needed. So, I became caught up by fears, doubts and procrastination. Getting to know about the use of intention has been a happy incident for me, and the results are great.

I have been repeatedly told by professors, colleagues and friends that finishing an M.A. thesis is not at all difficult and that all I need is to "do it." Because I really wanted to finish, I tried that new strategy of having my intention work for me. So, I made a sincere intention to get my degree that same semester. This simply means that I am honestly ready to do all the work needed to finish the thesis: the fieldwork, the rest of the writing, and everything needed to make the thesis ready for submission on time.

The outcome is that in a semester's time, all the work was done with excellence, all the problems that had unexpectedly sprung up were settled, and the submission of the thesis took place on time. I graduated the same semester. That was a moment of outstanding success, a moment when I felt a rush of energy going through my veins. Ever since, whenever I want to get things achieved, I use the intention strategy.

I then, took different jobs: research assistant, tutor, facilitator and others. However, I have never felt as successful and fulfilled as I did when I held a copy of my first published book. At that moment, I realized that writing and communicating my thoughts, feelings, and experience to you, Reader, is what I love to do best. However, I knew I had completely cracked the success code when I started applying the strategy of learning from true experts and of dealing with the best people in my field.

Dear Reader, as you can see, I managed to change my situation from one point to its opposite: from being just a housewife, to creating success for myself and identifying my point of excellence. Today, I am working on fulfilling my potential.

If I have managed to achieve all this, you can certainly do the same. You can positively do better.

Any goal you want to achieve you *can* achieve. Just follow the strategy I have described to you.

If you have a goal in mind, just go for it. If you are not sure about your goal, pick any suitable goal that could lead to success and get started. As you move closer to success, you will acquire a clearer vision and you will be able to choose the right goals.

Get ready to crack the success code by following the strategy I have described here. The following strategy has worked very well for me; it will definitely work for you too. You may call it a resolution to success.

Keep Your Self-Image As Best As You Can

What is the common thing between a mirror and the universe? What is the difference? Both a mirror and the universe neutrally give back to every human being a reproduction of that human being's reality. The difference is that a mirror gives you a reflection of your outer figure while the universe gives you back a manifestation of what you think and believe about yourself—what you are, what you will be and what you are worthy of. So, if you want to be successful in something, you need to present to the universe the self-image you wish to see realized, not the other one. Outline an extremely successful version of you in front of your mind's eye or even in a sketch. Just repeat and confirm, "This is me."

Fall in Love with Your Goal
Have you ever been in love? Remember those feelings of being thrilled and excited by love? The best thing you can do to reach your goal is to relive such feelings while putting your goal in place of the beloved. In this way, you can have the passion and the patience you need to move from the point (B) where you stand to the point (A) where your goal is. If you are in love with your goal, you will work for it no matter what; you will implement the daily steps of your plan—defying procrastination and fear. Besides, when you are in love, you are already out of your comfort zone. When you achieve your present goal, remember to fall in love with your next one.

Have a Realistic Plan
What makes your dreams different than those of a daydreamer is the fact that you already have, or are in the process of having, a plan; while a daydreamer doesn't think of one. In order to put together a working plan, you must do your homework and educate yourself well. Study everything about your goal and the different methods to achieve it. Gather all information possible—particularly, how successful people have become so.

Learn from the Best
To make your path shorter and easier, just find out who are the true experts, the top people of your field and learn from them. Look at what they do and follow their footsteps. Always learn from true experts and deal with the best.

Intend to Be Successful

Are you *really* ready to *do* whatever it takes to achieve your goal? The use of intention is a highly effective method to achieve your goal. All you need is to sincerely repeat the following statement between you and yourself: "I will achieve that goal of mine no matter what. I am honestly ready to do all the work. I am ready to face all the problems that may happen and to find solutions for them. In short, I am true to my goal and I am ready to do whatever it takes me to reach it." It is as simple as that.

Make the Decision to Start

The most difficult part in any new project, career, job, etc., is the beginning part. When you want to start something new and you believe it is worthwhile, don't hesitate in making the decision to start. If your decision ever turns out to be wrong, never regret it and remember that for every failure you go through, a proportionate step is erected in the stairway that will make you reach success.

About Sahar

Sahar Aref is an Egyptian social researcher, translator and writer. She is a Ph.D. candidate; her dissertation talks about the Salafi trends in Egypt and the impact of their becoming considerable political players on society, particularly on women.

Sahar Aref is interested in studying personal growth from Western and Islamic perspectives and topics concerning Islam and women. She published her first book in Arabic in 2007. It is a short research study that draws from and combines Western and Islamic personal growth principles.

She publishes Arabic articles on her homepage: www.sahararef.net and will soon publish her first book in English. It describes her personal experiences in overcoming hardliner attitudes about women in Islam.

Sahar Aref is a wife and a mother of a son and two daughters.

She earned her Master's degree at The American University in Cairo, in sociology/anthropology, has studied Arabic/English translation at The American University in Cairo, and earned her B.A. in English and comparative literature at Girls' Colleges, Riyadh, K.S.A.

CHAPTER 13

Perform Like a Black Belt Champion: Develop the Right Mindset, Skill Set and Take Action

By Tommy Lee

The clock was ticking. The coach was yelling from the sidelines. You could see the sweat building on both competitors' foreheads, and you could almost feel their hearts pounding. Everyone watching could hear a man, clearly the father, simply shouting, "Go son."

The coach was intently focused … so focused that you could tell he was unaware of the number of people in the crowd who were cheering for the boys. After all, it was the national championship match with more than 2,000 young athletes nationwide. And the national championship gold medal match was between Alex and his younger brother, Matt. Both from the same martial arts school and from the same family.

Everyone thought Alex had a competitive advantage over Matt since he had earned his black belt one year before, and usually in these types of competitive matches, that makes a difference. Both boys had performed well; however Alex was a few points down at the end of round one. His coach gave Alex pointers on how to relax, how to focus on the way Matt leaves his body open and specifically how to score.

Alex went back out for the second round but was clearly not focused. He was not performing to his potential. He wasn't doing anything the coach had told him, so it was almost as if he had mentality given up. His coach was yelling advice to him with a loud yet caring level of intensity. But Alex didn't hear him. What made it even more difficult for Alex to focus was the fact that the audience was cheering for his brother; they were surprised that Matt was winning.

One minute into the second round Alex was still behind. There was a break in the match, so both fighters went to their coach. As Alex walked toward his coach, his back was slumped slightly, his arms dangling and his hollow eyes met the eyes of his coach. The coach reached out, and patted Alex on the back. He could tell that Alex's confidence had faded with this unexpected score and the crowd cheering for his brother. His coach could feel that Alex had lost the fire in his belly. Alex was wearing his emotions on his sleeve, and everyone could see and feel his dismay, the discouragement and his own disappointment.

His coach kept pushing him, encouraging him and attempting to pump him up. But Alex was in such an unfocused mental state that he hadn't even heard his coach's advice. Alex's glazed eyes turned from his coach as he walked back onto the mat for the final minute of the match.

Once again, the match unexpectedly stalled. There were only fifteen seconds left in this championship, and Alex was still behind. Coach wasn't sure if Alex simply hadn't heard him with all the noise in the arena. Then he looked into Alex's eyes, and he could see that Alex had stopped trying. Coach roared, "You need two points in five seconds." Then, at that moment, the coach grabbed him by the shoulders, shook him slightly and said, "Think about this. If your little brother wins, you will hear about it for the rest of your life. The effort and focus you put forth right now will last 15 seconds; however the result will last forever. Your lifetime memory will be of these next 15 seconds. If you try your best you will not regret the outcome, if you don't, you will never be able to change what happens."

Coach would never normally say anything like this, but somehow, he knew that Alex needed a pattern interrupt … something to rattle his brain and get him to refocus with the passion and fervor of a champion. It was as if the coach's words had awakened Alex. He went out and scored a point to the body and an additional two points to the head in less than five seconds. The crowd went crazy cheering. The roar was intense. Alex, in those 15 seconds, was able to win the championship and learn something that would last the rest of his life.

Alex's story illustrates that having a particular skill set isn't always enough to achieve success. Winners need the proper mindset and a strong coach to overcome inevitable and often unforeseen challenges that can threaten their potential. Alex not only benefited from his coach's advice and won the national championship, he also will use these principles throughout the rest of his life.

That day, the coach on the sidelines was me. It's my job to know how to change the mindset of those I coach. To help each recognize and overcome obstacles and to identify and maximize opportunities. I do this for fighters in the ring, and I do this for fighters in their business. Sometimes it takes a coach to determine the best strategy to use to ensure victory.

A COACH'S EAGLE-EYE PERSPECTIVE

In class, I use a short story when teaching my students this principle. I share that the hunter in the forest can only see what's directly around him but can't see everything fully surrounding him like as can the eagle circling above. It is the same with business owners. They usually know what to do and how to do it, they see what's in front of them, but it takes the right coach to share a new perspective and help guide the business owner in a winning strategy and direction.

The first role of an excellent coach is to get the athlete, or business owner, into the right mindset.

In business, a coach is critical because most business owners are not held accountable to anyone and they don't always have the consistent driving push to get to the next level. That's the role a coach and master-mind group can take. Look at franchises, they help an owner be more successful because they provide a system, continued training and the accountability factor that is critical. Franchises measure the performance daily, monthly, quarterly and then mentor on how to increase the overall performance.

For an entrepreneur, not having accountability can be the downfall of a business. To get your business to the next level, you must have a business coach. Think about it, every athletic team and professional athlete has a coach. Your coach can help you maintain the accountability, assist you in achieving the next level of training and most importantly, help you maintain the right mindset.

I knew that when Alex began the match, he had the right mindset. Then something happened. Just like a business owner whose mindset can be shifted as a result of a lost deal, financial blow, personal situation or even a temporary state of complacency. This mental shift often directly results in losing the fire in the belly, which causes a business owner to back off.

It wasn't that Alex couldn't do it. It was merely that his mindset was not in the right place. Have you been to a seminar, got all fired up, felt great, were motivated, had a positive mindset and then when you got home you allowed life to get in the way and you chose to do nothing? You need a coach, just like Alex needed a coach. It's not what you learn that counts, it's what you apply. Having a solid black belt mindset means you do what's expected without being told and when no one is watching.

A BLACK BELT MINDSET

The right mindset means practicing your skills until they become second nature with quality and without being told. In martial arts class, we always say "repetition is the mother of skill." It takes thousands of repetitions for the body to recognize the skill and make it reactive. Remember, it's not practice makes perfect, it's practice makes permanent. If you practice your technique the wrong way, you will get better at doing it wrong. If you practice it correctly you will get better at doing it right. Doing it right will have a positive impact on your bottom line.

The right mindset also means that you follow up with what you promised. The first sale is easy because anyone can get lucky once and win a sale, but servicing that client and providing what you promised is key to getting another order.

It also takes skill to keep a business on track. A business is like a rocket going to the moon, it's off course 99 percent of the time and needs statistics and coaching to stay on track. Even if you get a little off track, the longer it takes to realize or fix, the longer it will take to get back on the right path. An athlete practices every day while monitoring and honing technique for better performance. When this is done in business, the business performance will be better as well.

I have explained the mindset and skill set that is required to be a black belt, but I'd like to share with you what a black belt stands for and how you become a Black Belt Business Performer.

When someone comes into the studio to become a black belt, she or he must first learn respect. In martial arts, we bow to show respect, and this foundation is taught from day one. Do you have respect for yourself, your business and your clients? It is the foundation for you, just as it is in martial arts.

Next a student learns each individual movement and how to perform them correctly. Then it's just a matter of putting those movements together to perform the graceful martial art forms, combinations and self-defense techniques.

Business owners often learn how to perform a skill, but just as in martial arts, it's not just about learning to perform an individual skill, it takes practice to learn the proper way to combine those skills to achieve the desired outcome. In business, most people spend 90 percent of their time selling and 10 percent of time training or practicing. On the other hand, most athletes spend 90 percent of their time training and 10 percent of their time performing.

Let's take blocking a punch and compare it to overcoming an objection in sales. It's not just OK to know the block or the way to overcome the objection. You must know how to move and be able to apply the technique regardless of the situation or condition. Can we block the punch even if the opponent is faster and stronger? Is it possible to block it if it's dark outside? Can you overcome the objection when it just pops up or if it's delivered in a manner you haven't heard or seen before? Each of these factors matter, and knowing just one answer (skill) doesn't always work.

The next step is to practice the skills. Perform different reaction drills so the skills become instinctive. When training, we have some drills that pit two or three athletes against one. The one athlete clearly will not win, but he or she becomes more emotionally and directionally focused. Why do this? If a fighter is paired with one person, then the skills and performance will only rise to a specific point. When the athlete trains with multiple fighters, and then two are taken away it will seem much easier to fight only one.

In business, it is important to become reactionary and instinctive as well. It is important that you learn familiar objections and get to a reactive point so that each move becomes automatic.

If you are selling and there is an objection where you have to think about the answer before you give it to your prospect, the prospect will likely not believe your answer. On the other hand, if you are trained to a point so that you are prepared for each potential objection, then your reaction becomes part of you and there will never be a situation where your prospect will doubt your answer. Remember, an athlete can only win if the reaction is inherent and innate. If a fighter is going to strike you with his right hand, his left shoulder must move back first. If you know this, you see the signal of what will be done before it's even performed and you have a better chance to counter. In business, when you can recognize things before they happen, you are in a prime position to WIN.

Athletes don't need 1,000 moves, they need just a few they can perform really well. I teach my students to study their opponent to find the right moves. In business, you need to study your competition. If you know their moves inside and out, then you will be able to find one move you can counter; hone and use that move as your competitive advantage to win consistently.

Most businesses are good at one or two of the three black belt performance keys, but very few have all of them. You may have the right mindset and take action, but do you have the right skill set? Or you have the right skill set but know you need to take more action and work on your mindset.

Excellence mastered, staying focused and sharp requires you to surround yourself with the right people. Who do you spend your time with? Are you in a mastermind group, where you have the opportunity to brainstorm with like-minded Black Belt Business Performers to help you improve your game? Do you have the right coach?

Strive to be like Alex, who won the championship because:

- He had the right mindset—he had to believe in himself, even though the pressure and stakes were high.
- He had the right skill set—he had trained for years on a consistent basis so once his mindset was focused, his skill set was easily accessed.

- He took action. Once his mindset was focused, and he lost all fear of failing or getting hurt, he mentally committed to take action and win.

Goals don't fail, only the implementation of goals can fail. We each have 24 hours every day; what distinguishes each of us is how we use them, and how we use our resources.

Whether you achieve your goals or not is solely up to you. No one can do it for you. There are no promises or guarantees of what level of success you will or will not have. However, if you apply the Keys to Black Belt Excellence I have shared in this chapter, you will have a better chance of exceeding your goals. You CAN do it, but you need to start NOW!

It takes the same traits to succeed as a black belt and professional athlete as it does to succeed in business, so be a champion! Empower yourself and your team. Get an EDGE and make an IMPACT, and follow a formula to become an extraordinary businessperson.

About Tommy

After coaching hundreds of entrepreneurs over the last 16 years, Tommy Lee is proud to launch his Black Belt Peak Performance Business Program globally in 2012, which will be accompanied by an elite mastermind series unlike any other in the industry. He will be appearing on the Brian Tracy Show featured on NBC and CBS and has been recognized in *USA Today* as one of America's emerging business leaders. He also will have work published in two books in addition to this one in 2012: *Black Belt Selling: How to Sell with Respect and Integrity and Still Get The Knockout* and one co-authored with Jack Canfield (author of *Chicken Soup for the Soul*).

You can learn more about Tommy Lee and his programs at www.TommyLeeInternational.com. If you visit the website, you can use the code "Black Belt Success" to receive your free copy of "7 Steps to Become a Black Belt in Business." You took action by reading this chapter, so this is your reward.

CHAPTER 14

Retirement Is a State of Mind

By Rick Parkes

The other day I saw a clever illustration that was produced to show the progression of our lives from birth to death. It was a row of bottles, starting with a baby bottle, going to a coke bottle, a beer bottle, and finally a bottle of antacid medicine. I couldn't help but smile wryly as I reflected on how the phases of our lives could be so easily summed up by four bottles. Similarly, when it comes to how we view the acquisition, preservation and distribution of our money through life, there are three basic phases we go through. See if you don't agree.

Accumulation Phase. This is when we are in our younger years. We work hard to earn, accumulate, save and invest. Time is on our side. When it comes to investing we can afford to take greater risks. To us, the economy is a vast, if sometimes unpredictable, seascape on which we are sailing. As the swells approach our vessel, we confidently ride up the ridges and determinedly surf down the troughs, knowing that in the end we will come out ahead. To put it in factual terms, you can take any 15-year slice of the Standard and Poor's 500 index, for example, and the average gain is in the neighborhood of 8 percent. That statistic is very dependable. Start at 1958 and go forward 15 years to 1973, and you will see a gain of around 8 percent. Go from 1975 to 1990, and the gain will be about the same.

Preservation Mode. Here are the years when we begin thinking about retirement. Some of our friends have already retired. What were dreams 20 years ago have come to fruition because we have worked hard, and we have been good savers and careful investors. The goal now is not to lose it_by getting caught in one of those troughs and simply not having enough time to catch the next wave up. Our challenge now is to hold on to what we've got and make sure our nest egg will last throughout our retirement.

Distribution Mode. Now it's time to withdraw our money as we need it while we leave the rest to grow without unnecessary risk. It's a time to enjoy our money but spend it wisely so as not to outlive our resources or diminish the lifestyle to which we have become accustomed if at all possible. We view our resources as sand in an hourglass. They are finite. If we are judicious in our use of them and careful with our investments, they will last. Naturally, we are careful where we place and invest our assets because, at this stage of our life, we greatly treasure our independence. While we want our money to continue to work for us, we are not inclined to accept significant risk.

THE FORCE OF INERTIA

You may or may not remember this from your high school physics classes, but it was Sir Isaac Newton who came up with the law of inertia. Actually, I don't think Sir Isaac actually "came up" with it. He was just the first one to identify and explain it. "And just what does that have to do with finance?" you ask.

The law of inertia simply states that an object in motion will stay in motion until something pushes it or pulls it in another direction. It's the same way for sitting still. An object that is stationary_will continue to just sit there until an outside force makes it move.

When it comes to money decisions, all of us are affected by the law of inertia to some degree. Don't you worry; life will move us from one money phase to another whether we want to go or not. The problem is, we sometimes go kicking and screaming, which isn't good. During our accumulation phase, when the paychecks are rolling in, and we still have time on our side, risky financial behavior may be somewhat acceptable. During the preservation and distribution phases, however, it can be hazardous to our wealth!

I have a friend who loved to play basketball during his younger years. He is in his mid-sixties now. "I don't play anymore," he told me. "The last time I tried, I discovered that my mind knew how to fake left, dribble right and go for the basket. But with my bad knee and these extra pounds, all I did was lose the ball."

The point is, we don't always move easily from one money phase to the other. Sometimes we have to be jolted by reality. To illustrate the fact that we are all a bit resistant to change, try an experiment. When you are putting on your shoes, you will customarily put on either the left shoe or the right shoe first. Just reverse the procedure. If you are a "right shoe first" person, put on your left shoe first, and vice versa. It's what I call behavioral inertia. You have to force yourself to make a change sometimes.

Take for example moving from accumulation mode to preservation mode.

During the accumulation phase of our lives, we made a lot of money investing. We liked that. It was exciting. But we also lost a lot of money when those market corrections happened, didn't we? That wasn't fun, but we hung in there because we knew that in time it would come back, and it always did. In the 1990s the stock market made tremendous gains. The strategy of "buy and hold" worked quite well. In the latter part of that decade practically any strategy worked. We could hit the target without even aiming!

One of the most amazing periods was the time from January 1990 to March 1990 when the market grew an astonishing 455 percent. People were streaming to this new American bonanza in droves. Companies were starting up 401(k)s, and all of this money had to be parked somewhere. The market swelled so swiftly that a kind of euphoria overtook the nation. Many thought it would never end. But end it did. In March 24, 2002, a correction began that saw $9 trillion lost in 30 months. If you had $455,000 in the market, it would have dropped to $231,595, and $100,000 would have turned into $50,900. If you had retired in March of 2000 you would have seen a 49.1 percent decline in your retirement nest egg.

"BUY AND HOLD" NO LONGER WORKS

So is "buy and hold" for the long term the answer in today's market? No. Even if you could count on there being a steady 10 percent gain each year with no losses, which is unrealistic to the point of being silly to even contemplate, it would still have taken 82 months for your account to just break even and get back where you started. At a steady 5 percent growth, it would have taken 161 months to just break even.

What happened next? From October 9, 2002, to October 9, 2007, the stock market soared upward. We had a 102 percent return during that period. Your $50,900 would have grown to $102,818! Not bad, eh?

But then, starting on October 9, 2007, we had an $11 trillion decline. The Dow Jones lost 53.7 percent, and the S&P 500 lost 56.7 percent. Now your $100,000 is valued at $44,520. Do we see a pattern here?

The definition of a bear market is one where there is a decline of 20 percent or more. Since 1929, these bear markets have occurred every 4.8 years. That's the average. There is no way of pinpointing when they will occur or how long they will last.

The average depth of a bear market is a 38.24 percent drop. The average duration of a bear market is 17 months. The average time it would take to make up losses in a bear market is 60 months.

So that's why we say that a buy-and-hold strategy just doesn't work in today's economic environment. Managing a market portfolio success-fully today requires going to the strongest asset at any given time. In 2008, the strongest asset was cash. Successful money managers will not fear going mainly to cash when the situation calls for it.

It is important that both the fundamental as well as the technical sides of the analytical spectrum be looked at in order to decide where to position the assets of clients. What does that mean?

In financial analysis, the fundamental side can be likened to a movie re-view where the critic says the picture is horrible; whereas the technical side promotes the same "horrible" movie as being such a popular hit that the ticket lines go down the street and around the block. So, while past performance cannot guarantee future results, you may be able to avoid the full brunt of a major downturn by using tools to identify trends. If the major downturn doesn't happen overnight, you may be able to re-duce your exposure ahead of time.

So, it is just wise to weigh your individual risk tolerance carefully, tak-ing into consideration your age and your financial goals. That way you can sleep at night, knowing that, regardless of what the market does or doesn't do, your retirement nest egg won't vanish overnight.

HAVE AN "EMERGENCY FUND"

When I am called upon to speak to a group about basic money management, I usually always begin with one of my pet themes, which is "Have an Emergency Fund." It has been recommended that we have between three and six months worth of income, or living expenses, set aside in liquid cash or cash equivalent before we start thinking about investing or retirement. It is such a basic part of any financial plan. And yet, when I conduct my initial interview with clients, I am surprised at how few have one in place.

When I was in school, it was fashionable to wear "penny loafers." This is one shoe style that has stood the test of time. They were introduced to the world by a shoemaker by the name of John Bass in 1930 and have shod the feet of such celebrities as President John F. Kennedy and Michael Jackson. But what made them unique was a little slit on the outside of the shoe where a penny could be inserted. But at my school, we were too cool for pennies. We put DIMES in the slits of our penny loafers. How cool was THAT?

When I was in the ninth grade, I had gone to the movies with a pal. We had been dropped off by parents and were instructed to call them from a pay phone (this was way before cell phones) when the movie was over for the ride back home. The only problem was, we had spent every last cent of our money on candy and popcorn and neither of us had the money with which to make the call. We were working up the courage to ask the manager to borrow a dime when it occurred to me. I had not one, but TWO dimes. Problem solved!

Like the dimes in the penny loafers, our emergency money has to be readily available. It must be money we can put our hands on when we need it. It is advisable to have it placed in an account where it can be withdrawn by either going up to a teller window, an ATM machine, or writing a check. A money market account is the most popular type of account for this purpose, since you are at least getting some interest, albeit paltry. Since it goes without saying that we certainly do not want to trigger a capital gain or cause a taxable event if we have a sudden need, it would be questionable judgment to put this asset in anything that failed the liquidity test.

Why is it so important? Let's say you are in the accumulation phase of your life, and you have put an automatic savings plan in place. The emergency fund will help keep it on track. Let's say that you are steadily chunking away $100 from your weekly paycheck into your 401(k). That money goes to purchase shares of stock. When share prices go up, great! You made money in your account! When share prices go down, great! You bought more shares. That's called "dollar cost averaging." But if an emergency comes along for, you name it … car repairs, the orthodontist … and you don't have an emergency account, you will be tempted use that money you are saving for that expense. Your savings plan just got derailed. When you consider the effect of compound interest over time and possible matching funds, multiply by tenfold the amount you took from savings to meet that emergency.

In your preservation and distribution phases of life, the emergency fund will enable you to continue with the discipline you need to make your money last your lifetime. How? Let's say that prior to your retirement you set up a vehicle that would pay out a specific amount for life, with the caveat that you not touch the principal but let it grow until you needed to start your withdrawals. Your emergency fund would deliver you from the temptation to dip into your principal to care for… again, you name it. With a liquid, adequately funded stash of emergency cash, you will always have dimes in your penny loafers.

About Rick

Rick Parkes has been changing lives as a financial adviser for more than three decades. He helps people who have money keep their money and create a plan that will ensure that they do not outlive their money but live a comfortable life in retirement. He wants his clients to have a real plan instead of wishful thinking so they can Sleep Well At Night both when they are planning for and when they reach retirement. He calls it S.W.A.N. planning. Rick has been interviewed on ABC, NBC, Fox and CBS to explain the strategies that he has designed to help people weather the financial storms that lie ahead.

Many of these strategies are described in his new book, *Help I'm Retiring!*, released by Amazon publishing.

CHAPTER 15

Operating Your Business in Turbulent Times

By Gloria Taylor-Boyce

Let your imagination soar! Operating your business in turbulent times requires a different kind of vision and discipline. In order to achieve success it is almost always inevitable that you will make mistakes and encounter setbacks along the way. If you fear failure, you need to realize that setbacks are as much a part of achieving success as the euphoric feelings you experience upon your accomplishments.

Your miscues can teach you much, and you can gain benefits that will actually help you to become successful, provided you keep both your eyes and your mind wide open.

However, when you are operating a business in turbulent times, mistakes have to be few and far between as the circumstances are not very forgiving. Turbulent times call for attention to details. You must be aware of all aspects of your operation, and you must also be on top of industry standards. In real meaning, you must run a thinking operation constantly thinking outside of the box. You must also know internally that you already have what it takes to win.

The success of any business starts with desire. No matter what type of business or entrepreneurship you are involved in, there is a system to success. This coordination starts with a strong desire like an urge seeking a fuller expression. You must know within yourself that the possibility of its fulfilment exists within you regardless of outside influences.

The stronger the desire or inner urge, the stronger the conviction to succeed. In essence, you must have an awesome action plan to achieve your desired goals. If you don't have a plan, you will never achieve the goals that you desire. You have to be aware of what is working and what is not working. Don't hesitate to change your approach

PLANNING FOR SUCCESS

Without a doubt, success is a planned event. In this chapter, I will reveal the secret of operating a successful business when the economy is saying you should fail, when everything in your environment seems to be going belly up. You will remain standing with your head high above the waters. Remember, success does not happen by chance. It must be planned and deliberate.

I am taking this opportunity to introduce you to a cyber church called Zoe Ministries International—Canada (Zoe Canada) zoe canada.org. Against all odds, Zoe Ministries International—Canada is booming in today's uncertain economy when an estimated 3,500 to 4,000 churches in America close their doors each year. What is Zoe's secret? Fasten your seat belts—I am about to tell you!

Zoe Ministries International—Canada is a not-for-profit church ministry established to minister to communities, families and individuals globally. Zoe Canada incorporates the best in industry standards, from technology to social networking to reach God's people, while spreading his word and globalizing the prophetic. In its first year of operation, Zoe grossed $100,000. Not much money you say? Well consider that this is a virtual church with real people and real money. You'll be surprised to learn that its leaders know their parishioners by name and telephone number by memory.

What made Zoe Canada successful was entrepreneurial spirit and operating the church as a business while ministering to human souls. In managing a business for tomorrow one must enter the marketplace as a growth company with an entrepreneurial engine. An entrepreneur is a person who synergistically combines risk, innovation, leadership, artistry, skill and craftsmanship. To grow and stay ahead of the game in today's economy, your leaders and managers must possess an entrepreneurial spirit. At Zoe Canada, the entrepreneurial spirit is embedded in the philosophy, ideology and mission statements of the church. It is a way of life.

And this is only the beginning. To operate a successful business during difficult economic times, start with a spirit of love for your product or industry, which leads to the spirit of freedom, and freedom of the mind. You cannot afford to entertain fear or limitations. You must wipe those words out of your vocabulary. In essence, your life must be balanced and disciplined; you must be able to control your time and thoughts and not be easily moved by fear or emotions. In turbulent times, quick decisions often have to be made on the spur of the moment, and this calls for a disciplined mind. Your mind must be free to make right choices quickly.

What do I mean by freedom? Freedom is in being able to control your life and in making it what you want it to be. What I am leading to is this: freedom is not living an obsessed, undisciplined life. This calls for a balanced lifestyle, hard work, exercise, good diet and plenty of rest.

Another key principle is in communication. The way you communicate affects the response you get. It is important to understand that people arrive at the meaning of words based on their experience while communicating with you. This is based on the fact that people will pick out the way you communicated the message rather than the actual context of the message. It is not what is said but how it is stated during the conversation. In solving problems in turbulent times, it is important to remember that every behavior has a positive intention. Furthermore, people will make the best choices available to them at that time. Remember: our choices are always driven from our beliefs, attitudes and values.

As a result, we must pay close attention to feedback and make necessary adjustments to our message. In doing so, you are giving the people what they want. We live in an increasingly complex society which demands strong determination in order to be successful. There is a fine line between determination and intimidation, and you must find it. We must be determined without intimidating others. So remember, the task of communication is never ending. At Zoe Canada, leaders are constantly thinking of new and innovative ways to reach their partners.

Anyone can be a success in times of plenty. However, in today's tentative economy, communication must be tight. Everyone in your organization must be singing from the same hymn book. In real meaning, there must be no dissension; you cannot afford a Judas—not in these times. Traitors must be dealt with quickly to avoid damage. Everyone at all levels must buy into the vision of the organization and stick with it.

MANAGING KEY RESOURCES:

There are four key resources that must be managed like clockwork, thoroughly and faithfully in order to remain in this competitive market.

Labor

The main resource in any business is labor. The truth is running a successful business, no matter what size, means effectively managing your staff. This principle applies whether you have one or 1,000 employees and requires that you know the strengths of your people and particularly of those with a proven record of performance. It is necessary that the manager knows the answers to these questions concerning employees in his or her department. *What do they do well? Where do they belong?* It is imperative that, as far as possible, managers assign staff where they can maximize their strengths.

There are two kinds of beliefs: empowering and limiting. Knowing which category your employees fall into is critical. Your beliefs shape your principles and how you view yourself. Your beliefs also filter how you hear, what you see, and even how you feel. These beliefs, whether empowering or limiting, determine your actions, which in turn verify your beliefs as true. If an employee's belief system is not in line with the ideology of the company, they must exit.

Develop Your Own Operational System

There are a lot of management systems out there. It is important that you do not mold your business to suit someone else's model. These are different times we are operating in. While these principles once were good, today's market economy calls for a different approach. However, having said that, you must not throw out the baby with the bath water. By all means, adapt the best of any system. However, it must fit with your own vision.

Cut Back on Bricks and Mortar

With the use of technology and social media, we live and operate in a global economy. Virtual assistance and offices are key resources when operating a business in today's volatile market. Virtual offices and virtual office services include local or toll-free telephone and fax numbers, digital voicemail, electronic fax, email, an online command center, unified messaging, voicemail to email, fax to email, professional live receptionist services, virtual assistants, live call answering, screening and forwarding, outbound calling, customer service, and appointment scheduling. You can acquire all these services without paying for a mortgage, heat, electricity, telephone connections or transportation to and from an office. While you focus on making your business grow, virtual assistance will handle all of your office needs.

However, while I am a great advocate for virtual solutions and your customers will deal with and through them, it is important that you maintain a physical location, even if it is a home office. This also applies to post office boxes; ensure that your customers are writing to a person—not just an organization, in care of a P.O. box.

Discipline

Most problems arise because we are not controlling our ideas. Self-control consists of an organized thought direction and well-defined objective. So remember, running a successful business in turbulent times takes discipline. To rise above any limitation, we must organize our thinking along constructive lines. You cannot afford to do whatever comes along. In today's uncertain economy, one must plan that something definite will be accomplished toward your aim. To do otherwise is to be deemed a drifter. In today's competitive marketplace one cannot support drifters—only builders. Each day our work must be carefully planned so that your organization will steadily become more disciplined and cooperative until all employees are working as a single unit.

Let me ask you a simple question. Did you ever ask yourself, which is more prevalent in your life—competition or growth? In competition, there is much stress, but in growth you find balance, harmony and equilibrium; therefore, *growth and knowledge* must be your foundation. You owe it to yourself to know that success is finding your voice, and failure is simply not having a voice. The truth is the greatest challenge, and the greatest changes ahead pertain to top management.

It's no secret that one of the errors many businesspeople and executives commit is that they believe the competitive fight takes place in the present and so do not worry about the future. However, what happens when the rules of the game are modified, and you are faced with market uncertainty caused by changing government economic legislation, rapid technological changes, unexpected competitors or a host of other factors? Are you equipped to redefine your markets with new strategies? And if so, how do you design the future without knowing what is going to come back and bite you on the butt?

Creating strategies necessitates foresight as well as being able to clearly articulate industry trends that threaten your continued success. Uncertainty prompts the frightful thought that there may not be enough supply or that you will not even be able to survive. Time and nature teach us that each cycle passes. Change leads to stability, which sooner or later returns to change. In short, we must never stop learning! We must dedicate ourselves to constant and never-ending improvement. We must always strive to better ourselves every single day.

In closing, these are challenging yet exciting times, and if I could leave you with a few thoughts it would be that confidence is the test when operating your business in turbulent times; also, do not be afraid to promote the young people in your organization because they are tomorrow's leaders. So remember, life's battles do not go to the strong but to the one who thinks they can win. Are you a winner?

About Pastor Gloria

Pastor Gloria Taylor-Boyce is the author of the books *Why Are You Here?* and *Watt's in Your Hands*. A writer of occupational health and safety material by profession and now an ordained minister, Pastor Taylor-Boyce is a team builder who possesses amazing leadership skills and is a strategic and long-range planner and lover of emerging and advancing technology. She has more than 25 years of occupational health and safety experiences.

Pastor Taylor-Boyce is a consummate values-driven professional with a reputation for driving quantifiable advances for her organization. She and her husband, Pastor Ralph Boyce, are pastors of the church Zoe Ministries International—Canada. (www.zoecanada.org).

For her work in occupational health and safety, Gloria was featured in numerous health and safety magazines and was nominated to receive the Canadian National's Railways President's Awards for Excellence. As a matter of fact, Pastor Gloria Boyce cornered the rail industry with respect to the development of occupational health and safety training material with organizations such as Canadian National Railway, Canadian Pacific Railway, Ontario Northland Railway, Via Rail and Canadian Pacific Railway Soo Line.

Gloria Taylor-Boyce started her early education in the Caribbean and then moved to Ottawa where she became a registered nurse. She is also a graduate of the Labour College University of Ottawa, class of 1991. She has worked on a number of election campaigns in Ottawa, Nova Scotia and Brampton. Gloria and her family live in Brampton where she serves in executive positions on a number of committees. Gloria also serves in her community and has held positions of director and also co-chair on the local training board.

The first Sunday in every month Pastor Gloria Taylor-Boyce conducts a series of online lectures called "Millionaire Consciousness Expansion." Please join her every first Sunday of the month from 8 to 10 p.m. EST. To hear the lecture series by telephone on our conference call line, call 1-712-432-0075, use pass-code 793755# or 1-805-360-1075, then enter 712-432-0075# and pass-code 793755#.

Pastor Ralph Boyce and Pastor Gloria Taylor-Boyce are ordained pastors of Zoe Ministries International—Canada, a prophetic church located in Ontario, Canada. They are ministers of God after God's own heart. They are also prophets in the Prophetic Order of Mar Elijah. Pastor Ralph Boyce and Pastor Gloria Taylor-Boyce are builders of the kingdom of God and love God's people. They are lifestyle coaches and motivational speakers. They are also communication specialist masters and neuro-linguistic programming (NLP) masters/trainers. Their desire is that God (the great architect of the universe) would use them mightily in building his kingdom through the globalization of the prophetic.

ZOE Ministries International-Canada has weekly prophetic church services on Thursdays and Saturdays starting at 8 p.m. EST. You can listen in on these live interactive services and/or the rebroadcast which run 24/7, by telephone on the Telephone Conference Call line: 1-712-432-0075, pass-code 793755# or 1-805-360-1075, then enter 712-432-0075# and pass-code 793755#. You can also join us from anywhere around the world, via the Internet using www.skype.com. Skype contact is: feeconferencing, pass-code 793755#.

Contact information: Zoe Ministries International—Canada, c/o Pastor Ralph H. Boyce, 3938 Cottrelle Blvd., P.O. Box 80069 Brampton, Ontario, Canada L6P 2W7. Telephone: 1-800-441-0239 or 1-905-794-7358.

CHAPTER 16

Stay Bitter or Get Better

By David Montelongo

Imagine being on top of the world, young, full of energy, spiritually connected, rich, influential; with a loving and passionate spouse, beautiful kids, an incredible house, fine cars and a solid real estate portfolio.

Now imagine what it would feel like to lose the financial stability you had built, almost overnight.

Can you imagine the cumbersome thoughts that could possibly creep into your head, the self-doubt, the nerves, the pit in your stomach?

In 2007 this is where I found myself. By the age of 30, I was married to my beautiful wife and had two amazing kids. I had built a multimillion dollar real estate portfolio and was featured on a nationally aired hit TV show, "Flip This House." Soon after, I took a major hit when the real estate bubble burst.

Millions of Americans faced financial strain over the past six years just like I did. When this happens, people find themselves at a major crossroads. A decision has to be made either to stay bitter about things lost or get better and create a new way to reach your inner brilliance.

Cracking the Success Code is a topic near and dear to my heart. I am honored to be able to share what has actually worked in my own life with you. You know, once the mind expands, it is extremely uncomfortable to settle for anything less than the excellence you know you are capable of.

If you have ever faced challenges in your life you know that it can become easy to be cynical and to allow self doubt to take over. If you don't proactively take steps to improve, the negativity can become a way of life.

To me, the definition of success is very closely aligned with happiness. This is the case because "success" has different meanings to different people, and ultimately the higher the level of happiness you reach, the more successful you feel in life.

Here is the really cool thing: "happiness" is a choice. It is not about what happens to you in life but about what you choose to do with what happens. Your reality is directly affected by how you choose to view the things that have happened or will happen in your life. So if happiness is a choice, then success is also. We all have the power to create success in our lives. It is up to each of us to determine the level of success that we reach.

10 KEYS TO DETERMINING YOUR LEVEL OF SUCCESS

1. **DECIDE** to create success in you life. It must not be a whimsical idea or notion. Truly deciding with every fiber of your being that you will achieve success in your life will kick the domino. After you decide, write it down, and share your vision with as many people as you can. Share it on a public level, Facebook, Twitter or your blog. By making a public declaration, you allow the public to become your accountability partner.

   Speaking and sharing your vision for success will begin to transform your vision into your passion. When you are passionate about your journey to success, you will begin to see that others will be magnetized by your passion and want to get involved with your growth and expansion.

2. **CHOOSE** a vehicle for success. My vehicle is real estate, which also happens to be my passion. What are you passionate about?

   Some people are very clear about their passion, so building a business or life around that passion comes naturally; for others it is an ongoing discovery process.

   Many times success comes in steps because what we are passionate about today may grow and change as you develop as a person. If you are not yet clear on your passion, don't let that be an excuse for you to sit on the sidelines and do nothing. Find something you are interested in now and pursue it with the same level of energy as you would pursue your passion.

Don't be the person who wakes up 20 years from now scratching your head and wondering why you never found your drive in life.

By waking up every day excited about the opportunities that will arise, you will actually open yourself up to attract more opportunity into your life. By playing full out now, you will condition yourself to perform at the highest level so that when you do find your passion it will feel as if you are showing up to play—not work—every single day.

3. **DESIGN** your life; what do you want your life to be like in one year? Three years? Five years and beyond?

It can be easy to get caught up with "setting goals," but I like to work backward by planning the outcomes for my life. Try this exercise.

Sit in a quiet room or even outdoors as long as it's quiet and you won't be disturbed. Now close your eyes and allow all of your worries, busy thoughts and anxieties to go away.

Focus intently on what you want your life to look like one year from now. What improvements can you make for yourself in one-year's time? What do you want in your relationships, your business and your finances?

Then, consider what you want your life to look like in three years. Understand that you can make dramatic improvements in three-year's time. What do you want your relationship to look like? What kind of car will you drive? What will your house look like? How much money will you have in the bank?

After spending some time looking three years into the future, focus on what your life will look like in five years.

Once you are clear on what you want for your life in one, three and five years, you can then design your life backward by laying out the action steps you will need to take to help you reach your desired results. So many people never reach the level of success that they believe they want because they never set a clear intention or outcome for their life.

4. **DEFINE** the actions steps that you must take daily, monthly and yearly to reach your desired outcomes.

Once you have clearly designed your "outcomes," it will be easier to work backward from those outcomes to map out the action steps you will have to take to get there. Here is a simple example of how I work my real estate business backward.

Outcome: In the next 12 months I will make $1 million with one of my real estate investing strategies called "deed flipping." My average profit per deal with this strategy is just over $11,000 per deal, so I will need to complete 91 of these deals to accomplish this "outcome."

On average, I have to look at 10 leads to close two or three of these deals, so my team and I will have to look at 455 deals in the next 12 months or 38 deals each month for the next 12 months. On average, I need to send out 1,000 direct-mail marketing pieces to motivated sellers to get 10 to 20 leads. Thus, over the next 12 months, I will need to send out 45,000 direct-mail pieces or 3,750 mail pieces per month.

Knowing my desired outcome allows me to project the exact action steps to take in my business that will give me the results I desire. If you are clear on your desired outcome, it will be much easier for you to lay out a plan of action for your success.

5. **CREATE** your "action plan" or blueprint so that you are crystal clear on what you have to do every step of the way.

In traditional business, you are taught to develop a "business plan"; however a business plan without "action" behind it is just a well thought-out collection of ideas.

When I am launching a business, I like to write an action plan that allows me to create an "action step" to back up every idea that goes into my plan. After all, it is the "action" that gives your business or idea life and energy to gain momentum and bring results.

6. DEVELOP "laser beam focus" so intense that nothing will lure you off of your path.

Losing focus is very easy to do; in fact most people walk around with no focus. There are so many distractions around us every day with phone calls, texts, and emails, not to mention that the average Facebook user is logged on for almost 19 minutes at a time every day.

Developing focus is like exercising a muscle: if you don't actively work to develop a particular muscle, it will not grow. If you don't actively develop focus, you can be carried away every time a new, shiny object catches your eye.

What should you focus on? One of my personal mentors taught me to focus on the highest and best use of my time. You can get caught up with plenty of small tasks, but you need to constantly ask yourself this question: will spending my time doing X bring me closer to my desired outcome?

If answering emails, lingering on Facebook, sending texts, mowing the lawn, or picking up dry cleaning is not getting you closer to your desired outcome, then DON'T DO IT!

7. NURTURE a "deep belief" that you can accomplish anything and everything you desire. This belief is also known as self-confidence or swagger! Confidence in business is critical; if you are unsure of yourself and your abilities, it is going to be extremely difficult to get others to believe in you.

One of the best ways to build your self-confidence—or swagger—is to wake up every morning and repeat daily affirmations. In our family, we call them I AMs.

- I am brilliant.
- I am beautiful.
- I am a genius.
- I am healthy.

- I am strong.
- I am deeply loved.
- I am creative.
- I am a leader.
- I am blessed.
- I am successful.
- I am a money magnet—money comes to me freely.
- I am a positive being.
- I am compassionate.

For a full list of affirmations go to my blog, www.davidmonte-longo.tv.

8. **RECOGNIZE** your past mistakes as life lessons and let them be stepping-stones on your path to success.

We all make mistakes; how you view those mistakes will deeply impact how the mistake affects your life. If you beat yourself up over your mistakes, they will serve to tear you down, break down your self-confidence and leave you feeling very fearful of trying new things in the future.

If you choose to see your blunders as life lessons and learning experiences, these experiences become stepping-stones to future success. After all, if you learn from your mistakes, you will not continue to make the same mistakes over and over. Life lessons give you personal power, serve to make you a stronger decision-maker and reinforce your confidence and swagger!

9. **SERVE** as many people as you can; having a positive impact on others will positively impact you tenfold.

Your journey to success is a life lesson in of itself; as you go through the process, document the things that work for you and the things that do not. Share your learning experiences with as many people as you can so that you can positively impact as many people as possible.

By positively impacting others, the law of reciprocity will kick in, and you will notice that others will more freely share their learning experiences with you.

10. BE an action taker!

The most successful people in life are always action takers! It is not enough to have good ideas or to learn new techniques or strategies. Without action, an idea is just an idea; with action, an idea takes on a life form of its own and will release new possibilities that will lead you closer to your desired success.

What I know is this: in order to enjoy your life to the fullest extent and feel success and ultimately feel happiness, you have to love the process and the journey. You have to be willing to get up 10 times if you're knocked down nine. Most importantly it's OK to make mistakes, and it's critical that you learn from those mistakes so that you don't make the same ones twice.

Michael Jordan said it best when he said: "I've missed more than 9,000 shots in my career. I've lost almost 300 games. 26 times, I've been trusted to take the game winning shot and missed. I've failed over and over and over again in my life. And that is why I succeed."

You have the ability to do and be anything that you desire. With hard work, faith in your divine source and confidence in yourself, you will *Crack the Success Code*!

About David

David Montelongo's incredible story of riches to rags to riches is one that makes him the real estate mentor that aspiring million-aires are seeking out. His remarkable journey from creating a multimillion dollar real estate portfolio at the age of 28 and flipping over 536 houses in his career to building a legacy for his young family is truly inspiring.

David's business grew so fast that he caught the eye of America and was featured on A&E's hit TV show "Flip this House," where more than a million viewers a week watched his business explode!

After his time on "Flip This House," the housing bubble burst, and David found himself unprepared for the economic fallout and lost most of his multimillion-dollar portfolio. David faced the decision that so many Americans face today: be bitter about things lost or get better by creating the solution that allows for a comeback. David knew that being wealthy was first a state of mind. He sought out financial, spiritual and physical mentors to reinvent himself and the strategies he uses to become a problem solver to many. He took inspired action and began to reinvent the way the modern investor would create a fortune in real estate and serve their communities.

David's determination enabled him to rebuild his real estate investment firm bigger than before and has allowed him to have the reach to inspire thousands of real estate investors across the country. David's multifaceted business, which tests strategies before releasing them to the public, has helped many accumulate hundreds of thousands of dollars in spendable cash and million-dollar portfolios.

David has produced and developed a home-study course and membership site where he teaches his five key strategies that include his hybrid cutting-edge house flipping system, "The Deed Flipping Blueprint."™ He also coaches and consults with students across the country in building a multigenerational legacy in his Millionaire Apprentice Program.™ In this program, he shares how to use YOUR mental strength to fireproof your business in today's changing economy and for the rest of your life.

David's keys to success are his highly converting marketing initiatives that bring in a consistent lead stream and having a strong belief that he can make money in any market regardless of current market conditions!

The David Montelongo Companies' team allows him to be able to focus on his real estate deals and help others learn how to "crush it" in today's economy.

David is an internationally known real estate entrepreneur, mentor, speaker, educator, whose passion for his divine source and family—wife, Melina, and two children, Zion and Eden, are his driving force. His mission is to help anybody who is coachable and willing to learn how to become financially independent with mental fortitude to create generational wealth. In his spare time, he enjoys training Brazilian Jui Jitsu, reading, writing, wine tasting, and vacationing with his family.

Connect with David,
www.DavidMontelongoTV.com
www.DeedFlippingBlueprint.com
1-888-406-2088 or support@davidmontelongotv.com.

CHAPTER 17

Successful Intelligence for Great Leaders: A Road Map To Creating Your Leadership Abilities

By Dushan Vaithilingam

The journey to define the ideal set of characteristics that describe the *successful leader* began around the time of Plato, approximately 400 B.C. Much has been invested in this effort in the thousands of years since that time. By some estimates, in the year 2001 alone, 8,000 books were published on the topic of leadership. To this day, this massive and important human venture remains unfinished. We are still in desperate search of the ideal suit of characteristics that define the successful leader.

WHY THE GARGANTUAN EFFORT TO DEFINE SUCCESSFUL LEADERS?

Experts in the area of leadership theorize that humans have a fundamental human need to follow. Now, more than ever, the need for successful leaders has become critical to the survival of major organizations and businesses, as we have come to know them over the past century. In this context, recent global and catastrophic events have made the quest for successful leaders critical.

A 2007 survey of leadership in 16 global companies from a wide range of commerce, including banking, insurance, technology and food, with ownership in the U.S., U.K., Japan, France, Switzerland and Holland revealed that fewer than 25 percent of these companies were comfortable with the growth of their leadership talent. This survey was taken just prior to the global financial crisis.

Since the demise of Enron, public opinion surveys have shown a growing regulatory, shareholder and public examination of leadership. This has in turn led to mistrust in our public governing institutions. There is less trust now for governments worldwide than ever before, regardless of a country's political system.

The highly competitive aspects of globalization combined with changing labor costs, diminishing resources and constantly shifting distribution networks have placed a steady pressure on the structure of businesses and organizations. This pressure has led to the quest for highly informed and cutting-edge leadership.

Major shifts in market share within short time frames driven by technology now require that companies make rapid adjustments in organizational frameworks to maintain a profitable edge.

The greater need to generate shareholder value due to increasing investor demands, now, also focuses on "intangibles," not only market capitalization. This factor alone demands more successful leaders.

The need for increased productivity by the individual worker and the concurrent stress that accompanies this demand is thought to relate directly to leadership behavior. The ever-changing landscape of corporate structures to meet local and global social responsibilities requires insightful leaders to maintain the trust of their followers.

Competition is heightened for high achievers in the worker pool, and this in turn requires that leaders of organizations and businesses maintain gratifying and competitive organizational work environments to attract and keep talented workers.

WHAT SHOULD THE NEW GENERATION OF LEADERSHIP LOOK LIKE?

In today's world, leaders are required to be dynamic, cognitive entities that spontaneously tap into a multitude of skills, knowledge and experience to involve team members in decision making and the deployment of strategies that are most appropriate for the moment, in their local and global environments. This is essential to facilitate optimal outcomes for enterprises while keeping those enterprises in a state of readiness to conquer the next moment. These calculated actions are a series of forward-and-backward movements. Successful leaders know when it is in their organization's strategic interest to advance and when to retreat and regroup. And while seeking to position their output beyond the competitive edge, they also need to maintain a constant state of harmony in their organizational space.

Today's successful leaders must display constancy, plasticity, inventiveness, knowledge and skills; a sense of purpose, consideration, unambiguous priorities, honesty and good listening to flourish. Successful leaders are the products of their own dynamic creation through time. During the process, leaders employing successful intelligence use the combined approach of their own personal strengths and expertise and leverages the strengths and expertise of others to create the desired result for the collective whole of the organization.

THE THEORY OF SUCCESSFUL INTELLIGENCE

R. J. Sternberg, in the 1996 book *Successful Intelligence* (published by Simon Schuster), introduced the theory of successful intelligence to more accurately represent the basic nature of human cognitive abilities. In essence, successful intelligence theory benefits individuals, organizations and society—both in the short and long terms. Successful intelligence incorporates the abilities essential to reach achievement in life—however a person defines achievement within personal life context. Individuals are successfully intelligent if they can recognize their strengths and make the most of them while also knowing their weaknesses and finding ways to correct or compensate for them. Both are important. Finding success in life requires matching one's set of abilities to the requirements of a given task or series of tasks in the real world. Successful intelligence focuses not only on how much information a person knows but also on how much and how much wisdom has been acquired from experience.

THREE ABILITIES ESSENTIAL TO SUCCESSFUL INTELLIGENCE AS DEFINED BY STERNBERG

Analytical abilities are compulsory to assess and weigh challenges as they appear. Analytical abilities help a person be able to identify existing problems, define the scope of these problems, create processes that solve these problems, and evaluate the value of the solutions utilized.

Creative abilities are needed to spawn solutions prior to problems arising. Creative leaders have the courage to facilitate bold new innovations whether or not those innovations are popular. They have the ability to convince sufficient numbers of individuals to buy into their ideas, despite the lack of certainty of success. In Sternberg's model of successful intelligence, creativity in one domain of life does not imply inherent creativity in other domains—that is to say an artist need not make a great engineer.

Practical abilities are vital to put strategies into action and facilitate success in a timely sequence. Practical abilities are best seen when intelligence is applied to real-world problems. Essential to practical intelligence is the attainment and use of implicit knowledge, which is the hidden knowledge a successful leader needs to know to thrive in a given environment. Research shows that inherent knowledge is obtained through attentive exploitation of life experience; that it is relatively domain specific and independent of conventional abilities; and that it predicts leadership success.

PROOF THAT SUCCESSFUL INTELLIGENCE WORKS

Although the concept of successful intelligence was born in academia, it has been tried and proven in real-world settings. Sternberg and colleagues devised various tests of successful intelligence in real-world simulations for individuals across a wide spectrum of careers including business managers, college teachers, salespeople and army leaders. These simulations utilized complex situations individuals might face while at work. The test subjects were then required to appraise these situations. For example, a test subject might be given a long list of tasks to prioritize in a limited time. The successful intelligence model was proven highly effective in predicting individual performance outcomes.

However, it is fundamental to the model of successful intelligence to generate successful outcomes in the real world by real people, not in a laboratory setting by test subjects. In this regard, two studies used the theory of successful intelligence to boost scores on the SAT, often used to predict college achievement, and the GMAT, a test often used for admission into graduate business programs. "In the first study, the theory of successful intelligence was used to broaden the range of skills tested by going beyond the analytical and memory skills to include practical and creative skills; while in the second study, the theory was used to incorporate measures of practical abilities to complement this analytically orientated test. In both studies, the theory of Successful Intelligence was able to demonstrate that it effectively predicted the likely performance outcomes of future college students."

WHAT IS THE REAL WORK OF A LEADER?

Leaders delineate an organization's framework by a shared approach under their direction. Successful leaders are also visionaries. They construct joint visions by including as many players as possible in mapping the future path of their organizations. They are masters of goal setting, which is instrumental for them to complete their organizational missions as framed. Along the way, actions that are not consistent with flow toward the vision or the mission are seen as a drain of time and energy and must be eliminated.

Team players who become unfocused in an organization's vision are quickly identified as liabilities. Core values are established to provide reference for the conduct of organizational players. Recently, leadership models have focused heavily on emotional intelligence (the capacity to measure and control one's emotions and appreciate the emotions of others for the purpose of promoting superior relationships) to develop successful leaders. Emotional intelligence theories lie beyond the scope of this chapter and can be prone to unethical use that distracts from organizational success.

WHAT ARE REQUIREMENTS FOR TODAY'S LEADERS?

Leaders today are required to possess and manifest many or all of the following characteristics and mindsets.

Competency and talent for tactical data acquisition and analysis. A good leader uses knowledge (their own or from others) as required to achieve desired goals.

Vision. A leader needs the ability to see the future and have a clear and powerful framework that guides him or her to the place of achievement.

Mindfulness. A leader always maintains a presence of mind and has the ability to listen to others while sensing internal and external environments. The leader remains "in the flow" for the purpose of constant acquisition of new knowledge and execution of strategies.

Risk taking. A leader is willing to take risks but also encourages a consensus to support a vision that will empower all stakeholders.

Innovator. A leader is an agent of change who thinks out of the box.

Tenacity. A leader must possess a powerful drive to work through problems to achieve goals and possess an innate ability to overcome adversity and handle difficult situations spontaneously.

Self efficacy. A leader needs a strong belief in self and also the ability to be realistic in evaluating her or his own strengths and weaknesses.

Strategic planning. A leaders should have the ability to define a clear framework to guide team efforts and the skills to effectively identify the right person at the right time for the right action.

Support structure. A leader needs to be able to maintain a sense of compassion and remain constantly supportive and fair-minded even while inspiring team players to feel a sense of importance for his or her vision.

Great communication skills. A leader has the ability to deliver powerful messages and engage each team player in understanding the vision and the importance of their contributions to the vision.

Creator of positive work environment. A leader empowers the talent of team players and creates an environment in which these can be released.

Developer of talent. A leader works with team members to continually upgrade their capabilities and provide the means for them to make inspired contributions.

Developer of trust. A leader is a great listener who is open to real dialogue with those involved in the organization and encourages free and frank debate of all issues.

Authenticity. A leader is genuine—not attempting to "play a role," not acting in a manipulative way. She or he avoids unethical practices and stakeholder manipulation.

Integrity. A leader remains consistent in words and deeds.

Ability to be role model. A leader demonstrates ethical emotional intelligence.

Self-awareness. Leaders possess a realistic understanding of "who they are," how they feel and how others see them.

Putting It Together: Successful Intelligence for Great Leaders		
Analytical Abilities	**Creative Abilities**	**Practical Abilities**
Can identify problems and know who owns which problem	Innovative, generates new ideas	Applies the right knowledge at the right time
Sets up strategies to solve problems logically	Has ability to convince others to believe in leaders' ideas	Goal setter, knows exactly how to work toward measurable, explicit goals
Has ability to monitor the solutions process	Visionary, able to use imagination	Highly motivated but knows when to quit
Is able to identify problems that are worth the effort to solve	Leverages others to cover weaknesses and inspire reciprocation in kind	Possesses high self efficacy—a strong belief in the ability to get things done
Is able to assess team players' abilities and behaviors	Creative in designing work flow and strategies of success	Knows own strengths and weaknesses well
Provides effective criticism of work quality	Has ability to find alternative solutions	Takes responsibility for problems they own
Can see all points of view	Can see what others miss	Translates thoughts into actions
Is excellent at communicating ideas and processes to others	Is inventive	Has excellent problem-solving ability
Has ability to sort and group		Able to learn via hands-on activities
Can always follow through		Able to resolve conflicts
		Is a good adviser
		Works well with others
		Adapts well to change

WHY SUCCESSFUL INTELLIGENCE IS THE BEST MODEL FOR DEVELOPING GREAT LEADERS

Successful intelligence is what great leaders require to create desired positive outcomes in the real world. Successful intelligence embodies the analytical, creative and practical aspects of intelligence, in addition to the memory and affect. The beauty of successful intelligence lies in the fact that it can be developed through life experience. You do not have to have perfect genes to develop successful intelligence. Experience can make it available to all who wish to seek personal growth and development. We have utilized successful intelligence to lay the pathway for the development of great leaders. Leaders who master successful intelligence will acquire the ability to adapt to, shape, and select environments to accomplish organizational goals with positive societal and cultural outcomes. Everyone wins.

About Dushan

Dushan Vaithilingam (B.Sc. [Hon], M.D., Ph.D.) is a physician-scientist who currently works as a medical director for two health-care companies and serves on a government steering committee that facilitates the development of innovative health-care delivery systems. He also serves as a practicing physician with a focus on the health of senior citizens and is also involved with software development and the development of innovative products and services for health-care and related industries.

In the past, he has served on several university student committees and the governing council of a major university that provided leadership in various aspects of biomedical research. Dr. Vaithilingam has addressed several international and local conferences both in the U.S. and Canada and has received several awards related to his work.

He says that his goals are to develop sustainable charities that support the work with orphans worldwide, providing them with much needed health care, education, nutrition and love.

To learn more about Dr. Vaithilingam's current innovative work in leadership development and personal development, email: dushanv@gmail.com. A website on leadership development is expected to be launched soon, and several of Dr. Vaithilingam's books on this topic should become available in the near future. Anyone who has expressed interest through the email address listed above will be notified of the developments.

CHAPTER 18

Turn Your Passion into Action

By Genevieve Kohn

There are risks and costs to a program of action. But they are far less than the long-range risks and costs of comfortable inaction.
~ John F. Kennedy

Kennedy's words contain such wisdom and truth. The program of action that I have come to live by today came neither easily nor quickly. It came from years of learning, growing, and yes, often struggling. Looking back, I wouldn't have it any other way. Now I get to tell you what I have learned with the intention that it will make *your* program of action easier to develop and follow.

Just over 10 years ago, I was diagnosed with multiple sclerosis. Having come from a medical career background, I had suspected for a few years that I had MS—I had many of the classic symptoms, such as leg weakness, occasional numbness and tingling and others. When the official diagnosis finally came, I had thought I was already used to the idea.

It didn't quite work out that way. In the spring of 2002, I had my worst MS flare ever. I could barely walk and lost much of the use of my right leg and foot, so I could not drive. To say that I was scared and depressed is an understatement. Fortunately, I was able to see the gift that my husband had been (and continues to be today). By this time, I had been on the path of personal development for years, and I quickly realized that I could either let my diagnosis define me and control my life or start to look for ways to manage my condition and keep living my life to the fullest. The risk of the former option was simply not worth it for me.

It was not easy. More flares hit me, but, fortunately, I was able to get excellent medical care (living in the Boston area has its perks). Even so, these flares sometimes created lasting nerve damage.

My job at that time was certainly beneficial; it was in a large Boston hospital, with great medical benefits (plus, I had met my husband there). However, not too long after my diagnosis I came to another realization: being in a high-pressure, stressful environment was not helping my medical condition. I am a firm believer in the mind-body connection, and had also started energy-healing school that year. So when the opportunity came to work at my school, even though it meant a 60 to 70 percent pay cut, I knew I had to grab it.

FOCUSING ON GIFTS

Another part of my resolve to live life to the fullest also included our decision to start a family. I had always wanted to be a mom, and there was no way I could let MS stop us. When I was about five months pregnant with my first child, I had another MS flare. I had left my hospital job by that point, so I made sure I got enough rest, took a day off when I needed to, and was able to recover. This time in my life really made me appreciate all I had. Why? Because feeling sorry for myself would have been extremely non-productive, not to mention put a strain on my marriage and pregnancy. My son Brandon was born that summer at full term, in perfect health.

I experienced another uneventful pregnancy and healthy delivery two years later when I gave birth to my second son, Jason. Then, another MS flare hit me when Jason was about two months old. As difficult as that experience was, I once again had to rest and focus on my gifts: I had two beautiful, healthy children and an adoring husband. For me, focusing on the gifts in life is the only way to be.

This philosophy has also been vital to my success in business. I have heard from many business owners that it often takes several tries at different businesses before one becomes successful. This has definitely been the case with me.

I first went into business for myself almost eight years ago after graduating from energy-healing school. I absolutely loved that school and the inner growth I had experienced during my education there, and the healing work I learned was so helpful for my physical condition. Also, the school included several classes about business development in my chosen field. So I figured I would be all set to go out into the world and build the business of my dreams.

I am by no means minimizing the field of energy-healing nor the training I received. The bottom line was that I simply was not ready to put in the time commitment required to grow my business. I was so involved with being a new mom—even though I had only Brandon at the time—that my brain was literally not there.

I had not put many of the necessary elements for business success in place. The basics such as consistent advertising, building a solid professional network and getting a regular schedule in place were not there at the time. When I did get an occasional client, all I could think was, "That's it? Where are the others? Why isn't my business taking off?" (Lack of patience might have also been an issue here.)

Energy-healing also had not quite caught on yet. So I decided to go back to school to learn massage therapy. This was also fantastic training, and I fared much better offering combination sessions. A friend from energy school had started a wellness center, where I was able to get a steady stream of clients in 2006. However, because very few middle-class folks can budget regular treatment sessions, there wasn't much return business. Once again, I began to wonder why I was not doing better. I had never practiced gratitude for any business growth I did have, nor had I given myself credit for generating a decent part-time income. So it wasn't long before I began my search anew.

To save money on day care, we decided to keep Jason, my younger son, at home for almost a year. This was a great bonding time for me and him. Brandon was only in day care twice a week, so I got to be with him a lot also. Being a stay-at-home mom was fun yet extremely challenging. (Full-time stay-at-home moms, in my opinion, deserve all the credit in the world.) I occasionally saw a weekend or evening client, yet I still had this hunger deep within to do work that was my true passion.

FOCUSING ON PASSIONS

During this period, I really began to reflect. I had spent thousands of dollars on advertising yet had never found my true niche. I had not identified the element that would separate me from the pack—leading to accumulated debt and more bills. Having some time at home, I spent too much time in reflection. Once again, I focused on what went wrong instead of what had gone right.

After a few more years of searching and striving, I learned my lesson the hard way: I really needed to focus on what I loved, what was profitable, and to get coaching and support to build my business.

My journey took an amazing turn due to this lesson. In 2010, I became a wellness and business coach with a large nutrition company. I appreciated many things about this business. I learned how to follow what the most successful people in the company had done before me. This development was huge. It confirmed my growing suspicion that trying to do things all by myself was just that: trying. I never really reached my business goals.

I gained many tools then: the knowledge of how to find my target market, the resources required to advertise to that market, and ideas about how to really communicate with clients. I will always be extremely grateful for these.

However, as much as I gained from this company, the experience was also extremely stressful, not to mention draining. Though at first I was thrilled by actually finding people who were interested in what I had to offer, the price was ultimately too high. I was getting paid, but I was still investing way too much and going further into debt—by the beginning of the second year, I had spent almost 10 times what I earned. Also, most of the people on my team quit before really giving their new businesses a chance.

Spending 12 hours a day on work, along with taking care of my family, did not leave me enough time for rest or even a decent night's sleep. I became irritable and impatient, frequently yelling at my loving family. My MS symptoms worsened, even though I was taking the best nutritional products on the planet. I came down with a nasty sinus infection that lasted more than a month. I kept asking myself: why am I attracting so many people who don't want to do the work? It wasn't long before the answer hit me like a thunderbolt: *I* didn't want to do this myself!

I had started networking with people who were making a very profitable living by doing what they loved. Thanks to some of these folks, I was able to fulfill my lifelong dream of becoming a published author. So I guess *it had to be painful enough to make me finally take action.* Writing has been one of my passions since I was in grade school. I also dabbled in public speaking during my twenties, and I felt very comfortable and connected to my audiences.

Once I followed my heart and allowed myself to do what I truly loved, the results were amazing. I am now able to reach many more people than ever before with my message and experience—and I am climbing the mountain right up to that summit of financial freedom. My family sees how much happier I am, and the tension around the house has dissipated. The gifts just keep on coming!

I will never be certain why it took me so long to develop the action program that I am sharing with you here. Maybe it's because, for me, the lessons best learned are the ones that take the longest!

TAKING SEVEN HELPFUL STEPS

My story is not unique: success is a journey, not a destination. These seven steps will put you on the right path.

1. **Find your true passion.** If you have already found this, congratulate yourself. If you are still searching: What have you loved to do during your lifetime? Go back through your life, beginning with childhood. Often the things that give us the most joy can stem from the time in life when we were most in touch with our joy. Perhaps early-to-mid adulthood years are when you found what you really love to do.

2. **Find ways to turn what you love to do into a way to make a living.** This is not as difficult as it seems, for it is literally a labor of love. You can look into careers that would be up your alley, or you can start a business of your own. If you are not sure of how to do this, working with a life coach or business coach can help you monetize your passion so that you love the work you do each day without accumulating massive debt.

3. **Get organized.** The best way to turn your dream into a success is to know where everything is in your home and workspace. This will save you countless hours of searching through the mess, which in turn will **free up your time and energy** to focus on your new venture. This is where the fun really begins!

4. **Get your time organized also.** Obtain a daily planner, desk calendar or online calendar that can preferably be synchronized with a smartphone. Following a daily schedule is vital to your success. This way, you will not miss appointments or deadlines and you can stay sharply focused.

5. **Get into social networking.** This can include Facebook, Twitter and LinkedIn, among others. When you are plugged into online groups, you are availing yourself of an endless source of people who share your passion and goals, as well as people who can advise and inspire you. This is also FREE!

6. **Keep growing your network of people, resources, and ideas.** This network will take on a life of its own, where opportunities abound. Some of my greatest success has come from branching out in directions that would not have occurred to me had I been brainstorming by myself!

7. **Always take time to relax and celebrate every milestone.** For example, when I had my first article published online, I told everyone I knew about it. Then I took a couple of hours to relax and be grateful that, although it wasn't a major publication, something I created had gone "live." I now do this after each writing I complete. It brings such feelings of peace and joy! For me, gratitude is the way to go. This creates space for the universe to bring in even more success.

About Genevieve

Genevieve Kohn, also known as the "Yes I Can Coach,"™ is a best-selling author, success coach and public speaker who writes, coaches and gives workshops with her online, at-home business and all over the United States, sharing her experience and expertise, as well as teaching others how to create the lives of their dreams. She has developed a system called Parent-GOALS™ for parents who are also entrepreneurs. This system helps parents balance their family and work lives so they can take care of themselves, their families AND build their fortunes while helping others.

With the simplicity of the Parent-GOALS™ system, parents have a clear roadmap to their destinations that also reminds them to enjoy the journey.

To learn more about Genevieve Kohn, The Yes I Can Coach™ and how you can receive the free, special report, "Finding Your Own Happiness with Mom-GOALS" (can be used by dads too), visit www.triadsuccesscoaching.com or www.genevievekohn.com.

CHAPTER 19

Protect Your Business Secrets: Seven New Information Security Principles for Successful Entrepreneurs

By Paulius Petretis

Have you ever thought that you never really know who is reading your emails? Or why you have started losing contracts?

Recently one of my clients called me and said: "Paulius, I know you've been for a while in what do you call it? Information security business? … So maybe you could help me?"

"Well, what is the problem?" I asked.

"I have a feeling that someone is stealing my clients," he replied.

Apparently, one of his employees was selling customer information to his competitors. Two months later, the same guy called me and said he has just signed a major contract.

What is most valuable in your business? In some cases it might be your car, but more frequently, it's your business secrets! Your precious business ideas, a customer list, product details, secret formulas, information about a failed project (which I guess you are not proud of)—you name it.

Now, think about your competitors for a minute. What information would you like to know about them? Wouldn't it be what I have just listed as your most valuable information? That is why I would like to share with you my seven new information security principles for successful businesses!

1. LIST YOUR SECRETS

If you want to protect your secrets, first you have to know what they are. So the first step is to list any important information you have in your business. At this stage, people usually include sensitive financial, client- and product-related information. You should create a list of 10 to 20 of the most valuable information types in your business.

Sometimes, some types of information can be like the elephant in a room—so obvious that no one can see it. The first time I made this kind of list I was surprised at what kind of information I really had. Double-check to ensure you have not missed information which is owned by your customers and which you are using in your business. For example, I spend most of my time consulting clients, and I have information which is owned by my customers – like their product details, business plans, procedures, and service descriptions and so on. I am sure you might have customer information as well. In this case, you should treat your customers' information the same way you treat your own information, or even better, as the customer is the key in any business.

Then evaluate the value of any of the items on your list. One aspect is monetary value: How much it would cost you if this information were to be disclosed, or how much it would cost you to create that information once again, if it were damaged or destroyed.

Consider other aspects, such as goodwill or relationship with your customers or suppliers. Also, consider how much a security breach could affect you in general. Once, when I asked a client what the possible consequences might be if a certain type of information were unintentionally disclosed, he paused for a while and then said, "Consequences would be global." Be honest with yourself, and don't overestimate or underestimate possible consequences. Try to be as accurate as possible.

2. FIND YOUR SECRETS

Having defined which information is valuable to you, the next step is to find out where that information is. Understanding and identifying where information is can be one of the most difficult steps. Your information could be stored electronically, for example, in your email, customer relationship system, and website. It might be stored in one of your social media pages (like Facebook, Twitter, LinkedIn) or blogs.

Another type is paper information. You should know where it is and who can access it. Finding your cell phone somewhere in your house can be easy—you just need to phone yourself. Unfortunately, this cannot be accomplished with your information.

Also think about information you carry with you: information in your laptop, cell phone or any other devices, even paper documents in your briefcase.

After locating your information, you can consider labeling it according to its sensitivity to your company, e.g., whether it is public or sensitive. You need to label but not to mark your valuable information. In other words, it should be clear for the employees in your organization which kind of information is sensitive and which is not, but labeling should not attract any unwanted attention.

I often see a sign on a door stating "SERVER ROOM." In other words— "Down here is where we keep valuable information, please, be so kind, come in and take it." You can consider labeling your files with colors like "blue," "brown," or "green" instead of "public" or "confidential." You can label rooms with names like "tiger," and "lion," or "Venus," "Jupiter," and "Mars" instead of "Server room," or "Archive," etc. This way you would not attract unnecessary attention to the file or the room, but it would be clear for those who knew the system.

3. KNOW POSSIBLE DANGERS

The third principle is knowing what can happen to your information. Who and how would someone benefit from having your information or from destroying it, or maybe from altering some figures in your reports?

There are three basic types of dangers. First, your information could be stolen. Think of who might want to steal your information and why.

Second, your information could be damaged or destroyed. This could happen due to several reasons, for example, natural disasters or technical failures. Third, someone might have unrestricted access to the information, which means, information could be disclosed unintentionally.

Work out any possible scenarios and think of how and why it could happen. You should include scenarios related to people, technical equipment and natural events. Also, think about physical access to the information and the environment in which it is stored. The basic rule is that if one has physical access to your information, one has it all, no matter if it's electronic or on paper. Just to prove my point, I can tell you one hacker said it takes her about five minutes to completely overtake a computer if she has physical access to it.

4. SET RULES

Knowing what, how and why an incident might happen, it is necessary to apply certain rules and technologies to prevent negative actions. To ensure that everything is on the right track, you need to set certain work hygiene rules.

You should set your own specific rules. But here are some essential ones.

Treat all communication mediums with caution. If you think you can share very sensitive information via cellphone, email, or fax … think twice. Just to give you an idea, if you have ever seen at least one of James Bond film and think that all those gadgets he uses are fictional, you might be misled. Choose carefully how to transfer your information to your clients, partners or colleagues. There are secret cameras, recording devices and other means that you surely might not know about. Only if you know that you have taken the necessary steps to secure your environment can you be more confident.

Think of any laws and legislation related to information processing or information security. At this point, you might want to consult your lawyer. It is very important not to miss anything, and of course, not to break any laws. For example, personal data related laws may vary from country to country, so consultation with an expert is highly advisable.

Be prepared to react. Do you know how you would react in case of information loss or disclosure? Just think about it. In this case it might be a good idea to consult with your lawyer and to discuss it with your public relations consultants. Remember situations when something bad happened but at the end it was perceived not so bad? That might inspire you.

Browse the Internet securely. There are various webpages that can harm your computer, so avoid webpages that do not have a good reputation. The less you know about a webpage the less you should trust it. Use antivirus systems. They can protect you from the majority of bad things when browsing.

When writing an email, make sure you know whom you are sending it to. I often receive emails that are not intended for me. A lot of email software guesses e-mail addresses just from the beginning of a name. For example, you intend to write an email to someone called John Smith. But after you write "John," the email program fills in the name as "John Johnson." Have you ever faced this issue?

Do you know that most people still store their passwords in the upper left tray of their table or behind their keyboard or mouse pad? Some even stick them on the wall or monitor. I am sure you do not do this. Select passwords that contain both letters and digits, both upper case and lower case so that they would be more difficult to guess. You can use a sentence as a password, such as, "My password is 7 times stronger now." Sentences are easy to remember and more difficult to guess.

Liking the saying, "don't eat any food from the hands of the stranger," you should never install any software that comes from an unknown source. If you do, you could be unwittingly installing software that will monitor your activities, store your passwords, allow remote control of your computer and so on. The same is true for your smartphone and other handheld devices. If you leave your phone unattended for even a few minutes, it is no longer your phone. There are many types of spyware that can be installed into your phone that will grant access to hackers. Your activity can be tracked and your emails and other sensitive information can be read.

Decide what kind of information can and cannot be posted on your blogs and social media posts.

5. PEOPLE ARE THE KEY

The most important part of security is dealing with people. First of all, if you have anyone working for you, know who they are. Be sure that you are employing people who can be trusted. Ensure that information protection is everyone's business. Be aware that there are many ways to influence people using manipulation and psychological tricks to make them do something against their will. Second, know your suppliers—IT staff, cleaning services, etc. Be very specific about your rules and requirements for information security.

We often forget about our family and friends. It is a rather tricky part, because you want to be open and share some parts about your business with them. But they might not realize if the information could be shared. So if you still prefer to share business secrets with your friends and family, make it clear when it is confidential.

6. KEEP IT SIMPLE

Keep information security as simple as possible so it becomes a habit, a lifestyle. Don't make compromises with yourself, but do not become overly paranoid either. Information security is a means for achieving business objectives and control risk, but not a goal itself.

7. MAKE IT SUSTAINABLE

The protection of business secrets should be sustainable. Set goals for improving information security and align them with your business goals. When the rules you set become a habit, add new rules and improve existing ones to control your business secrets better. Be sure to review your rules at least once a year. Know what is changing in your environment.

Business secrets are the most valuable part of your business, and they deserve your proper attention. These seven information security principles are the best starting points to protecting your business secrets.

About Paulius

Paulius Petretis is an information security expert and has been helping people, small businesses and government organizations in Europe protect their business secrets for more than 11 years. He is a Certified Information Security Manager (CISM®), Certified Information System Auditor (CISA®), Certified in the Governance of Enterprise IT (CGEIT®) and Certified in Risk and Information Systems Control (CRISC®).

Paulius has been a guest speaker at various conferences and seminars and a trainer at information security related training courses provided by different companies.

Paulius thinks that information security must help businesses achieve goals but not vice versa. To learn more about Paulius Petretis and how you can protect your business secrets, visit www.petretis.com.

CHAPTER 20

How a 30,000-Foot Perspective Can Position Your Business as the Best and Only Choice

By Rik Villegas

Flying in the Air Force provided an interesting three-dimensional perspective that opened my mind to the big picture in business. While flying between Abilene and San Angelo, Texas, I could see both cities on either side of the cockpit. The 90-mile distance between the two cities would normally take me about one and a-half hours to drive; however, flying between them at a 30,000-foot perspective allowed me to see both cities at once.

Time seemed to slow down as I looked at the speck of cars traveling on a thread of road because the cars seemed to be moving at an ant's pace, and I could easily see most of the landmarks and intersections they had passed or would eventually encounter. Their limited perspective from ground level only allowed them to see a few thousand feet ahead or behind them, and it would take more than an hour before they could catch their first glimpse of their final destination.

Driving is a two-dimensional process that can be planned with a map to travel from a starting point to the end location. Intermediate transition points, such as geographic landmarks, cities and intersections act as reference points to gauge a traveler's progress.

Business planning is similarly looked at as a two-dimensional planning process that has a starting point and a final destination. Milestones along the route help gauge the progress of the business as transition points are passed.

Part of the planning process includes identifying groups of potential customers in various target markets and then developing a strategy to effectively entice them to buy from your business. The marketing section typically takes a two-dimensional approach by looking at individuals who have an immediate need for your product. The plan also tends to use marketing messages and media that are very similar and easily accessible to your competition.

Using the driving analogy with your prospects moving along a road that symbolizes a timeline, they would approach a busy intersection where you and your competitors are gathered. As they continue to move through the intersection, all of your competitors are trying to grab their attention by waving brightly colored signs and screaming for the prospects to stop and buy from them. This creates confusion because of the numerous and similar messages that are promoted in the same media, and it positions each business as a commodity very similar to every other business vying for their attention.

VIEWING YOUR PROSPECTS FROM A 30,000-FOOT PERSPECTIVE

What difference would it make in your business if your message was the first and only one your potential customers noticed, and if you and your staff were viewed as trusted professionals who could best satisfy their wants and needs? Obviously, that's a dream position to be in, and here's how it can become a reality for your business: You need to look at your future customers from a 30,000-foot perspective and understand how you can distinctively position your business *before* they need what you have to offer.

Business is ultimately about attracting and keeping customers by offering solutions with goods and services that uniquely satisfy wants and needs. Those wants and needs will change as your customers move through life, and specific events at the intersection of a person's life will create added stress and require additional solutions. I refer to these events and changes as "life transitions," and they act as milestones, or intermediate reference points in a person's life.

The starting point for everyone is birth, and their final destination is to have lived a fulfilling life when their journey is complete. In between those two positions are numerous transition points throughout life that challenge a person to look for businesses that can provide better solutions to their wants and needs. Some of the major life transitions that many people will travel through on their life's journey include parenting, starting school, employment and career development, engagement and wedding, pregnancy and birth, celebrating special events, moving and relocation, purchasing or renting a house, starting and growing a business, taking care of health issues, retirement, divorce, and coping with the death of a loved one.

When you view the lives of your prospects from a heightened perspective, you'll see how each life transition is part of the continuous journey your prospects will encounter on their timeline road. The transitions also create stress in a good or bad way and act as catalysts to trigger new needs and wants that were latent or did not previously exist. This drives individuals to seek out goods and services that they are motivated to purchase soon.

For example, when a couple becomes engaged, the event triggers a slew of needs and wants that will be satisfied before the eventual marriage. The bride, groom, and families will need rings, a cake, announcements, decorations, tuxedos, dresses, a bridal gown, photos, catered food, etc. Some businesses earn a large portion of their revenue catering to couples who are experiencing this particular life transition.

BUILDING BENEFICIAL RELATIONSHIPS WITH COMPLEMENTARY BUSINESSES

At the present moment, many of the prospects in your target market may be experiencing a specific life transition that connects them with you. Imagine, though, if you could figuratively use Google Maps to view your prospect's life at the ground level, and then increase the altitude to an elevation that allows you to view all their life transition intersections that are before and after the ones you best serve.

Often, the specific life transition that you and all your competitors center your marketing efforts around is preceded by one or more transition points that are the focus of other non-competing businesses that are gathered at the intersections your prospects just left. Instead of doing what all your competitors do by figuratively standing at your prospects' specific life transition intersection and just waiting for them to show up and take notice of your business, you could also develop beneficial relationships with those noncompeting and complementary businesses.

I call them complementary businesses because they are focused on the same prospects as your business, but they are positioned earlier in the life transition intersection. In the wedding example, after a ring is purchased at the jewelry store and the bride accepts the proposal, many other businesses will be visited prior to the wedding date, such as flower shops and reception centers, to complete the process that ensures a successful wedding. It makes sense that a complementary business that is visited later in the timeline should develop a mutually beneficial relationship with those businesses visited earlier.

At the lower level of a business relationship, the jewelry store will have the business cards or brochures of the other companies on their counter for couples to take. At the highest level of the business relationship, the owner and staff would highly recommend the services of a business they trust to assist the couple with the success of their wedding.

A key concept is for you to work with trusted professionals who are reputable because of their excellent customer-focused orientation, are respected by their peers and clients, and whose recommendations are warmly welcomed. Nurturing a mutually beneficial relationship with a trusted professional will allow you to be associated with a strong center of influence that refers qualified prospects who already trust you to offer the best life transition solution to their wants and needs.

As you develop more relationships with complementary businesses that cater to your prospects at a life transition intersection prior to the transition point you serve, you will create an ongoing stream of referrals. You will also begin to position your business as a trusted source because of the regular recommendations from other trusted, complementary businesses.

Years ago, before the Internet became a powerful marketing tool, I noticed that many of my clients served engaged couples as a common customer. They were all advertising in the same media with about the same message as their competitors and waiting for the couples to contact them. I worked with them for about a year to fine-tune a program that got the names of newly engaged couples and asked them to complete a checklist of the items they were still planning to purchase.

The couples were mailed a packet that included a checklist, useful information, and coupons from the businesses I worked with, and my clients received a useful database of names and the items the couple still needed so they could be contacted directly. Each of the businesses worked collaboratively to pre-empt the marketing efforts of their competitors, and the competition didn't even know what was happening because we didn't use conventional media to promote it.

This is a more complicated method to establish cooperative relationships with several businesses in a strategic alliance. However, you can develop simpler life transition relationships working one-on-one with complementary businesses. Once you grasp the power of harnessing life transitions in your business and how you can become a part of your prospect's life prior to their need for your goods and services, you'll easily identify ways to keep customers loyal to your business and create a greater lifetime value from your customers.

SEVEN STEPS TO MAKE EACH CUSTOMER'S LIFE TRANSITION THEIR BEST

Here are seven things you can do to start harnessing the power of life transitions for your business and become an important part of your customers' lives.

First, identify the specific life transitions your current customers may be experiencing. If it's not obvious, ask them questions to learn more about their situations and what motivates them to seek your products and how those products benefit them. If you discover more than one life transition, prioritize them and examine the effectiveness of your current marketing strategy to attract individuals in the various transition points. For example, if you own a furniture store, you might identify these prior transition points: Moving to the area, buying a new home, birth of a child, etc.

Second, examine the life transitions that precede the one that motivates your customers to come to your business. Draw a timeline and label the specific transition points in relation to the one you primarily service. You may notice that some points are directly connected and occur shortly prior to the life transition that motivates your customers to come to you, or they may be at the same transition point and much earlier in the process. Other transition points will occur over a longer period of time on average. If new move-ins is the primary life transition that motivates people to buy from a furniture store, then they will have bought or rented a house recently.

Third, list the business categories and specific businesses that serve each of the life transitions identified in the second step. Using the example of a new home rental or purchase from the second step, you could list realtors, apartment complexes, and property management companies as the business categories. Once you've identified the categories, look through your local directory to list specific businesses serving each category.

Fourth, identify what's in it for them to work with your business. This will vary for each type of business and each business owner. Some professions do not allow a financial reward, while it may be the standard practice for others. Some may be more than happy to refer their customers to you once they feel you will deal with their customers professionally and provide outstanding service. In other words, you must sell yourself to the business owner, and then discuss how the relationship can be mutually beneficial.

Fifth, contact the business owners or managers to discuss your proposal to work together. This can be an informal visit over the phone or in person that is concluded with a handshake, or it could involve a letter of agreement to formally establish the relationship and expectations of each other. Make it convenient to refer your business by providing business cards, brochures, and other materials that will make it easy to recommend your business.

Sixth, follow-up frequently and keep the relationship active. Just like any other relationship, you must continue to make contact and communicate the results of the individuals or companies referred to your business. You are building an ongoing relationship to develop greater trust and benefit among everyone involved.

Seventh, analyze the life transitions your customers experience during or after you have served them. You want to do this for several reasons.

By fully understanding and empathizing with what your customers are experiencing, you can provide better service to them and also refer them to other highly qualified businesses that will take care of their additional needs.

You could earn some form of a reward if the customer makes a purchase based on your referral. Again, this will depend on the type of business and the laws that regulate compensation.

You may expand the products or services you provide to better satisfy that specific life transition and earn additional income. Using the furniture store example, you may discover that new parents are buying rockers, but many of them are complaining about the lack of quality cribs and other related furniture, so you could expand your product line to include baby furniture.

Your ability to work with complementary businesses in the same or different life transitions will improve as you continue to build a strong network where each business benefits. Over time, you'll receive more qualified referrals, your marketing will be much more effective, and your profits will increase.

The 30,000-foot perspective offers a greater view for your business to serve your customers better by being there before they need you. It will also allow you to gain a competitive edge by positioning your business as the best and only choice for a successful transition, even in a crowded life transition intersection.

About Rik

Rik Villegas is a business owner, author, speaker, trainer and business coach who works with business owners to develop consistently profitable businesses that can operate without them. His personal goal is to add another zero to the bottom line of those clients he decides to partner with, while creating their dream lifestyle in the process.

In the past 30 years, Rik has started, managed, or turned around 11 organizations. He has also worked closely with more than 400 businesses ranging from small, privately owned companies to large multinational corporations as a consultant, coach, trainer and strategist in numerous industries. This has allowed him to gain a broad understanding of the procedures, practices and processes of many different types of businesses.

His career has ranged from being a captain in the Air Force, marketing director of a regional mall, manager of a business incubator, college business professor, and director of a Small Business Development Center. He has also worked with medical professionals, government, and nonprofit organizations.

More than 500 of Rik's business articles have been published in newspapers and magazines, and he is also the author of *Your BizGrowth Challenge: Implementing Solutions in the 7 Strategic Dimensions to Take Control of Your Business Growth, Even During Tough Economic Times.*

Rik was working with more than 20 clients when he stumbled onto the concept of building strategic alliances around moments he calls life transitions. He went on to develop a website that provides businesses with an automated, lead-generation system by focusing on over 17 major life transitions most people will experience on their life's journey. His clients in each life transition are positioned as trusted professionals who offer outstanding solutions to the challenges experienced by people during each transition.

In addition, he has developed a unique, inside-out customer training program that helps his clients create loyal customers who love to return more often, and refer more of their friends, family, and associates.

Rik has personally experienced most of the life transitions during his life's journey, where he has learned some powerful lessons on how to crack the success code in life transitions, as well as the business transitions of starting up, growing and exiting a business successfully.

To learn more about how life transitions can benefit your business, go to *BestLifeTran sitions.com* and click on the "Business Stages" Life Transition link where you'll learn how to position your business as the best and only choice, before your prospects even enter a crowded Life Transition intersection. You can also contact Rik directly with any questions at: *RikVillegas@gmail.com.*

CHAPTER 21

Taking Charge of Your Attention

By Dr. Barbara Walton

At any given moment, life is offering you a myriad of circumstances competing for your attention and energy. Where you focus your attention has a huge impact on what action you will take and will yield a defining influence on your life. Thus, being intentional in how—and where—you focus your attention is paramount to your success. Recognize that whatever you give your attention to you also give your power to.

As you contribute energy—positive or negative—to anything, it will grow. Decide to give your attention only to those aspects of life that you want to see more of and to minimize the amounts of energy and attention you give to aspects of life that you do not want to be your focus. Give those aspects of living just enough positive energy and attention to keep them in good working order and conserve the remaining attention and energy for the parts of life that you are committed to influencing.

It's very easy to get so overwhelmed with all the events or circumstances surrounding you that you aren't choosing where to focus your attention. When the exterior events and circumstances are directing your attention, you are operating at the whim and fancy of everything and everyone around you. There is never any sustainable satisfaction or serenity in operating in this "externally prompted" manner. You will feel like life is bombarding you and that you are always behind the curve.

To take back your own power and ability to direct your attention, to live a life of greatness, each individual must become "internally directed." This is a lot like reversing the flow of energy—instead of all the energy rushing at you and overwhelming you, you "plug in" to a source of energy that is bigger than you. Choose what you believe reflects the source of energy—God, Universe, Source, Nature, Imagination—and allow that energy to flow through you and out to your circumstances. When you do this, you create something like a buffer around you. I often correlate this buffer to having a moat around your castle, which means you have to lower the drawbridge to invite in what you decide you want to let in, that is, whatever you decide you want to give your attention to.

When you operate in this way, life becomes much more manageable. It's not that the circumstances outside of you have changed; it's simply that you have changed the way you engage with the circumstances of your life. Recognizing that your attention is a limited resource, choose wisely what to focus on as you take action to create the life that you desire.

FOUR AVAILABLE OPTIONS

When you are actively deciding what you give your attention to, it is important to understand the choices, or options, you have and the actions you might take to address whatever you are giving your attention to. To deepen your understanding of the options available to you, it may be helpful to categorize the possible actions. There are four overarching categories: to react, to resist, to resign, or to respond.

When you are surprised or overwhelmed, you are likely to react. This is most often fueled by unprocessed emotions and includes little to no conscious thought or choice. The emotions take over and fuel the actions taken. This can look very similar to a temper tantrum or an outburst of unexpected emotion. A reaction will often lead to regrets and damage to relationships that you must repair later. When circumstances appear to be going in a direction other than you have anticipated, or are comfortable with, you are likely to resist. While resisting includes slightly more conscious choice, it is also quite emotionally charged and is likely to result when emotions are mismanaged or less than fully processed. Active resistance is often easily identified, especially in others. Passive resistance is a bit more subtle, and therefore more of a challenge to identify and change. Both types of resistance take a lot of energy and become hindrances to creating your desired outcomes.

The third possibility, becoming resigned, is a surrender of sorts. It is most likely to happen when you have exhausted energy resources through reacting and/or resisting. It is also possible that you may have a habituated drama state that feels very normal and acceptable to you. In this case, it looks like the character Eeyore, from Winnie the Pooh, who is known to say, "Don't worry about me, nobody else does." This strategy occasionally works, as it guilts others into giving you what you want. It will back-fire even when it works though, so it's a temporary fix at best, as it is manipulative and people who have been manipulated will avoid further interaction with the offending party.

Ideally, being a conscious creator and choosing how to respond is the goal. The first three (reacting, resisting, and resigning) are sure-fire ways to increase drama and confusion while consuming huge amounts of energy. Unconsciously, one may use these less-optimal strategies to temporarily feel better or postpone uncomfortable personal action. It's a risky strategy though, as it will generally involve giving one's attention to what belongs to others. When you give your attention to what you believe others ought to be doing differently, you may be distracting yourself from what you are able to control and could do differently yourself. Unintentionally, when you tell another what you believe they should be doing, you will initiate a power struggle as they will resist being controlled and try to prove how they have a right to act in the way they have chosen. This drama and confusion is predictable when distract yourself from what you can control and give your attention to what belongs to another person.

If you know that you are 100 percent committed to your success and creating it with integrity, responding is the choice that will most often support your goals. A response is a well thought out and consciously chosen action or path of action. It may include considering several different scenarios and choosing the one that is going to get you closer to your desired goal without creating drama or confusion for yourself or others. Your ability to consciously choose to respond, and to stay response-able, is a masterkey to cracking the success code.

TWO FUNDAMENTAL ELEMENTS

Two fundamental and supportive elements allow you to direct your attention and choose your response. These elements are basically precursors to your being able to focus your attention and respond well at any given point in time. These two elements are the mindset you operate with and the meaning that you ascribe to events/circumstances. Both of these are deeply influential in creating the results you aspire to. Deficits in either of these areas will increase drama, deepen your struggle, and add difficulty to your experience.

Your mindset is basically the way you see the world, and what many people find surprising is that you can *choose* the most appropriate mindset to carry you forward. If you aren't consciously choosing your mindset, then a default mindset will be in operation. Any actions you take, when driven by default mindsets, are not accurate reflections of who you are or who you are capable of being. Default mindsets are derivatives of your innate personality, your past experiences, or mindsets you've seen modeled by others. The most detrimental default mindsets tend to be negative: fear, judgment, scarcity, pessimism, or sarcasm. These default mindsets will quickly take over, influencing your actions/behaviors, at any time you are not consciously choosing your mindset.

THE BEST MINDSET

A consciously chosen mindset is far better than any of the possible defaults, or unconsciously adopted mindsets of significant others or our past experiences. I guarantee that if you are not consciously choosing your mindset every minute of the way forward, that one of your default mindsets will finagle its way into the "drivers' seat" of your experience. A successful person is one who consciously chooses the mindset that will be most supportive of the desired results, as well as the desired experience on the way to creating the desired results.

The single most powerful mindset that one can choose is one of pure gratitude, and a secondary backup mindset is one of curiosity. Be willing to hold a mindset of gratitude for your ability to take another breath, live another day, and have another chance at getting it all right. There is always, always, always something to be thankful for. In times of deep challenge, when it becomes difficult to maintain the attitude of gratitude, I always tell my clients that curiosity is your "life jacket." When you find yourself leaving a mindset of gratitude and sinking into the negativity of current world circumstances or some difficult or painful experience of reality, it is most important to get really, really curious.

Life is too short for allowing what is predictable to dominate; one must stay committed to the mindset and the stories that will support you in being part of transcending what is predictable.

Gratitude and curiosity will serve as the most stable, most consistent foundation for creativity and innovation. When you consciously choose to come from an attitude of gratitude, you will see the world through a different lens. An attitude of gratitude can make the best of any challenge, can create possibility in any set of circumstance. You set yourself up for creating more of what is positive, right, and good when you hold a mindset of gratitude and curiosity.

THE STORIES YOU TELL

The meaning you ascribe to events/circumstances is simply the story that you tell yourself, and others, at any given time. These stories reflect your beliefs about life and what is possible. Without revising the stories you would be doomed to creating more of the same, over and over. When you commit to creating a new and different experiences, you have to be willing to upgrade your storylines to support the improved outcomes you desire. Often your stories will be a reflection of your past experiences from which you gain your wisdom. Wisdom is a wonderful possession until you allow it to taint your view of possibility or limit potentiality in your life. When you are able to consistently challenge your own stories— your wisdom derived from experience of what has already been achieved or created— you are most able to transcend what is predictable.

At this point, you can begin to shift what appears impossible to make it possible. This is where each of us has the broadest opportunity to impact the final outcome, and thus this is the area where one must continually revisit, revise, and choose to stay response-able. Additionally, your experience of circumstances will likely yield a whole range of emotions which are very real for you, and contributing to the story you tell. It is important for you to recognize that while each emotion is important for you to experience; not every emotion you experience is worthy of your expressing it nor will that expression support you in creating the outcome you desire.

At times, each of us must choose from our experienced emotions what is most important and necessary to express to others. This is a choice of leadership, of serving others, of responding to the needs of important others in our lives instead of always responding to our own individual needs. Make this choice consciously, without regret, from a place of service. Albert Einstein is known to have expressed that idea when he said, "Life begins when a man can live beyond himself." I believe he was alluding to the opportunity that exists in recognizing what others need of us instead of allowing our own needs to drive us.

When you choose to express the emotions that will support your desired outcomes in language that supports staying engaged, then you are living beyond your own comfort zone and tapping into the zone where "magic" happens. You are responsibly delivering what the experience is asking of you to be part of creating success.

Cracking the success code happens when you are able to choose a healthy mindset grounded in gratitude, focus your attention on what you value and prioritize—the issues you have identified as most important and within your ability to control—and actively choose storylines that support sustained good action toward the ideal future. An intentionally chosen mindset and intentionally focused attention will yield intentionally successful outcomes. It's this version of you that the world is waiting for, to create the outcomes that will be your specific contribution to an improved world.

About Barbara

Dr. Barbara Walton is a highly experienced and successful Master Certified Coach. She is known internationally for her passion, energy, wisdom, and insightful ability to support her clients in business, leadership and relationships. Barbara is passionate about inspiring others to see the world with a deeper sense of awareness, compassion and love. Since leaving the field of clinical psychology, she has spent the last 11 years coaching a diverse group of high-profile people: physicians, business owners, senior executives, entrepreneurs, and domestic engineers. Her focus has been on supporting and challenging them in the building of sustainable, ethical and socially responsible businesses and happier, healthier lifestyles.

In addition to her coaching work, Walton has held leadership positions with the International Coach Federation (2004 ICF President) and the ICF Foundation; has taught coaching skills to students and managers internationally and locally; and has served as co-leader of team development workshops for NASA for the past seven years. Barbara has five grown children and three granddaughters who occupy her time and attention when she isn't coaching.

Visit Barbara at www.kansascitycoach.com; find her on Twitter @LifeConnoisseur; or call her directly at 816-456-6380.

CHAPTER 22

Living a Dream, Bridging Two Cultures

By Motoko Ishihara Evans

"KAORU KANETAKA: Hopping around the world"

It was my favorite travel show sponsored by Pan American Airlines. It inspired me to travel around the world and make friends with many people. With this dream in my mind, I kept learning English. At the age of 19, I started my journey overseas. At 22, I became an English teacher of junior high school students.

MY 20s

Everything went smoothly. My life seemed to be fully enjoyable, but there was one thorn; I didn't get married in my 20s like many Japanese women. In Japan, many women are conditioned and accustomed to marry at around that age. I was definitely in the minority on this. I even felt a little alienated and wondered why I couldn't just live like an average woman. What was wrong with me?

I had been influenced by traditional Japanese values, which is to do what the majority of people do—try not to stand out. When positively interpreted, this value can be seen as "harmonizing with others and being a team player."

However, instead of getting married, I devoted myself to working. I received an opportunity to study in the U.K.- sponsored by Japan's Ministry of Education for six months. My dream became true. I was on top of the world. But in reality I was very much discouraged to speak out because I was surrounded by many talented teachers from Japan and other countries. I wondered how others were able to speak English so well and look so confident in doing so. Why couldn't I ?

BECOMING A CHRISTIAN

"Run your own course given from God, and then the crown will be given." Do not compare your life with others. Everybody had his own course. "Live your own life," the pastor of my church preached. Then he continued, "You can be newly born and start a new life." What an inspirational moment for me! I was baptized in the name of Jesus Christ at IESU NO MITAMA KYOKAI (The Spirit of Jesus Church) in the U.K. and became Christian. It was in September of 1993.

I realized that I had tortured myself, trying to adjust myself in the eyes of everyone else. I had been comparing myself to others all the time. I completely accepted myself, and I could live my life with my chin up. The whole world looked completely different, so bright and full of hope, even though I had some difficulties in studying at the college. I made up my mind to just do my best. I just stuck to my dream——to become friends with people from all over the world, and then I tried to talk to one person every day, not waiting for someone to talk to me.

One day I went to London and stayed at a bed and breakfast. I met a lady working there. She was from Bosnia and had been a teacher but due to the civil war in her own country, she had come to London. She was 32 years old——one year older than me.

She said some children in her country could not go to school, and some of her close acquaintances had been killed in the war. Talking to her made me realize that war was still happening in the world. I thought studying overseas had been tough for me, but she had come to another country to just survive. What a big difference there was between us!

Why was I complaining about not being able to speak English fluently? I promised myself that I should not forget this woman and that I would share her experience with my students in order that they could appreciate their daily life and live to the fullest. I had always taken peace and freedom for granted, but there were so many other unforgettable people who gave me a different perspective of life.

WORKING AS A TEACHER

I worked harder with more passion. I wanted to be a window for my students to see the world. I encouraged my students to learn not only about English but also to know more about the world happening outside of school. I was not afraid to be labeled a little different from the other teachers. I worked in order to contribute to my students' learning so that they could contribute to society.

I wanted every student of mine to reach their potential to the fullest. I believed I was doing this. I worked at schools that had student discipline problems. This was a hardship, but I kept consistent with my teaching philosophy, believing every student wants to be better. I tried various ways to communicate with them and to develop a better relationship with them so that they received my support and guidance to get better.

MARRYING AN AMERICAN

While I was experiencing these ups and downs at school, I met my husband, an American. He had been educated in the United States. I'm fortunate now to have a family in the U.S. I cannot forget when I first met his family. They welcomed me as a new family member.

Every member of my new family was very positive and open-minded. They believed in always challenging oneself to be better. How different they are from my family in Japan! My family prefer to stay in their comfort zone. Although I have no children, and I am very comfortable with my family situation.

I have traveled with my husband to several countries around the world. I have someone to share the joys of travel. The more I traveled and visited my family in the U.S., the more I became conscious of my Japanese heritage.

MOVING TO THE U.S.

I thought I had lived my life to the fullest as a successful teacher in Japan for 25 years. But I moved to the United States in December 2010 with my husband, excited about my new life. Everything should have been happy and smooth for me. But again, reality was not on my side. I had no friends, no job. I just stayed home watching TV, alienated from society, and just waited for my husband to arrive home from work each day.

I have a very nice family here, but I became depressed and gradually lost my self-confidence and became disappointed about not even being able to say "hi" to my neighbors. I felt hopeless, while for other people America is a country of opportunity. I felt that my whole life experience was worthless because many employers want work experiences here in the U.S. Then I asked myself "why am I even here? Why did I spend so much money, time and energy learning English? Why am I so miserable?"

I lost direction. At that time, it was so hard for me to accept my hopeless life.

My only healing was to have my own Japanese day. I wanted to keep my skills and my culture, so I wore a kimono—a Japanese traditional dress—which helped me feel my parents' love. And I would perform a tea ceremony all by myself. Once a week, I bought flowers and arranged them in Japanese ikebana style. When I was doing ikebana and the tea ceremony, I could experience joy of quietness and peace of mind. I started to feel better and better. I became more comfortable when I did my traditional arts.

IKENOBO IKEBANA FLOWER ARRANGEMENT

Ikenobo ikebana has a 550-year history. Ikebana is one's expression— of a person who arranged flowers. The Japanese people appreciate its simplicity, beauty and harmony. Western flower arrangement is perfectly beautiful to everyone. The flower's color and condition is in their bloomed stage most of the time.

On the other hand, the Japanese style uses branches too. The flower's stage varies; a bud stage expresses hope in the future, a dried leaf expresses coming winter, for example. Not all flowers and branches have to be perfectly beautiful since the natural-looking arrangement itself is an expression of harmony of the person with flowers. That is what is enjoyable.

We can create our own world within a small flower vase. We must choose carefully which flowers to use. The positioning of the flowers at just the perfect angle is important too. The length of the stem, the color of the flowers, and the spacing of each plant are very important too.

My teacher often said, "Watch carefully; every single flower has face and its own character. This one stands out too much. That one looks shy." I watched carefully and listened to the voice of the flowers; I like to be placed here and contribute to a whole. My teacher would say, "Just cut one more inch and it will make a big difference."

Yes! That's right. Even one inch of length makes a big difference. "This branch has a beautiful curve, therefore why don't you use its beauty as it is?" OK!," I replied. I should not interrupt its extensive curve with another branch. She was very precise in her critique of my arrangements, but it was each critique that gave me the wisdom to improve my arrangement. She loved all flowers and enjoyed their uniqueness. I acquired some very important lesson unconsciously about how to discipline myself and how to communicate with students.

TEA CEREMONY

My tea ceremony teacher, who has learned the art more than 60 years, often mentions that this art is to be a well organized and sophisticated art form practiced by Sen no Rikyuu(千利休), who lived from 1522–1591. According to Rikyuu, the ceremony should be simple, and there should be no extra movements. The manners are reflection of his principle of *ichi-go ichi-e*: 一期一会.

According to a Wikipedia entry on the Japanese tea ceremony, *ichi-go ichi-e* literally means "one time, one meeting" is a Japanese term that describes a cultural concept often linked with Sen no Rikyuu. The term is often translated as "for this time only," "never again," or "one chance in a lifetime." Ichi-go ichi-e is particularly associated with the Japanese tea ceremony, and in that context the term reminds participants that each tea meeting is unique and is a once-in-a-lifetime encounter with people. A host must treat his guest with highest respect and hospitality because the present tea ceremony could be the first and the last in the lifetime for both the host and guest. This concept was confirmed for me when I remembered the people I had met in all my travels.

RECOVERING FROM DEPRESSION

During this time of depression, I continued to quietly pray and do just my day of Japanese culture. One day when I was practicing my Japanese traditional skills, I thought of a great idea. I decided to share my skills with people here, with any Americans who needed peace of mind or were interested in Japanese culture. I wanted to harmonize and contribute to American society with my knowledge and experience just as one flower contributes to whole ikebana arrangement.

In September of 2011, I learned about Brian Tracy. I decided to find a job in customer service. I remembered bringing a book from Japan written by him. This book is titled *Psychological Selling*. As a teacher, I naturally compared my lessons to sales presentations.

I read Brian Tracy's book again, and I watched him on the Internet. Then I bought his CDs and listened. The CD, "Change Your Thinking Change Your Life" was inspiring. I was amazed to learn new ideas and awakened to a new perspective on life. *I can paint my own life?* I wondered. *I can do it if other people can do it.* Really? *There's no failure, just feedback.* Wow! This is incredible.

These ideas woke me up. I've followed my dream, and now I am in the United States where many people have historically immigrated while trying to reach their dreams. Why should I stay at home?

Then I remembered another one of my dreams——to serve people like Mother Teresa did. I realized what I had been doing and laughed. What was I doing? If I'm not able to help myself, how can I help others? I said to myself, "Don't be afraid of making mistakes. Just get out there! Get feedback!"

ACTION

I set new goals for myself:

1. To share in the joys of Japanese culture

2. To introduce and spread the good words of Brian Tracy to more students of Japan and the world

3. To provide opportunities for needy children.

I picked up the courage to look for contacts and information; this involved sending out emails. I also applied to take an online floral certification course. I began helping my Japanese study group more. Currently, I am writing a chapter book that tells about my road to a successful life.

SUMMARY

When I was a young girl from Japan, TV inspired me to travel around the world.

I understood that English was the key to travel and so began studying English. It was English that led me to meet Jesus—which started my new life. It was English that matched my husband to me.

English allowed me to meet so many different people, which in turn allowed me to broaden my view and perspective on life. My experience of depression after moving to the U.S. allowed me to learn to appreciate Japanese traditional culture even more. During this low time of my life, I got to know Brian Tracy. He guided me to my promising new life.

I could now recover from difficulties and setbacks that had come my way. I can truly say that my life has been very enriched by all these experiences and all people I have met. Life is an accumulation of single encounters with people in one lifetime (一期一会:*Ichi-go Ichi-e*).

MY 3As

1. Accept yourself and your situation; tough out the difficulties. Then you can identify what past challenges were and stop worrying.

2. Appreciate what you have and what others have. Appreciate differences which enable you to respect others and learn from them. Don't be afraid to have a different view of life.

3. Act toward goals. Action will bring new experiences which will allow you to live your life to the fullest.

Finally, I would like to add that native English speakers already possess a valuable tool because they are able to open up the potential for endless experiences in the world. They are blessed with having the best tool for obtaining these experiences. This tool is the English language.

About Motoko

Motoko Ishihara Evans lives in Dallas, Texas. Her company name is MOTOKO Japanese Culture Consultant; you can find more information at www.motokojapaneseculture.com.

She taught for many years in Japan and won an award from Kurashiki City for educational contribution. She says what made her unique as a teacher was getting her students involved with projects outside of school as well as with academic tutoring. Some of their projects include visiting Kamedake Hibakusha Elder's Home in Nagasaki, exchanging English letters with Taegu Girls Junior High School, making quilts for AIDS babies, sending letters and toys to an elementary school in Vietnam.

She has been a licensed teacher of Ikenobo Ikebana with experience for 26 years, and has two certificates related to the tea ceremony she has been practicing for 12 years. She learned kyokushin karate and sodou, Japanese kimono and manners.

CHAPTER 23

Standing Up to Make a Difference

By Bruce Langford

"I hate going to school, every single day." The boy who said these words inspired me to set off on a journey I could never have imagined.

It was mid-May, and I was on recess duty following a busy morning of teaching instrumental music. As I watched the students on the school-yard talking and playing basketball, I noticed one boy standing over by the wall, alone. He didn't look very happy, and I couldn't help wondering why such an athletic kid wasn't playing basketball with the others.

Two days later I again noticed Adam hanging out by the wall, alone. I decided to ask him what was going on. The only answer I got was, "I'm fine." After a few minutes, I spotted a boy who knew Adam from the audio-visual club I led. I asked him what was going on with Adam.

"I think it's his accent," Jason replied.

"What accent?" I asked.

"He talks funny," Jason answered.

I started to watch and listen to Adam more intently and soon realized he had a minor speech impediment. He had trouble with the *r* sounds in certain words. A week later, as I was waiting for the students to line up after recess, I noticed that Adam appeared to be upset. I discreetly kept him back for a moment to talk. After an awkward silence, Adam started to tell me what was happening. Some students were picking on him because of his speech problem. They'd call him names, give him the cold shoulder and leave him out of games and activities.

I asked him how long he had been receiving such treatment, and he told me it had been happening consistently, even at his previous school. I felt for the guy. I told him how much I wanted to help him but said it was tough to do when I wasn't around. So I promised I would do some research and meet with him again in a few days.

By Wednesday, I was armed with pointers I had picked up from my research. I told Adam I would suggest three tips that I felt were important; I had more ideas but didn't want to overwhelm him with too much information. When we talked again the following week, he had some good news.

"Those things you told me to do are helping," he said. "I'm keeping my chin up, but I just keep thinking about some of the junk that happened at my other school."

"What happened?" I asked him.

"Well, we had this talent show, and so I decided to do my karate routine. I thought it would be cool to have a chance to do my karate on the stage for the whole school. I had the music playing and I did the routine just like I'd practiced. Then at the end, I did my final move and froze with the music. Guess what happened?"

"What?" I asked.

"Everybody booed. They booed and screamed. And they all made fun of me afterwards. It was the worst day of my life."

I could feel Adam's pain as he relayed his story to me. I told him to try not to let a past incident affect his life today, but deep down I knew that some events can have a major influence on a person, while other incidents seem to roll by and are forgotten almost immediately.

A SHOW IS BORN

At that moment, I made a decision to do everything I could to help Adam. After thinking about his story for the next two days, an idea started to develop in my mind. I would learn everything I could about bullying, share it with Adam and my other students and then use my knowledge to create a show to help kids. I was convinced his story could be the springboard to help thousands of others. I decided to share my idea with Adam.

Adam lit up when I told him my plan. He thought it would be cool if what happened to him actually ended up helping other people. I told him that I had come up with a way he could be a part of the process directly.

"I think your idea is great, but I don't see how I can be a part of it," he said.

"Well," I answered. "I've been thinking. How about if I made a video of you doing your karate routine? That would be a great way of grabbing the audience's attention and then you would start talking about what you have actually been going through at school. It would be a way of getting the audience to relate to you and create empathy. Then, I would continue to teach strategies about how to deal with bullying."

"Just a minute," he answered. I'm not an actor. And I don't think I could do that. I wouldn't know what to say. Let me think about it, OK?"

I agreed and then followed up with him the next week. "I've decided I'll do it," he said. "If I can help just one other person so they don't have to go through what happened to me, it would be worth it."

I was elated. I began to plan how to make the video happen. I decided I would shoot it like an interview, ask Adam lots of questions, pull impactful clips from the footage and film him doing his karate routine.

In the meantime, I thought constantly about how to make my show idea a reality. I had always wanted to do something that would make a difference in the world, and I figured I could use some of my skills and interests to create a show demonstrating how to deal with bullying while incorporating music, videos and drama that would make it appealing to kids. I decided to send out fliers to schools to determine the interest level in such a program.

I was supercharged and excited to get going on the project. I outlined the steps I would need to take and started on my mission. I had 66 days to complete the finished product before school started in September.

To present strategies that would be effective against bullying behaviors, I decided to create a persona who would be a bit crazy, silly and zany but could be serious when talking about the realities of bullying. I made up my mind to be a radio DJ who was doing a "live on-location broadcast" from whatever school I was visiting.

I decided to use the name and initials of my son, Ben, as my DJ handle and to also incorporate a bit of my past into the character. While attending university, I had played piano as part of my business called A Time For Music, and the acronym ATFM seemed to fit right in with my plan to be a wacky radio DJ. Thus was born Benny DL with radio station ATFM.

Skipping forward almost 10 years, I have now visited more than 1,400 schools and presented my message to more than 740,000 students. Students empathize with Adam in his video appearance as he explains his life in seventh grade, ending with his statement: "I hate going to school, every single day." Even after thousands of presentations, I am still pleased to share my knowledge about bullying whenever possible.

HOW TO STOP BULLYING BEHAVIORS

To deal with bullying, you need to understand what it is. Bullying is defined as harassment and repeated attacks intended to cause injury or discomfort to others. It is characterized by an imbalance of power between the bully and the victim, allowing one person or a group of people to victimize others. Awareness of the different types of bullying is an important tool to use when evaluating bullying incidents. There are four main kinds of bullying:

- Verbal
- Physical
- Relational
- Cyber

Studies have shown that bullying often begins with name calling or abusive language and that 70 percent of bullying is verbal. During the early stages of bullying, victims sometimes are embarrassed and don't know what to do about it. I encourage the targets of bullying to deal with the problem by talking it out with a trusted person or by keeping a private journal to express personal feelings.

Here are a few suggestions about how to handle bullying situations. These techniques won't work in every situation, but many of my students have had success with them.

Ignore the Behavior
People who bully are often seeking attention. Sometimes they have been bullied themselves or are looking for people they can intimidate. By ignoring the incident, I am encouraging targets to make sure the bullies do not know they are having an impact.

Use Humor
Many times being able to lighten up a situation can work wonders. People who are quick with a joke or are able to see the funny side of an incident seem to be able to more easily get through difficult situations. Kids who are being targeted by bullies should remember that people who bully others are looking for a reaction. I tell my students to stand up, remain strong and refuse to react in the predictable way.

Change the Subject or Activity
When an attack seems likely, the intended target can try to change the subject by beginning a conversation about a sport or an event that might interest the would-be bully. Sometimes changing the focus to another person or activity can also be very effective.

Ask The Bully To Stop
I tell children to use a confident, serious voice but to not let their request sound mean or nasty. The target should just ask the would-be bully to quit their troublesome actions and then walk away or change the subject.

Avoidance
Children should make every effort to avoid the person or group who is causing the problem. Although avoiding the bully or bullies is not always possible, it can be one of the most effective ways to end bullying.

Walk with Confidence
I believe confidence is the single most important attribute that can counter bullying. I tell kids to keep their posture straight and their chin up and to walk with purpose. By acting confident, they will begin to feel more confident and their self-esteem will improve as a result, making them less attractive to bullies.

HOW TO PREVENT A CYBERBULLYING ATTACK

Much of the bullying that happens today is related to technology and the Internet. Cyberbullying includes, but is not limited to, the use of texting, email, instant messaging, social networking and games as methods of attack. I am frequently asked to present my "Cyberbullying—Got To Go" presentation because it is filled with tips to help people stay safe online. As a parent myself, I know it is difficult to keep up with the ways our children are using technology, but it is absolutely crucial for parents to constantly remain aware of what our kids are doing on the Internet.

Here are seven key strategies to help prevent cyber-bullying and remain safe online.

- **S**urf in a central place
- **T**ell personal information to nobody online
- **A**lways leave the conversation if you see online putdowns
- **N**ever meet people you have met on the web (without an adult present)
- **D**o other things too
- **U**se friendly language and practice netiquette
- **P**asswords—keep them private, choose them wisely.

For more ways to deal with cyberbullying, visit www.standupnow.ca.

Since creating my original show called "Stand Up Against Bullying," I have developed other programs focusing on the topics of respect, cyberbullying and parenting. I am constantly busy presenting school assemblies, addressing parent groups, delivering keynote speeches and writing books and articles.

A DREAM AFFECTS REALITY

Something interesting happened recently when I met with a group of students who had been chosen as actors for the "Stand Up Against Bullying" assembly I was about to present. As the students walked into the gym, I noticed a boy named Jeremy who looked remarkably like Adam. Fortunately, I was about to find out there was one major difference. Jeremy chatted openly with the other students, mentioning how glad he was that bullying almost never happened at his school.

"We do a lot of assemblies about cooperation and respect and stuff like that," he told me. "The kids are really nice here, and so are the teachers."

I smiled to myself, knowing we are on a long journey, but glad there is evidence showing that with increased awareness and through joint efforts, we are gradually moving closer to the elimination of bullying.

About Bruce

Bruce Langford is a teacher, presenter, musician and writer who specializes in the topic of bullying prevention. He devotes his time to his company, "Stand Up Now Productions," through which he has created school programs for children on bullying, respect and cyberbullying. Bruce uses drama and music to help teach strategies that can stop bullying virtually in its tracks.

Also known as "The Stand Up Against Bullying Guy," Bruce firmly believes that we can work together as a society to eliminate bullying. He frequently gives keynote addresses and workshops on bullying and works tirelessly on songs and videos for new programs.

To learn more about Bruce Langford and how you can receive his publication, "Avoid Bullying Forever—6 Powerful Strategies," visit www.standupnow.ca or call 1-800-901-8831.

CHAPTER 24

The Success Within

By Diana DeMar

INTRODUCTION

We seem to be turning into an unhealthy society of overwhelmed and hopeless people due to a failed economy and hectic lifestyle. We tend to wake up, stare at the mirror and ask ourselves, "What else is there?" when we have felt so stagnant due to stress from work, family expectations and even relationship issues. Thoughts, plans, worries and even dreams struggle within us and cause us to be physically ill and somewhat unhappy. We are not even aware that what we are searching for is our very own souls.

We have certainly forgotten to love ourselves, to truly appreciate who we are. We forgot to trust ourselves that we lost faith. Steve Jobs said, "We don't know where it will lead. We just know there's something much bigger than any of us here." Now, this awareness and confidence in something we don't see and ability to hold strong to something we want but don't have yet is our faith, and whatever it is, we are here … and whatever is our purpose … it is happening now.

That is why now is the right time to reconnect with our own source of strength, which we have all been blessed with. And becoming the main cause in our own lives will bring in more desired effect.

According to Ralph Waldo Emerson, "Shallow men believe in luck or in circumstance. Strong men believe in cause and effect." This proves that strong men already know they have the strength within to choose their paths and hold strong to their decisions.

In this chapter, you will be exposed to the brand code to "Awaken the Source of Wealth in You,"™ through which you are able to easily decipher your own success code. Success is not identified by your race, your culture, your sex, your economic status. Success is the inner strength off of You. Begin in You, and the rest is easy.

THE SOURCE OF WEALTH IN YOU™

The most precious gemstone, the diamond, comes from a piece of charcoal that has been formed in extreme heat and continuous pressure from the earth to make it hard. Then the diamond is cut by laser to a specific shape and subjected to cool water and oxidized to make it sparkle. We are that diamond. We are like a charcoal in that we do not see our own value. We must dig deeper and are subjected to extreme pressure of realization before we can fully be aware of how valuable we are.

The secret to success lies in a man's ability to see beyond the obvious. According to Albert Einstein, "Imagination is more important than knowledge. For knowledge is limited to all we now know and understand, while imagination embraces the entire world, and all there ever will be to know and understand."

Even this man of science knew that imagination and creativity are part of our true identity although most people have blocked those parts of themselves. Imagination and creativity are what keep one young. Everyone has the gift to procreate, but to awaken the unique gift you're blessed with—to see the unseen, to imagine, to create—that is where true material aspirations can be realized. Man's highest power comes not from speaking but walking his/her talk.

"The Source of Wealth in You"™ *(SOWIY*™*) Gives You the 11 Codes to Success*

1. The SOWIY™ Principle of Cause and Effect®
2. The SOWIY™ Balancing Act Principle® (The Principle of Polarity)
3. The SOWIY™ Principle of Attraction®
4. The SOWIY™ Principle of Letting Go®
5. The SOWIY™ Principle of Planting a Seed and Life's Cycles®
6. The SOWIY™ Principle of Restriction®
7. The SOWIY™ Principle of Selective Desire®

8. The SOWIY™ Principle of the Opposite Action®

9. The SOWIY™ Principle of Transferable Energy®

10. The SOWIY™ Ego Principle®

11. The SOWIY™ Principle of Vibration®

THE BEST IS YET TO COME

There are things we cannot explain in this world, things that are beyond our control, but everything around us will gradually change in our favor when we take control of our attitude, our thoughts, our ego, which is the real secret of power. Mark Twain says, "Inherently, each one of us has the substance within to achieve whatever our goals and dreams define. What are missing from each of us are the training, education, knowledge and insight to utilize what we already have."

The SOWIY™ Principle of Cause and Effect® explains that nothing in the entire universe ever happens by chance. Everything, including every thought and every action, results in an "effect," always being associated with a preceding and directly corresponding "cause." Every thought that passes through your mind (Cause) will turn into action (Effect). The attitude (Cause) you have and how it's projected in your interaction with others will be how others react to you (Effect). This Principle is constant.

Let me tell you about how I was led to a charmed life. Not long ago, I was a nobody. I was stuck as I never knew what to do in my life. I barely existed in this world. Maybe such a feeling came to me because I had grown up in a dysfunctional family where I was exposed to alcoholism, sexual abuse and neglect. These experiences left me drowning in low self-esteem, depression and anxiety. I graduated as a physician's assistant but tried to find a sense of accomplishment elsewhere. I turned to modeling, acting, then became a singer-songwriter. I still wasn't able to find happiness.

Eventually, depression caught me once more. I was medicated while my inner turmoil, anger and self-destructive nature robbed me of any direction in my life. I became suicidal. But something in me still held on. I was desperately searching for a way out of my situation until I took a meditation class. During my class, I felt a transcendence like my body was a weightless feather moving up into the infinite. I was convinced then that there is more to life than there appears to be and spent the next three years in meditation and soul cleansing.

On August 7, 2007, at 11 p.m., I lay down to sleep and suddenly found myself gasping for air. I got very, very cold; shaking uncontrollably, I saw my body, which was perfectly horizontal, inflexible, straight and tight lifted up from the mattress. I was going through an out-of-body experience also known as a near-death experience. The next day, I saw beauty everywhere. Wisdom was flowing within. All of a sudden I was aware of who I was and why I was here. I woke up to my gift. It was miraculous.

Today, I'm content, confident, healthy, happy and successful. I exist from my higher self—the truth. This is the "Source of Wealth in You,"™ and each one of us is born with it.

RECOVER THE CODE WITHIN

Every creation has a creator. Anything present has a source. If success is a creation, it's therefore already present and has originated from a source. And such source is you. The only real and permanent source of wealth is already within humans. Awareness is the answer. There isn't anything to look for outside of ourselves because it's already inside us. All we need to do is reconnect with the source of wealth within by awakening ourselves.

There are times we feel so empty that it's hard to reconnect within ourselves. We feel the need to struggle. And yet we fail to realize that life here on earth is a cycle, a circle in which we go round and round. And the cycle completes itself when we awaken. With awareness, we are able to have a clearer objective, a concrete direction, a goal.

The goal is to transform; to shed peacefully what's not useful anymore, and become more of a pure energy. Such pure energy enhances our wits, makes our emotions clear and easy, and it is called love. When love envelops our innermost being, we are able to project love and attract the same love from others.

The SOWIY™ Principle of Attraction® claims that one attracts what one represents. That is why if you're feeling negative, negative people will very likely be attracted to you. If you are filled with love, loving people will come your way. And when you are giving, then generous people are attracted to you as well.

Now the journey toward completion of the cycle of suffering, also known as birth and death, means liberation from the boundaries that keep us chained and prevent us in becoming our true selves. Our purpose here on earth is to manifest our true selves; to develop ourselves through self-discipline, self-discovery and self-mastery. This is the key to success.

According to the song, "The Greatest Love of All," "is easy to achieve, learning to love yourself is the greatest love of all." The song itself shows that to be able to feel real love, you must be able to love who you are, because loving yourself is identifying and nurturing who you are. Maslow's hierarchy of needs claims that self-actualization is the highest point of the pyramid in which one would manifest the ideal happiness. In the Bible, God's commandment to us is, "You shall love your neighbor as yourself," which is rather contradictory realizing that love for others is actually a manifestation of love of oneself.

FROM WITHIN TO WITHOUT

This world is a world of appearances. However, knowing the truth in this spiritually ambiguous place, the material world, is not hard at all. Being aware of the connection between attitude, thought and action unlocks the code to success, the quality of the mind is what matters; logical intellect alone is not enough.

This is man's law: "Show me before I believe." Most of us are truly concerned with what we have. Though happiness is unseen, we need objects to remind us of this happiness. We need properties to help us visualize happiness. A husband and wife want to be fulfilled as good parents by giving quality education to their children, but how can such unseen things be verified? After their son's graduation, he is able to find a nice-paying job and care for himself. How can a lover prove he loves his fiancée? Yes there is the occasional passion of calling her, sending her messages and red roses ... but wait! The calling and the sending must be paid for.

The world is actually a material world. Everything a person does is already connected to a material entity to which we are obligated, such as paying taxes. And yet, there is more than being material. "The Source of Wealth in You"™ helps you to understand that material things are tools to attain the true wealth of being you.

The SOWIY™ Balancing Act Principle® (The Principle of Polarity) claims that everything in the material world is dual and that there are no extremes but only degrees of the same thing. All is charged with both masculine and feminine energy; recognize the two opposites in any situation and balance them against each other for a practical resolution. For instance, to balance the inner with the outer, the emotional with the physical—take the problem you're presented with (from the material world) and balance it against what is true for you (emotionally, spiritually) to find a practical resolution.

The same process allows you to balance the masculine with the feminine. When you say masculine, you want to see a concrete manifestation of the success you attained, and when you say feminine, you want to feel the success within. Unfortunately, we are more of the masculine. We want to see it all with our eyes. The inner power of yourself, the real thing, expresses usually on the opposite of what we're used to—from within to without. If you haven't connected to the source within, then you are without. When you have it from within, then you surely will have it from without.

The point is, believe in yourself. Doubts overwhelm our existence. A great example of someone who believed in himself is Bill Gates, who is now one of the richest men in the world. Bill Gates was not from a super-rich family. When he was merely 17 years old, he created his own program, a time tabling system. He sold it for $4,200. This helped him visualize, and he soon established Microsoft in 1975. The ordinary boy is now worth $56 billion. Most of us think that this is just his luck. The truth is, Bill Gates was able to see his purpose. What is stopping you from attaining the material wealth that reflects the wealth within you? Could it be because of self-doubt? Or is it because of your ego?

The SOWIY™ Ego Principle® explains that the human ego is a double-edged sword. It can help you build up some confidence, yet it is the biggest obstacle to true success and happiness. Why? Because too much ego clouds your reality of life, it disrupts your balance. You need to firmly ground your dream; to know exactly when and how the ego can serve you and also be aware of how it can cause irreparable damage. A very good example of a person who was able to control his ego is the world-renowned Filipino boxer Manny "Pacman" Pacquiao. A poor boy, he has been using the money he won through fighting to serve his countrymen as a congressman. Currently still a boxer, this rich and strong sports icon will still stoop humbly to be approached by everyone. That is true success when you master yourself. Don't let your ego get the best of you.

FROM DESPERATION TO ILLUMINATION

The SOWIY™ Principle of Letting Go® explains that when you let go what is blocking your progress, more space will open up for the new to come in. Such examples are letting go of a troubled past, of bad memories and experiences, of a destructive habit, of a relationship that cannot be saved, of foods and thoughts that are bad for your health or anything else that is holding you down. When you let go, you allow yourself to be cleansed. You are able to see the real situation in a broader perspective so that you can plan and prioritize your next moves.

CONCLUSION

Life is truly a game; play, make mistakes, learn from life and have fun at it. What you truly need will arrive. It depends solely on your readiness for it. "So, how do I begin?," you may ask. First, consider "what is" that can't be changed and accept it. It's a proven truth that no one can do it all on their own. Seek help, if needed. Second, connect with The Source of Wealth in You™ by daily conscious application of the 11 codes to success; they're your success applications (aka "SOWIY™ Success Apps") to unlock life's mysteries. Third, co-create and act upon in alliance with the universe's plan for you.

Remain strong with a positive outlook regardless of the circumstances. On this amazing journey of life, success and happiness are present and available. Consciously align yourself with it each day! At the end of the day, the expected results depend on the nature of your attitude and thoughts within this very moment.

Each one of us is unique. There isn't another person like you. An exact match does not exist. All dreams, ambitions and prayers will be answered depending on how you strongly believe in your capacity to attain it. When you stop to pray, you have confidence in God. And yet, only when we take charge of our lives and manage our problems can God demonstrate confidence in us. God helps those who help themselves.

About Diana

Diana DeMar, also known as "The Source of Wealth in You"™ is a best-selling author and life-success expert who is regularly sought out for her effective success strategies and applications to anyone looking to attain lasting results. Diana is an American author, speaker, inspirational teacher, actress and singer-songwriter. She writes extensively on the inner human wealth, promoting self-awareness, confidence and mind-power as the way to success and fulfillment.

Diana DeMar is the founder of "Diana DeMar Success" and "Huntress Records." She works globally with professionals, groups, organizations, and individuals to motivate people to act to achieve results. She also created *The Source of Wealth in You™* book series and *Awaken the Source of Wealth in You™,* which unveils the secrets on how to reconnect to one's ever- present strength in achieving success.

"The Source of Wealth in You"™ is the origin of strength, potential, hope and abundance each one of us is made of. The access to success lies in restoring the link to this place. Diana strongly believes that everything is made up of energy and all are connected through it. And because man is always distracted, such journey to perfection should then be redirected. This is the mission of "The Source of Wealth in You."™

Diana possesses a warm, playful personality, imparting energy to any project in which she becomes involved. She specializes in core energy coaching, which means coaching from within and assisting individuals and groups to improve their mental and physical well-being and happiness. She is a member of the International Coach Federation, Toastmasters International and the Screen Actors Guild.

To discover more about Diana, "The Source of Wealth in You,"™ "Awaken the Source of Wealth in You" ™ and to receive life-success technology, programs, courses, seminars, practical solutions from the inside out and *free* powerful tips, sign up at http://www.DianaDeMarSuccess.com.

CHAPTER 25

How I Turned My IRS Nightmare into A Dream-Come-True for People Who Need Tax Help

By Jack McDonough

I was about seven years into running my own little CPA firm in a bedroom community outside of Denver. I provided tax preparation services, bookkeeping and some business consulting. We were your typical neighborhood CPA firm, and my clients might run into me at church, school, kids' sporting events or in the local supermarket. We were a community. Most of my early clients came from word-of-mouth referrals. Life was good.

In my CPA firm, I had the luxury of seeing what my most affluent clients were doing to make more money from passive and semi-passive investments. I noticed that most of them had invested in mutual funds and real estate. At that time, real estate and the stock market were enjoying a great run. Earning 15 percent a year on stocks and 10 percent a year on real estate were no brainers. Or so I thought.

Based on this insider information, I decided to start buying residential real estate properties. I was a buying fool. The more I bought, the more the banks would lend me to buy even more. I went from owning my own condo to creating a mini real estate empire in three years. I was easily renting out all of the properties and enjoying additional cash flow each month. Life was even better. Or so I thought.

A funny thing happened on my path to becoming a real estate tycoon. The Colorado real estate market tanked when oil prices collapsed, sending the entire state into a tailspin as we experienced a regional recession.

I found myself losing tenants and not being able to replace them. I was faced with having to fund the mortgages on my rental properties by sucking all of the money out of my CPA business, borrowing on credit cards and not paying my payroll taxes. I felt like a hamster running on one of those little wheels.

My CPA firm was growing and making more money than ever, but I was spending all of it and then some to pay the mortgages on my vacant rental properties. After years of paying on empty properties, I saw no end in sight to the depressed real estate market. I wanted to get out, but there was no market for the real estate properties I owned, so I put my head down and kept plodding ahead. It was sucking the life out of me, my family and my CPA firm.

Because I wasn't paying my payroll taxes on time, I kept getting letters from the IRS asking for my returns and money. I didn't know what to do. I didn't have the money to pay the IRS because I using it to pay for the empty real estate properties. I guess I figured if I didn't file my payroll tax reports then the IRS wouldn't know how much I owed and somehow would leave me alone. Of course in the back of my mind, I knew this type of thinking was totally B.S. and flawed, but I had no other choices at the time. Or so I thought. What I came to realize was that I was wrong, very wrong.

The next thing I knew it was the middle of tax-filing season, and my office was jammed with clients waiting to see me. Then out of the blue, my secretary comes back to my office to tell me that an IRS revenue officer is in my lobby and wants to talk to me.

At the time, I was not representing clients with IRS problems, so I immediately knew he was there to see me about *my* unfiled and unpaid payroll taxes. I was shocked. I was sweating profusely. I had no idea what to expect. Everything running through my mind was negative. I was expecting the worst.

Figuring they would take my Mercedes 500SEL, my watch, my house, my CPA firm and maybe even me, I was stuttering and stammering when the IRS revenue officer showed me his badge.

He read me the riot act—real fire and brimstone stuff. It reminded me of growing up Catholic in Boston where every nun and priest constantly reminded you that if you do *anything* wrong you'll go straight to hell. I figured this was it. I was going straight to hell.

I had no idea if the IRS revenue officer was telling me the truth or just a bunch of stuff to scare me (later on, I figured out it was about 50/50). I knew I had not filed and had not paid, but he made it sound like my life was over if I didn't immediately come up with the payroll tax returns and the money.

I told him I'd see what I could do. The next day, he levied my CPA firm bank account and sucked out $3,000 or $4,000 that I really needed at the time. A couple of days later, he filed a federal tax lien. Everything was going downhill fast. My banker was looking at me funny; my credit was shot with the tax lien, and my spouse was ballistic.

For six months, the IRS revenue officer would just show up randomly in my office and shake me down for a payment. If he didn't get what he wanted, he would levy my bank account for more. He loved zeroing out my bank account. Life was not good.

Finally, I made the strategic decision to get rid of all the real estate rental properties and stop the bleeding. I'd had it and couldn't take it anymore. I finally let go of the American Dream of buying real estate as "it always goes up." What I had failed to realize is that it can also go down ... by a lot.

I was bummed, but I had no other choices. My next problem was how to get out of my real estate deals. There was zero market for rental properties; the market was already flooded with foreclosed properties. The Sunday newspaper had it own pullout section featuring pages and pages of FHA and VA properties for sale.

I negotiated with my lenders to take my rental properties back; some did, and others foreclosed. It was a mess, but at least I was out of all the real estate deals. Once out, I was able to get current with my IRS payroll taxes and get the IRS revenue officer out of my life. Life was OK—not good—but OK.

Before I filed my tax return for that year and reported all the real estate transactions, I did a little tax research to see how to report all the crummy real estate deals where I had basically lost everything – including my savings and credit . I found this IRS Code Section (I think it was Section 108.something), that would allow me to avoid paying taxes on all my real estate deals gone-bad.

I felt good about my research and filed my tax return based on that. Unfortunately, the IRS did not like the way I filed and decided to audit my tax return. For anyone reading this who has not undergone the scrutiny of an IRS audit—suffice it to say it's comparable to having a few root canals done without Novocain and a heck of a lot more expensive.

When I got the audit letter from the IRS, I thought, "no big deal." I knew my tax return had been filed accurately and that I would easily be able to explain my reasoning. But the more I tried to talk myself into believing the audit would be a breeze, the more nervous I got, especially as the audit date approached.

So I go to the audit myself (first mistake), and I'm thinking "heck I'm a bright young CPA and I know I'm right," (second mistake), and at the time I was probably still a bit arrogant (third mistake). All of this added up to the perfect storm.

The IRS auditor basically tells me in no uncertain terms that I am wrong, and my interpretation of the tax code as it related to my crummy real estate deals was a "reach" at best. She issues me an audit report showing that I owe tens of thousands of dollars in additional taxes, plus interest and of course some penalties. I'm angry. So I file for an appeal.

I get ready for the appeal by re-reading my original research. I know I'm right. The appeal date comes and I go by myself (fourth mistake). The appeal officer is nicer than my auditor, but after a couple of hours of discussion, I get nowhere. I still believe I'm correct.

I convince the appeals officer to keep my case open for a long as she can so I can obtain representation. She agrees and gives me five days. When I argue with her about the five days, she holds up her hand and says, "or

I make my decision today." I agree with her, five days will be fine.

The next day I meet with an attorney to handle my appeal. He quickly looks over my return and my research and agrees that I'm right. He tells me his fee will be $5,000. I'm shocked, as all the research is done and all he has to do is convey it to the appeals auditor. He says, "Well, if that was so easy then you should just do it yourself." I pay him the $5,000.

He schedules an appointment with the IRS appeals officer for a couple of days later. I pace around for days like an expectant father, waiting and waiting and playing what-if scenarios over and over in my head. Even though I know I'm right, I'm worried about what would happen to me and my family if I really owe all the money that the auditor computed. I was scared. Heck, I'm in the tax profession, and I have no idea what the IRS can do to me.

Most of my CPA clients who had me prepare their taxes either enjoyed their refund or attached a check to their tax return and paid what they owed. For the few who ever did get audited by the IRS, the proposed IRS changes were minimal, and my clients paid them and moved on. My clients didn't have problems like I had. My problems were serious; they were big and bad. I had the feeling that I was about to become a poster child for the IRS.

Finally I get a call from my tax attorney. He says that I was right. Upon further review, the IRS appeals officer agreed with my documentation and the IRS code section I had hung my hat on. I was ecstatic. I owed the IRS *zero* dollars. My IRS audit was written up as a no-change audit.

I realized what had just happened to me totally sucked and it had cost me untold sleepless nights, pounding stress and $5,000; but life was good again. And about to get even better.

In that very moment, the entire "IRS Industry" was created in my mind. I knew my attorney had not done anything special in representing me other than what I had done with the exact same information. He barely had time to read all of my documentation before meeting with the appeals officer.

What my attorney had done was so simple, it was stupid. He had represented me as an independent third-party professional. Before I retained him it was just me (uninformed taxpayer) against the IRS, and the IRS was having its way with me.

Almost like magic, once I retained a tax attorney the whole game changed. It seemed like it went from Jack McDonough—self-serving CPA trying to save himself—to Jack McDonough, who has hired a tax attorney to deliver a message to the IRS loud and clear.

AN INDUSTRY IS BORN

The big *ah-hah* moment for me was this: I realized that if the IRS could do that to me as a CPA, imagine what they must do to the average tax-payer who has zero tax knowledge or understanding of their rights with the IRS. Standing in my kitchen that night when my attorney called to tell me the good news, I knew that my life was never going to be the same. A giant new industry in America had just been born. It was the IRS representation industry.

I'm not sure the federal government is proud of the fact that its taxpay-ers need protection against their own government, but it is what it is. So I started getting the word out to any taxpayer suffering from IRS prob-lems should call me and let me help them out. I had a sneaking suspicion that many taxpayers who were dealing with similar IRS problems didn't know what I did.

I wanted to put every taxpayer on notice that solutions to IRS problems actually exist—but in most cases you need to hire a professional to rep-resent you in front of the IRS. I was living proof of what happens if you try to represent yourself.

My CPA firm started marketing our IRS services in the local newspa-per using some very small ads. The results were truly remarkable. The phone rang off the hook with taxpayers calling for help. Potential clients were crawling all over each other to get in to see me. We had to add more phones lines to handle the demand.

We were literally overwhelmed with taxpayers seeking assistance. I started seeing upwards of 14 people a day suffering from all kinds of IRS problems. With this overnight windfall of new clients, I had to add staff to keep up with the volume of work. We added more administrative assistants to answer the endlessly ringing phones as well as attorneys, CPAs and ex-IRS agents to do the work.

Our once seemingly spacious office became a little bit too cozy overnight. We had files on files to the point where you could not even see a glimmer of a desktop. The file cabinets were full, and we had no room to add more of them. We had to get additional office space during the busiest time of the year in order to keep growing at such a rapid pace.

Within eight months it became apparent that I would have to sell my CPA firm and my conventional clients because the IRS representation services had taken off so fast that I just didn't have time to provide my existing clients the level of service they deserved.

I found selling a professional practice to be a double-edged sword. I had formed a lot of great relationships, both business and personal, with many of my clients; and now I was forced to gather up all their files and sell them to another firm just to ensure they received the level of service they deserved.

The upside was that I was able to focus 100 percent on growing the IRS representation practice and create a cushion of savings from the sale proceeds. Life was great and going faster everyday.

The IRS representation practice was fun. It was exciting! It was like being taped to a missile launching into space. We grew and grew and grew.

We went from being a stodgy old CPA firm to a drama-filled office of taxpayers undergoing the worst part of their lives. Helping them was the most personally satisfying thing I had ever done as a professional.

The best part of all of this was helping so many taxpayers get their lives back. We saved countless marriages. We kept families together. Our clients loved us. They brought us food and gifts. They invited us to Thanksgiving dinner and expected us to come. We helped everyone who could make it into our office. We even tried to help people who in the end couldn't be helped by us or anyone else, but we still tried.

AN INDUSTRY GROWS

My second big *ah-hah* moment came when I realized that maybe this was not just a Denver problem, but that taxpayers in other parts of Colorado might need IRS representation as well. So I opened an office 67 miles away in Colorado Springs, which has a population of 280,000.

Overnight, we were busy. In the first 30 days, I then realized that this was a national problem—not just a Colorado problem. I knew millions of taxpayers nationwide were suffering from similar IRS problems.

Colorado Springs provided me some of the most colorful clients I could have ever imagined. I met gun-carrying clients, clients from the religious right and even tax protesters. Often the tax protesters tried to hire us, so we had to be careful not to accept them as clients. If one snuck through our screening process, we would give them two choices: apologize to the IRS and get in filing and paying compliance or we would refund any fees they had paid us and they could move along their merry way.

Things were going so well in Colorado Springs with our new, colorful clients that we decided to expand by adding three additional satellite offices in the Denver market. We opened the satellite offices to make it more convenient for taxpayers to meet us in locations closer to their homes or businesses.

The new locations made our business explode even more. We were representing thousands of taxpayers suffering from IRS problems. Life was better than good. But I had a sneaking suspicion that something was not right.

My suspicion was right—our success almost caused us to fail. The problem was that we really had few, if any, systems in place to handle the huge onslaught of brand-new clients. We did not have a database system robust enough to keep up with everything.

We finally had to stop dead in our tracks and no longer accept new clients while we wrote processes and systems to ensure that we professionally represented every single client. We hired an outside company to write a database to track all of our clients. It was tedious but completely necessary. I hated stopping but we were going to implode without it.

AN INDUSTRY GOES NATIONAL

My third big *ah-hah* moment came when I realized, while documenting all of our processes and systems, that we had created a great business model. We were able to offer extremely beneficial, professional IRS representation services to help our clients end their IRS problems and get their lives back on track ... all while we enjoyed a profitable business. It was a total win-win.

I already knew, or had a good hunch, that if I had uncovered this many taxpayers seeking help with IRS problems in five different offices in Colorado, that a national market for these services most likely existed.

Based on that hunch and our newly written documented processes and systems, I created a turnkey program to offer to attorneys and CPAs all over the United States. The program was an A–Z system, which allowed any savvy professional to add IRS representation services to an existing law or accounting practice.

So in addition to successfully operating my own IRS representation practice in Colorado, I was now helping attorneys and CPAs across the United States add the same service to their practices.

The demand for my turnkey system was almost as rabid as the demand from local Colorado taxpayers. We had created a bigger business than our original business. We ended up with thousands of professionals as clients.

Most, if not all, of the IRS representation companies that are advertised on TV, radio and the Internet today have purchased my turnkey programs, attended my seminars and consulted with me.

Many of these companies have grown into businesses that annually generate millions of dollars in fees each year. Unfortunately, some of them subscribe to unethical business practices and seem to have lost their moral compass (if they ever had one).

The worst thing about these unscrupulous companies is that the person who loses the most in dealing with them ends up being the average taxpayer who hires them. They fall prey to the firms' strong-arm sales tactics and then receive shoddy, unprofessional services resulting in no solution or relief to their IRS problem.

These unscrupulous companies extract high fees from the people who can least afford to pay for something and not receive anything in return. Often, after months or years of getting no relief from these companies, they must find a real professional to help them.

The fact that these companies exist and prey on people everyday bothers me to the core. I personally don't know how they can live with themselves knowing they've done little or nothing to help their clients. This awareness led me to my fourth big *ah-hah* moment. It was time to create a professional community of local, licensed, IRS problem solving attorneys. I called it BlackFin IRS Solutions.

AN INDUSTRY IS GUARANTEED

American taxpayers need a name and brand they can trust when it comes to solving IRS problems. They deserve a place they can go and know that their hard-earned money will be not be lost. So I've created an ethical solution for every American taxpayer who is suffering from an IRS problem and needs the help of a trained, local professional. I've built a community of local, licensed attorneys to represent local taxpayers.

This community of local licensed attorneys is called BlackFin IRS Solutions®. Each member of our professional community agrees to be bound by the BlackFin® code of ethics which is shown here.

BLACKFIN® CODE OF ETHICS

Adhered to by all BlackFin® certified attorneys.

1. To provide clients a 100 percent free consultation
2. To provide clients a written description of services to be provided
3. To provide clients a fixed fee for representation with the IRS
4. To provide clients a written copy of the BlackFin® Service Guarantee
5. To confidentially represent each client with their best interest in mind
6. To possess a current state license to practice law
7. To communicate with clients on a regular basis
8. To complete annual BlackFin IRS® problem-solving continuing education
9. To always uphold the BlackFin® Code of Ethics
10. To be an active participant in my local community.

At BlackFin IRS Solutions® our number-one concern is for the taxpayer. We promise every taxpayer who meets with one of the local licensed attorneys in our community that we will stand behind that individual attorney with our BlackFin® Promise.

BLACKFIN® PROMISE

We offer our clients a written promise of satisfaction with our services. We are able to make this promise because of our confidence in our skills, experience, judgment and commitment to delivering high-quality, client-focused service.

We promise to put our clients first by working with them to identify, address and effectively pursue their objectives. To ensure that we provide this level of dedication, we framed our guarantee in these terms:

We promise that as our client you will receive COST-EFFECTIVE Services delivered in a TIMELY manner. We promise to INVOLVE you in strategic decisions and to COMMUNICATE with you regularly. We cannot promise outcomes, but we do PROMISE YOUR SATISFACTION with our SERVICE. If at any time we do not perform to your satisfaction, we ask that you inform us PROMPTLY. We will then resolve the issue to YOUR SATISFACTION, even if it means reducing our legal fees.

COMMUNICATION IS THE KEY

Our promise is structured to foster an open, candid relationship with our clients. We pledge to provide services that effectively address each client's specific objectives. In return, we ask our clients to promptly inform us if they are dissatisfied with our services and to allow us an opportunity to correct any service related issues. This input from our clients helps us to improve all of our service relationships. Providing and improving value to our clients is the primary measure of our success.

As I said at the beginning of this chapter, I know what it's like to deal an IRS problem. I've been there and lived through that nightmare. I wouldn't wish it on anyone.

What I do wish for every American is that they can sleep at night knowing that if—for whatever reason—they find themselves face-to-face with an IRS agent or an IRS action which could result in the loss of their assets or ability to provide for themselves or protect their family or employees, that they can get help from a local, ethical, BlackFin®-trained, licensed attorney.

Remember what your mom told you years ago: "stay away from strangers." Especially ones in other states, on the Internet, or the ones that call you.

If you are an ethical, local attorney who is seriously interested in helping local taxpayers end their IRS problems, contact me for more information about becoming a professional member of the BlackFin® community.

About Jack

Jack McDonough, also known as "The IRS Guy," has been helping taxpayers solve IRS problems for 20 years. Realizing he couldn't save the world by himself, Jack has taught attorneys in every state how to solve IRS problems and add IRS representation services to their law practices so that more taxpayers can obtain local legal representation.

Jack is a best-selling author and coauthor and can often be found speaking on live radio shows, as a keynote speaker or presenting seminars to tax attorneys. Regularly sought after by the media, Jack has appeared on ABC, CBS, NBC and FOX. Over the last decade Jack has published *The IRS Times & Inquirer Newsletter, The Attorney Next Door Newsletter, The Attorney Exit Strategy Newsletter* as well as hundreds of articles and blogs about the IRS representation industry.

In 2009 Jack founded BlackFin® IRS Solutions, a community of local, licensed and specially trained tax attorneys who provide professional solutions to local taxpayers while adhering to the BlackFin® Code of Ethics and the BlackFin® Promise. The company believes that all taxpayers should have affordable and easy access to trustworthy, local and licensed attorneys.

In addition to his professional endeavors, Jack founded Camp BlackFin®—a program that identifies families who are currently enduring significant IRS related stress/problems and places their children in summer camp. Selecting local children from local families is an important part of helping communities ease IRS-related tension.

If you are a taxpayer suffering from an IRS problem or if you just want to learn more about BlackFin IRS® visit www.blackfinirs.com.

Attorneys who would like more information about Jack McDonough and how he can help you should go to his website www.blackfinlicensing.com or call his office at 303-904-1451.

CHAPTER 26

The Seven Elements of Success

By Jennie Brown

When I was born, my parents lived in a rented garage, on the wrong side of the railway tracks, in a little country town in Australia called Parkes. Parkes is in central New South Wales, close to the edge of the great Australian outback.

We were poor. My parents had access to a car—owned by the sales company my Dad worked for. He traveled all week, driving from country town to country town, so we only saw him on weekends.

Soon after I was born, my baby brother came along, and we started moving around—through rental properties and government housing.

When I was about five, we moved into the first home my parents owned. Dad had a dream ... a dream of financial freedom, owning his own home, and investing in what was considered to be the best investment of the time—a piece of property.

That property was the first of many, and throughout my childhood I learned many skills, particularly in real estate—skills that would take me into life as an adult and form part of my own success story.

Success means many things—and different things—to different people.

It was these formative years of poverty that instilled in me my biggest dream, my own personal success goal, to be a millionaire by the time I was 30.

Alas, at the age of 30, I was a long way from success. I was unemployed, had recently left a disastrous marriage, was facing a serious health scare, and was barely hanging on financially. A long way from the millionaire status I had dreamed about.

I had some serious choices to make. Quit, give up and wallow in misery or get up and make something of myself.

I chose the second option, and from the depths of ruin I fought my way back. Using the real estate skills learned earlier in life, against all odds and all advice, I built a house. I worked two jobs, and I poured everything into the project. A few years later I sold that house for a profit—giving me the choice to never have to work for someone else again.

Since then, I have undertaken a number of successful and profitable property projects. I have even completed a couple that were not profitable!

Today I live an extraordinary life. I am an Australian real estate investing expert, a published author, a speaker, and a mentor to many in the areas of property, lifestyle and mindset.

Life has its ups and downs; succeeding is about choice, survival, hanging on, pushing through and triumphing.

FINDING THE ROAD TO SUCCESS

Success is whatever you wish it to be. For you it could mean being the most amazing parent. It could be rising to the top of your career. It could be measured in wealth—perhaps being a millionaire. It could be related to health, knowledge, relationships or charity. It could be any number of things.

Only YOU can define what success means for you.

But I have discovered that however you define success, several elements are integral to achieving it. With your permission, I'd like to share seven of my favorite elements with you.

Sacrifice
I have a huge goal board next to me in my office. On it I put many things—photos, goals, dreams, mementos of successes achieved, a million-dollar note (fake!), messages from friends and family, meaningful articles, poems and quotes …

One of my favorite quotes is from Blair Singer: "Most people fail rather than succeed because they give up what they really want for what they want at the moment."

That sums up sacrifice for me. It's about giving up something in the short term, in order to succeed in the long term. Every single moment of our lives, we are making choices. And those choices either take us toward, or away from, success. A moment in time, a choice, and the consequences are huge. The result can be negative or positive. We can be sent sliding into despair or into pure joy and fulfillment. Every choice we make determines either our failure or our success. There is no in between, no gray area, no place where we mark time.

We make thousands of choices every day—most of them with little or no conscious thought. Become conscious of the choices you are making. Will this choice take you to where you really want to go? Or will it stop you, slow you down or, worse yet, take you in the opposite direction of your success?

Be willing to sacrifice in the moment to achieve the success you really desire.

Spirituality

Sometimes I watch a video of myself running a seminar or listen to an audio recording of myself and think, "Wow, I really didn't know I knew that!" Or "I remember that, but I had forgotten it."

Other times I'll be with a client or a friend, and I'll open my mouth. And as I speak I think to myself, "Jennie, are you really sure you want to say that?" And a voice inside of me says, keep speaking. And ultimately, inevitably, the words will trigger something in that person, the walls will come crumbling down, and their reality comes tumbling out.

Then they can move on, deal with the issue, fix the problem, or just feel better. Regardless, the result is great. And most of the time the person is grateful that I cared enough to keep moving them forward.

You can call it what you want—conscience or intuition—I personally believe it is God. I believe this is him with me, helping me, guiding me.

And I believe that we all have access to this guidance. A knowledge we didn't know we had, a feeling that something isn't right, a fleeting glimpse of bad character. A feeling that everything is all right, even though circumstances are indicating otherwise.

It has saved me many times, and the times I have failed I can clearly see where I haven't tapped into it!

In the toughest of times, this guidance gives you peace. It embraces you and allows you to move forward. It gives you the strength to keep going, even when you are not sure of where you are going or what you are doing. It brings people and opportunities to you. It shuts doors you shouldn't go through and opens other doors wide.

Encourage it, practice it, seek it, and use it wisely.

Strategy

As mentioned previously, when I was around the age of 30, I went through a very painful time in my life. I had no money, no husband, no job and no visible means of supporting myself. I was close to having nowhere to live, and I had health problems.

It seemed that there was absolutely no way through. The good thing about hitting bottom is that the only way you can go is up!

So I got another job, lived in a travel trailer at a friend's place, pleaded with the bank and got through the health scare. I started to put my life back together.

And I became focused on just one goal—my next property project— building a house. The goal was to live in it, then sell it, and make a profit. I never considered failure. It just had to be done. And I did it.

I moved into the house—a beautiful new home. The first morning in that house, I was lying in bed, looking out big sliding glass doors at the Australian bush—blue skies, trees waving gently in the breeze. I should have been ecstatic, but instead I felt empty. Hollow. Miserable.

It took me months to work out why.

First, I had had a BIG goal. With a strategy, a plan to achieve it. And I threw everything at it.

Then I achieved the BIG goal.

But I had no new goals to focus on. And I felt empty.

You have to have a strategy, or a plan, or a goal or whatever you want to call it! And this starts with having a clear outcome, or end, in mind. And clear directions on how to get to it.

Then you have to take action—throw yourself completely into it. Don't give up. Don't be distracted. Don't deviate. Just go for it as if your life depends upon you succeeding.

And when you succeed, make sure you have another strategy, or plan, or goal, ready to go.

Speech

At the beginning of 2011 I made a statement: "I will work hard for the first six months of the year, and then I will go play for the second half of the year."

By May I was tearing my hair out. I was working hard, but I really wasn't getting anywhere. Then it dawned on me. I was getting exactly what I had said: "I will work hard." But what I really wanted was to work smart, make profits and then enjoy them! What I should have said was something like: "I will work smart for the first half of the year, making huge profits, and having fun."

What you think, is what you speak, is what you think, is what you speak … is what you receive … and this just keeps on repeating and repeating. So be careful what you think, and be very careful what you speak.

I am sure you have heard the saying "be careful what you wish for." Make sure that what you say is really what you want.

If you want to change what is happening in your life, choose different thoughts, and change the way you speak.

One of my clients decided to stop using inappropriate language. She implemented a fine system whereby every time she used inappropriate language a gold coin went into a jar. Her coworkers quickly became aware of what she was doing, and they "helped" to pull her up. Those gold coins added up very quickly!

The cost of negative thoughts and speech is huge. It takes a toll on your emotions, physical life, relationships and many other things. Changing your thoughts, speech and actions, however, costs you nothing (unless you fine yourself!)

The result of positive thoughts, speech and actions is priceless. It is not something you can put a price tag on.

As to the second half of 2011 … "I will go play …" I took four overseas trips— heaps of vacations, loads of fun!

You really do receive what you ask for!

Stamina

When you start making changes in any area of your life, the results flow into other areas.

For example, if you wake up tired and grumpy, you are more likely to be rude to your family, which starts the day off wrong. Problems seem to multiply and escalate, and your stress levels skyrocket.

However, if you are excited, you will be more likely to be positive and happy. Then you will find that problems are easier to handle and less likely to stress you out. That means your day is easier, you smile more, your relationships are easy, you achieve lots, and life feels great.

One of the easiest ways to make your both your inner and outer body smile is to take care of it. Eat good food and do some exercise!

The changes will flow into all areas of your life, and you will be surprised at how good you feel! And how great life really is! And how much you can achieve!

Smile ☺

One of the things that I absolutely love about my husband, Warren, is that whenever he sees me, he lights up and smiles at me. The delight on his face is worth everything. It makes my day!

When I call him on the phone, I can hear the smile and delight in his voice when he answers. A smile costs nothing. But it can change somebody's world.

So smile, and have fun.

In addition, smile your way through your both your trials and your successes. A smile in the midst of trouble lightens the load.

And Celebrate! Celebrate the wins, and celebrate the steps you take along the way. Enjoy the journey, reap the rewards and share with others.

Service
Out of your success, the best rewards come from serving and giving to others. The Bible says "It is more blessed to give than to receive" (Acts 20:35).

Being of service to others comes in a variety of ways. You can give your time, your experience, your skills, your knowledge, your contacts, your money.

Like a smile, it does not have to cost you anything. A smile is free, and we can change the world one smile at a time!

Of course, money does help! My friend John says "You can never have too much money." When he first told me that, I must say I was taken aback. After all, we really do not need a lot of money to live a comfortable life.

But John believes "you can never have too much money" because, when you have met your own needs, everything else is for sharing and blessing others. You can never have too much money for that!

Look for ways and opportunities to serve, gift and bless others. You may never know the results of your service, but I guarantee that you will change someone's life. You may even *save* someone's life. What an amazing gift!

When we freely serve others, we have reached the pinnacle of success. And the pinnacle of success is available to you, right now. Just reach out and serve someone!

IN CONCLUSION … I WOULD LIKE TO GIVE YOU A BONUS!
Why do you want to be successful? What does success mean to you? Each one of the seven elements is important to YOUR success.

However, not one of them is worth anything unless you *step out and take action!*

And now, YOU have a choice.

Work out what is important to you, listen to your inner voice, get a plan, be positive, prepare yourself, have fun, share with others. And take action!

Choose success. YOUR success depends on it.

About Jennie

Jennie Brown is a speaker, writer, mentor and experienced real estate investor. She is an "Aussie" and lives in the "sunny" state of Queensland – where it's "beautiful one day, perfect the next!"

Jennie is highly sought after by the media and regularly writes for Australian magazines. She is also a contributing author to the Australian bestseller *Property Millionaire*.

With a passion for helping people achieve their goals and attain financial freedom, Jennie travels the world, mentoring and educating others about mindset, lifestyle and real estate investing.

While Jennie is extremely serious about changing people's lives and making a difference, she firmly believes in fun and lifestyle, particularly her own! She travels extensively and enjoys vacations, "works" from home, takes her business calls sitting with her feet in the pool, loves animals, supports a number of charities and philanthropic organizations and has the typical Aussie sense of humor.

She is passionate about facilitating positive, lasting life change in people and inspiring her clients to be proactive in the legacy they leave with family, friends and the people they come in contact with.

Jennie's speaking and seminar business aims to educate people on how to live a more purposeful, extraordinary and inspired life, and to live the life of their dreams. Her events are run in a variety of different settings, including a one-week overseas experience called "The Wealth Retreat," which has received rave reviews.

To learn more about Jennie Brown, her events, invite her to speak or receive her free special report, visit www.JennieBrownEvents.com.

CHAPTER 27

Partnering with God in Business

By Brenda Byers-Im

"Praying you prosper in all things" is my signature on most correspondence. It is inspired by a scripture that says, "Beloved I pray you prosper in all things, even as your soul prospers." (3 John 2, NKJV). My experience in living according to scripture, partnering with God and allowing him to reign supreme in every area has brought me so much passion, purpose and peace. And results! Time and time again he shows me that every area of my life matters greatly to him.

BIRTHING A COMPANY AND LEARNING TO PARTNER WITH GOD

When our eldest daughter was a year old, she had a reaction to her immunizations that caused a serious auto-immune disorder. The doctors said nothing could be done to help her. We could not find answers or hope in either traditional, Western medicine or alternative treatments and therapies.

In desperation, we turned it over to God in prayer, saying, "This is your little girl. We have done all we know how to do." Amazingly, that's when the answers began to arrive. Hours and hours of research, a multitude of long-distance calls and international travel that included meeting more than 200 scientists, researchers and nutritionists around the world resulted in a nutritional formula that synthesized wisdom and ingredients from three continents. We mixed these ingredients in our daughter's applesauce and saw improvement within weeks. Little did we know than that this formula would go beyond helping our daughter to become a best-selling product that God would use to bring healing and hope to thousands of people.

We named this miraculous formula EnerPrime and created a company, IMPaX WORLD, to distribute it. As we began, God was working on the outside and on the inside. He had to break down limiting beliefs that kept me from experiencing the fullness of all he wanted to do in our business. For years I had the concept that money was the root of all evil (a biblical misquote) and that somehow being broke was holier than having money. This mindset caused me to press simultaneously on the gas pedal and the brakes in my business. Further compounding the problem was my concept of "sacred" and "secular," which labeled church and ministry as sacred and work as secular, a malignant necessity to pay our bills.

I couldn't conceive of God being interested in my business let alone the idea of partnering with him in business. Wow, was I mistaken! I have since discovered that God wants to be my partner—in business and all of *life!* As I have learned to yield to this partnership, he has given me far greater potential than anything I could have done in my own strength. I have filled more than twenty journals with the miracles that I have seen *in the marketplace*, and I can confidently say with God as CEO, I have more creativity, more boldness and more resources! A new God-sized vision that includes hospitals, universities, homes for children, libraries, and retreat centers worldwide has replaced my original just-get-by vision. The God-sized vision of will requires total reliance on his power, grace and resources. And what he orders, he pays for.

We have seen so many miracles that one of our staff members recently commented, "Even an atheist would have to believe in God after seeing all the miracles here." We certainly have learned that prayer works and miracles happen! Some of the most amazing miracles I experience are "divine appointments." In other words, the right people just seem to appear with just the right answers at just the right times. What seemed impossible suddenly becomes possible!

FAITH, HOPE AND LOVE IN THE MARKETPLACE

Prayer not only led to our best-selling product, EnerPrime, but also to our second best-seller, delta-E. After much prayer, delta-E appeared in a dream! In the same way, our company IMPaX WORLD, was created not in a board room but from 12 people praying every Wednesday night for a year and a half. Prayer has played a vital role in every aspect of running our business—from praying for resources to praying for our customers. It has not been unusual for customers to walk in with a prayer request or phone in to share their prayer needs or recount answered prayers to our staff. We have seen many answers to prayer. We have been blessed to see a number of physical healings at our office and corporate events.

Having God as CEO has also inspired a "culture of honor" which recognizes each individual as a being created in the image of God, worthy of respect and dignity, and filled with unlimited potential. An overall sense of family brings people together with an attitude of serving one another. One recent example touched me deeply. A couple who had lost their home in the economic downturn met another member of IMPaX who had undergone a painful separation from a long-term relationship. The single gentleman offered the spare room in his house to the couple who had lost their home. I almost cry when I see how beautifully God worked in this humble act. They are living like a family; he is becoming like a son to them and they like loving parents to him.

I have also witnessed this sense of family in the prayer/Bible study I host at the office every Tuesday morning. Our staff, customers and many locals from our community come together at 7 a.m. at the IMPaX headquarters or via conference call to listen in from cities and states across the country and sometimes from as far as the Philippines! Many of those attending have lost everything—homes, marriages, children—even their sense of purpose or desire to live! Arriving without hope or passion, they are discovering how much God loves them and the unlimited potential he has placed in them. Hopelessness is being replaced with hope and lack of purpose replaced with purpose and passion.

One woman who was burned out after losing her home and her marriage told us she was going back home to the Philippines to rest. While in the Philippines, she decided to visit the home of a couple raising 45 orphans with support from IMPaX WORLD. That visit would forever change her life. Today she is filled with a passion to see that no "stray" will remain on the streets of the Philippines.

At our Tuesday prayer meetings, we often study and discuss three pivotal concepts:

1. Identity—who we are

2. Whose we are

3. Our purpose.

Discovering the answer to these questions results in transformation and brings new meaning and purpose to life. Each person in our group has touched my life in profound ways. Tuesdays are the high point of my week!

FINDING MEANING AND PURPOSE IN YOUR WORK

Many people I meet feel fragmented and fried as they try to hold together compartmentalized lives. They have one life on Monday through Friday, another with their family, another on the weekend and still another at their place of worship. All of these tug and pull at each other, often competing for time and energy. Each area of their lives requires specific roles and masks. For example, one mask for Sunday morning and another mask at work while trying to get that promotion.

The endless juggling and balancing is exhausting, but some, including myself, are breaking free! Books such as *God@Work* and *Anointed for Business* represent a grassroots movement that is rapidly gaining momentum. This movement proposes that ordinary people no longer want to separate their spiritual selves from their everyday work selves. Individuals today want to find moral meaning and purpose in their work. For them, God is more than just a concept. He is a living reality affecting every aspect of their lives. People we meet at our conferences often come up and thank us and tell us how refreshed they are to see us sharing and living our faith openly in the marketplace.

We have found hypocrisy (words with contrary actions) will always be rejected, but true love for God and fellow man is magnetic! St. Francis of Assisi once said it beautifully, "Preach the Gospel at all times, and when necessary use words." As humans, we all make mistakes, but by God's grace I pray my life will demonstrate God's power, forgiveness, hope and love to every person I meet and am privileged to work with.

STEWARDING PEOPLE AND RESOURCES

While I was soaking up the sun on the beach and praying on a recent trip to Hawaii, I felt God speak, "Your life is My gift to you. The life you live is your gift to Me." These words have profoundly affected me. Since hearing them, I awaken each morning with the realization that my very breath and the day ahead are gifts from God. The thought of this not only fills me with gratitude but also a sense of responsibility. All that I have is a gift. The people and resources that come into my life are to be managed in such a way as to be a blessing and to bring increase.

The biblical parable of the talents is a picture of the fact that we all are given a measure of resources to manage and are expected by the giver to use and invest them to produce increase. Although those given the talents brought different returns on their investments, only one was reprimanded by Jesus. He was the one who walked in fear and buried his talent. To create wealth is to empower people to have resources for the basic necessities of life and much more.

Scripture gives us this assurance: "And you shall remember the LORD your God, for it is He who gives you power to get wealth." (Deut. 8:18, AMP). As the source of wealth, God empowers us to use wealth wisely to improve the quality of life— body, soul and spirit. Wealth becomes a tool for advancing the well-being of others. When abused, wealth creates pride and arrogance. When stewarded with an attitude of thanksgiving, wealth becomes a tool to bless others.

THE LAW OF SOWING AND REAPING

"Out of Africa" wasn't just a great film. We personally experienced it. In the middle of our prayer and searching, a pastor approached us about helping an orphanage in Tanzania. He had heard of the immune-enhancing properties of EnerPrime. Having recently lost their medical support, 70 children in this orphanage would be left to die of AIDS. The question came, "Would we be willing to donate EnerPrime?"

Although this happened at a difficult and inconvenient time, we felt God saying "Do it!" Within a month of sending EnerPrime to the orphanage, we received a letter from their doctor saying the children had improved tremendously. Their hair was no longer orange. They were out of bed.

They were back in school and playing again. What we didn't know then but have since come to learn was the lesson of sowing and reaping. This Tanzanian orphanage would be among the first of many "seeds" sown into the lives of others that God would use to produce a "harvest."

Our global vision was birthed out of this experience in Africa. IMPaX WORLD was to become international. In going to the nations, we would be sowing into the lives of individuals physically, financially and spiritually. God was teaching us an important life lesson: part of stewardship is sowing.

"Don't judge each day by the harvest you reap but by the seeds that you plant," Robert Louis Stevenson once said. Sowing produces a harvest of natural and spiritual health and abundance. We had to take a step of faith and trust God by sowing into Tanzania. Scripture declares, "Faith without works is dead (James 2:26, KJV). It's one thing to say that we trust God and are surrendered to his control. It's another to actually risk money, time, resources and a business. *Sowing involves risk.* But, risk with faith can produce an abundant harvest. Not only were the lives of the children in the orphanage changed, we were changed. When the leaders of a business change, life and business both change. We are living testimony of that truth.

And Love Never Fails

About Brenda

Brenda Byers-Im is a highly sought speaker and coach who inspires and mentors others to develop their greatness within. She is unique in her ability to touch people on all levels of body, soul and spirit. High school speech and debate students coached by Brenda have won national championships. Corporate leaders and entrepreneurs have increased their income exponentially with her mentoring. She is frequently a keynote speaker at business networking events and fundraisers. Brenda has created and led cutting-edge sales and marketing events, weekend training seminars and retreats for the past 25 years.

Brenda holds degrees in business, nutrition and exercise physiology. She and her husband are founders of IMPaX WORLD, a successful direct-selling nutrition company. As vice-president of her company since 1994, Brenda has coached and inspired highly skilled independent distributors while maintaining IMPaX WORLD as a vibrant and progressive company offering the highest-quality products. Her vision and foresight in the field of health and wellness have led top doctors, athletes, and fitness coaches to seek out Brenda and the IMPaX WORLD products for their personal and professional use.

Brenda is an accomplished author and creator of numerous articles, blogs, CDs and magazines. She has been featured on local television stations, ABC, CBS, Fox and NBC. As a daily devoted student of the Bible, Brenda has helped individuals discover their identity and purpose. She believes God to be her partner in life and business. Her life's purpose is helping others recognize and develop their God-given gifting while inspiring them to expand their vision, goals and to celebrate their inner greatness.

To learn more about Brenda Byers-Im, follow her on her blog, www.prosperinallthings. com and on Facebook www.facebook.com/brendaim. To order her motivational tapes and CDs, go to www.impaxworld.com.

CHAPTER 28

Understanding Clients a Key to Success

By Dr. Jonathan Woodman, D.V.M.

No matter what business you're in, communication with others is essential to your success. You need to communicate your message to every client or potential client who walks in your door, visits your website, or makes contact with you in any way. But more importantly, you need to hear your client's message. I have recognized three levels of client communication, and mastering all of these with each and every client that you deal with is essential to your success.

In my first year as a veterinarian, my boss told me a story which has stuck with me. He related to me how an elderly gentleman had visited the clinic with his dog who was having ear troubles. My employer examined the dog, diagnosed an ear infection and dispensed medications. He explained to the customer that he was sending home two medications. An antibiotic tablet and an ointment for the ear.

A couple weeks later, my employer went on, a very angry, elderly woman came in to the clinic with the same dog. She said something to the effect of, "I've been lubing up these pills with that cream and sticking them in my dog's ears, and they're still not getting any better."

Obviously, the tablets were to be given orally, and only the cream was to be placed in the ear. My boss' point was that we need to communicate clearly with our clients to make sure our message is heard and understood.

UNDERSTANDING NEEDED FOR COMMUNICATION

I would take this idea further. I would say that we need also to understand our clients. And not just in the superficial sense. In our example, the veterinarian clearly understood the original message and acted on it appropriately. The dog had an ear problem; the problem was diagnosed as an infection, and an appropriate treatment was prescribed. However, the outcome was a failure. Why? Because my boss did not fully understand his client.

In his *7 Habits of Highly Effective People*, Stephen Covey lists his fifth habit as "seek first to understand, then to be understood." In order to accomplish our goals and effectively serve our clients, we must be able to fully understand them on multiple levels.

In my experience, I have recognized three levels of understanding when it comes to client communications. The most basic is understanding exactly *what* has brought them to you. In most cases, you've learned this information fairly early in your initial conversation.

The next level would be understanding *why* they have come to you in particular. Knowing this is especially important because they may have specific expectations about you.

And lastly, it is vital that you understand just *who* your client is. Understanding just a piece of their life story can help you cater specifically to their real needs. And it is this point that bonds them to you and your business.

THE WHAT

Let's look at these three levels more closely. First off: *What* basic need, desire, complaint, or motivation has brought them to you? "I need a _____." "Great, we've got those right over here." And that may be just about all they need. Sometimes you may need a little more detail. But rarely will it take a Sherlock Holmes to get that level of information from the client.

THE WHY

Once we understand our client's most basic need, we can move on to the second level. This takes a little more effort. But learning *why* a client has come to you can help you focus more specifically on their needs. It may be as simple as price, location or a referral. Great, we need to know all these things.

But perhaps it is due to a specific type of product or service that you offer. In my practice as a veterinarian, I've found that having this information really helps me to focus my services for a client better. This definitely makes for a happier customer.

Another point here is knowing if your customer has been referred by a specific person who is already your client. Knowing this can help you tailor your approach to this new client, as they've probably been sent to you for a particular reason.

The other side of this idea is that if they're looking for something that your business does not or cannot offer, you can quickly set them on the right path. While it can be unsettling to drive customers away, it can save the client time and frustration. Serving the client in this manner tends to make them look favorably on you, which is likely to drive more business in your direction anyway. They're going to realize that you are someone who will search for a solution for them, even if it doesn't directly benefit you. In my own experience, these clients are usually very happy to come back to us in the future or refer their friends to you.

THE WHO

But the one level of communication that has made the biggest difference in my 18-year career has been gaining a deeper understanding of *who* my client is.

Recently, in our clinic, we had a client come to us with a very sick cat. We ran several tests on the cat and tried several treatments. Ultimately we were unable to arrive at a specific diagnosis or to improve its condition. The cat's owner followed every suggestion we gave her very faithfully, even beyond what the vast majority of pet owners would do.

Eventually, she came in for a final evaluation to see if anything else could be done for her cat. We had done all that we were able to do, and the only thing further we could offer was referral to a specialty hospital.

That's when she finally gave us the piece of information we really needed. It turned out that the cat was the last link she had to her husband who had died some years before.

In this particular case, we had served her well and done everything we had been asked to do. However, knowing the level of importance she placed on the cat could certainly have helped us to serve her better. Whether it meant being more aggressive in our diagnostics from the start, or referring her to a specialist right away, we would have been making sure we were doing everything we could do to alleviate her concerns as well as we could right from the start. Of equal importance would have been to make sure that she knew we understood her priorities.

HOW TO GATHER INFORMATION

So now we need to consider how and when we collect this information and how best to act on it.

The simple answer to these considerations is to say you should do it in every way you can and all the time!

Surveys, Forms

How you collect that information will depend on your particular business, although a number of tactics can be utilized. In this day and age, where a lot of contact occurs online, asking clients to fill out questionnaires or short surveys is essential. In an online situation, this may be the only way of getting good information from your client.

But these same formats are quite useful for more traditional businesses also. In our practice, we utilize a number of forms to help us determine why our clients are in our office, what their concerns are and even some of who they are as people. If any of these are possibilities that could work for you, I encourage you to pursue them.

However, this is only the tip of the iceberg, and of course, not everyone will put a lot of detail on forms and surveys. So the next step is certainly verbal communication. Again, in a more traditional business, this is a lot easier.

In businesses where much of client contact is indirect, this can be a little more difficult. Online chat services can help, as can personal email contact with the client or potential client. Many larger companies have live chat available to pursue their customers concerns and questions. This is an ideal situation to find out more about them and to hone in on some of the things that are concerning to them. For instance, Zappos.com uses chat services to great effect in this manner.

Face to Face

What I use, whenever possible, is straight face-to-face interaction with my clients. That is the ideal situation in learning more about your client's story. From the first time they come in to your business you should make a point of engaging a client in friendly communication. While this is an opportunity to promote your business and your products, it is best to make a point of being non-pushy and just simply friendly.

I cannot stress this point enough. It is very important to make sure your client understands that you really want to take the time to get to know who they are and to fully understand them as a person. This is what it takes to earn their trust and to let them understand that you are committed to helping them.

In this fast-paced world of today, most customers will approach any business with a degree of suspicion. You're a business owner, and you're only in it for the money, they feel. While we're all in it to make money, I think we all realize that the important thing is fully serving our customers. We've entered the business we are in to help people in some way or another. And it is this point that we need to get across to them. That requires taking the time to get to know who they are and what they are truly after.

So I try to make it a point in every contact that I have with my clients to spend some time talking about a subject that has nothing to do with business. No matter how small of a time that is spent on such conversation, the effort to just be a person with your client is critical. It's what takes your relationship with that person to a whole different level. And most importantly, it is what will bond your client to your business.

There are certainly other ways that we can implement this, too. Many businesses will send out cards on special occasions to communicate with their clients. This is an opportunity to not so much sell your goods to them on a different occasion as to show them that you understand them. Nonadvertising cards on birthdays, for instance, show you know something about them and that you care. And I stress the point that it should be nonadvertising. Make it something personal.

The same goes for holiday cards. Make them personal. Show your clients that you care about them as a person, not just as a paycheck.

These methods are the most basic manner of developing a layer of trust. And its from here that we start to learn more about our clients. On each subsequent visit, you'll find your clients more likely to open up to you.

WHEN TO GATHER INFORMATION

By now you probably also understand that the "when" of implementing these communications is answered simply with: All The Time!

By striving to understand more of our clients at each interaction we have, we can learn more and more about what factors are inherent in their lives and how those apply to what brings them to us. Or at the very least it will help us to be more pointed in the things that we recommend to them. At the end of the day, that's the point of all of this. Finding ways that we can use our knowledge of the client to better serve them. We want to implement our knowledge of who our client is by designing our services to better fit their needs.

Knowing that a client has particular tastes or needs in their lives, for instance, may save us the trouble of recommending something that they would never go for. It also allows us to recommend extra services that can be of additional benefit to them. When it comes to add-on services, many customers tend to shy away from spending extra money if they don't need to. But if we know which clients would prefer to hear about the extras, we can better tailor these things to them. "I know you're concerned about X, so this would be ideal for you."

They say knowledge is power. The truth of the matter is that the appropriate collection and implementation of knowledge is power. Once we learn who are clients are, we can learn to serve them in the manner that will benefit them the most. And really what we are after is a happy, devoted client. By serving them as a friend, someone who knows them, and not just as a business owner, we can truly mark them as a lifetime client.

About Jonathan

Dr. Jonathan Woodman, D.V.M., is cofounder and head veterinarian at Town & Country Veterinary Services, P.A., a companion animal veterinary clinic in Hastings, Minnesota. As a veterinarian., he's worked in emergency medicine, farm animal ambulatory care, exotic animal medicine, and general companion animal medicine and surgery. As a business owner, he has grown Town & Country Veterinary Services from a part-time, one-doctor ambulatory service to a thriving full service clinic and hospital employing two additional veterinarians, four veterinary technicians, along with five other staff members. The clinic business has grown steadily each year since its founding in a very competitive marketplace, with the greatest expansion occurring during the last couple years in spite of the recession.

Dr. Woodman is a 1994 graduate of the University of Minnesota College of Veterinary Medicine. He also holds a B.S. In biology from Allegheny College in Meadville, Pa. (1990). He is a member of the AVMA, and his primary specialty interest is in canine and feline nutrition.

CHAPTER 29

Seven Things To Do for Your Business That Don't Require an MBA

By Kevin Johnson

I am not a scholar. I don't have an MBA. I don't even have a college degree from a prestigious university. I have a ninth-grade education and a very strong faith in God. I own and operate a very successful janitorial company that has grown exponentially despite what the news likes to refer to as a "down economy." Even as I have watched other businesses like mine fail, I have been able to grow my business. I don't believe in keeping the secrets of my success a secret at all; I want to share with you the seven things that have shaped my business most so that your business can benefit from them too.

HAVE FAITH

Several years back my business was struggling, and so was I. I had reached a crossroads where not enough customers were coming, and I wasn't certain whether or not I should stay in business at all. I am a man of faith, so the first thing I did was give it up to God. I basically said, "God, I don't have any idea what it is you want me to do with my business. I can't figure it out, so I am giving up control of my business to you."

Now, I don't know whether you believe in God or Allah or Fate or some other force in the universe, but I do know this: what you put out into the world you will get back tenfold. So many businesspeople want to grow their business so badly that they become cut-throat to get it.

For example, I have known people who are incredibly worried that someone will find out the "secrets" of how they run their businesses. My advice? Put some positive energy out there into the universe. Share your "secrets" with someone who is just starting out. When you trust people to do the right thing, I really believe that God then trusts you with more.

Have faith that if you build your business the right way and look out for those around you that you will be blessed with a bigger business than you can imagine. When I took myself out of the center of the equation, my business began to increase.

KNOW YOUR BUSINESS

I know this idea seems too ridiculous to mention, but I see examples all the time of people who don't know their own business. Know every little detail of your business. I am not telling you to micromanage your employees. You do need, however, to know what they do. You need to know the answers.

My cousin opened his own janitorial company and received an invitation to bid on a large, university campus project. He called me to find out how to price his bid. I quickly asked him a few questions as to how many buildings, how many floors, square footage etc. I then explained to him on the telephone, without benefit of calculator or computer, how many people he needed for each building and for how many hours. I keep that information in my head, not on paper. When you know the details so well that you can rattle them off and not waste time researching them you will have more time to build relationships with people.

BUILD RELATIONSHIPS

The product you sell or your fancy office might catch some people's attention, but any business is really built on relationships. People have told me, "Kevin, you're a people person." I guess that is true. I like to take the time to talk to customers and get to know them before I recommend services to them.

People are never as interested in what you sold them or what you did for them as they are about how you made them feel. Did you make their day easier? Did you answer their questions? Did you take time to really listen to what they were saying and to do your best to *understand* their needs? If you did, then, they are likely to tell their friends about you and your business.

I love the phrase that God gave me two ears but only one mouth so that I would listen twice as much as I talked. That's an unbelievably important aspect of your business. Be known as the person who fills a need, not sells a product. I had a client call me recently to tell me that I needed to bid on a business because she had told that business about us and recommended us for the job. Let happy customers sell for you.

If you have a start-up business, realize that you ARE the business your customers see until you have built a reference base. The more satisfied customers you can get, the more the word-of-mouth about your business will spread. Some of the best advice I got early on was to take jobs as a subcontractor to the "big dogs" in my industry. By doing so, I was on those big job sites, and I was the one those businesses saw working hard for them every day. When it came time to bid on my own jobs, those customers were happy to be references for me and my business.

Building relationships can also mean taking on business that you don't really think you want. Trust me, answer the call.

ANSWER THE CALL

Have you ever had one of those phone calls come in when you didn't really want to take the call? Maybe you thought the job was going to be too intricate? Or the order was too small? Or the person on the other end of the phone was just not your favorite person?

I want you to take that call (or make) that call for two reasons:

You have a chance to be the best part of that person's day.

You don't know yet why God, or the Universe, has put this job or this person in your path!

If you take the call and become the best part of a person's day, you are building relationships that build your business. Plus, that bid you are dreading submitting because the job seems too hard, or too small or too time-consuming might be a job that leads to the contract of your dreams.

I don't care if you want to thank God or the universe or whomever, but I believe that nothing happens by accident. The people and jobs that are put in your path are there for you. If you ignore them, you could be ignoring the call of a lifetime. It's best not to ignore those blessings.

BE A BLESSING BUT NOT A PUSHOVER

It's one thing to be blessed with a successful business; it's another to be a blessing to the people you come in contact with. In every relationship you develop either with customers or employees, you must create a win-win scenario. You must find a way to be a blessing to that person. Some people are leaders; some are followers. If you own your own business, chances are that you are a leader, as I am. The world needs both.

I do believe it is important to take care of the people who help fill your coffers. However, taking care of your employees cannot come at a sacrifice to your business. Make your employees understand that while you are willing to help them out with the hours they need or other matters that you also have a family and bills to pay and that your business pays all those bills. All your employees make up a big family, and every family has its challenges. But the communication in the family can make or break the family. In my business—and yours too—if we lose an account, the entire family suffers.

For example, I had an employee tell me after he was hired that he needed Wednesdays off to attend church. I had to be honest with him that I, too, would like to attend church on Wednesdays, but that I had a business to run with customers who need their buildings cleaned on Wednesdays just the same as on the other days. While I could appreciate his position, I could not agree to give him every Wednesday off. If I lost an account because nobody would clean a building on Wednesday, then the wages of other members of our work family would be affected as well.

Your work ethic sets the example for your employees. In the beginning, my business was me and one other employee. We worked from 6 a.m. to 6 p.m. landscaping. We would then take a little dinner break and have a little family time before we went back to work from 7 p.m. to 12 a.m. cleaning offices. You're the leader. Your employees emulate what they see you do.

Now, sometimes you get good workers who do crazy things—just like you get in any family. Bad days can happen to anyone; bad months can kill your business.

ONE BAD APPLE

As I said, a bad day can happen to anyone, but a month of bad days or bad attitudes will affect your business. Remember that one bad apple will spoil the bunch! Don't be afraid to do something about the bad apples.

In my business, if an employee is not happy at a certain job site (in your office maybe it is an employee unhappy with certain tasks) I have several choices. First, I can talk to the employee to see if the issue is just a bad day that will pass. Second, if the situation seems unlikely to go away, I can move the employee to another building to work or move him or her to another task altogether. If the employee has been trained and is a decent employee then it makes more sense to place that employee somewhere else and keep them on staff. Some industries, like the janitorial field, have an employee turnover rate as high as 70 percent. Every employee that you lose costs your company profit when you have to hire and retrain someone else for that position. It behooves you to keep an employee when feasible.

But, remember the one bad apple. If the employee is not moved or terminated, his or her unhappiness can cost you other valuable employees or even the customers that you have worked so hard to win. Use your common sense. No one likes to fire an employee, but loss of revenue can cost many employees their jobs as well as jeapordize your business long term.

INTERVIEW, INTERVIEW, INTERVIEW

How can you find the best employees? Honestly, sometimes when you are starting out in a field, you really don't have much choice other than to hire the warm bodies that walk through the door. Some of them will rise to the challenge and become outstanding employees. Some won't last long.

I have learned that how I interview potential employees has a large impact on how many of them I can retain longer term. I use a three-interview process. During the first interview I find out about their employment track record. Do they tend to spend years on a job or do they change jobs frequently? I build a rapport with them by finding out about them and their families. I get to know their personality a bit.

If their work history and experience are decent, in the second interview I will talk to them with another employee present. Because I have previously spoken with them they will have their guard down a bit. This gives me an opportunity to get to know the real person a little better and to see how she or he might interact with another employee. During this interview I try to find out why they want to work for me. Let's face it, few people wake up and say, "I think I will go get a college degree and become a janitor!" It's essential that I weed out the temporary employees as much as possible. A person who wants the additional income for a vacation will likely leave once that additional money is saved. A person who needs the income to pay for their child's education will probably stay on longer, thus costing me less in the long run.

Employees I am seriously considering hiring will get a third and final interview. If you don't currently operate with a multiple interview process, consider this. If I interview the potential employee multiple times, it is mainly my time that has been wasted. If I only interview once, hire the person, and they quit or are fired very quickly, I lost not only the wages it cost for that employee to work a week, but it ALSO cost me the wages of the employees who trained that new worker.

Your business is your baby. Have a love for what you are doing. Operate your business in the faith that whatever you put into it and put out into the world, you will get back tenfold. I know you can change your business and your life for the better by utilizing these seven simple ideas. Don't let the media hype about a "down economy" keep you from building the business that you want and deserve.

About Kevin

Kevin Johnson has been the owner of A thru Z Janitorial Service & Supply Inc. for more than 18 years. Unlike other successful entrepreneurs, he didn't start his company after receiving a business-school education or training from another business partner. In fact, he says he knew absolutely nothing about business when he first started.

Although he never dreamed he would one day own his own business, Kevin's family and friends say he has had business sense from the time he was a little boy. They remind him of times when he would buy candy from the neighborhood store, take it to school and then resell it for a profit; or when he cut grass in the summer, pushing his lawnmower from yard to yard around town. Growing up as the only child of a single mother who sometimes struggled to make ends meet, Kevin says he learned early that a little hard work won't ever kill you.

That lesson has served him well in running his own business, where he has put in long hours and worn many hats and then watched his perseverance pay off. During hard times, Kevin saw his mother stretch old "George Washington" a long way and learned to do the same in his business. Kevin believes management skills can be learned along the way but that the most important aspects are to do to others as you want them to do to you; be fair but firm with your workers; and make customer service a priority. To stay number one in your business, you must offer your customer the best service ever and solve any problems that arise so that your company's name will be passed along to potential customers.

Kevin says he believes his success in business truly stems from his belief in God. The word of God says put God's Kingdom first and he will take care of all your needs and desires (1 Peter 5:6-8 and Psalms 37:4), and Kevin believes that God's wisdom will always lead you into true success and prosperity. He encourages you to try it for yourself and see. He would like readers to email him at Kevin@athruzbm.com to describe how that plan worked.

CHAPTER 30

Fear Is a Gift in Disguise

By Diana Todd-Banks

New unexpected dilemmas, hurdles, pleasures and achievements occur throughout our lives, and sometimes lurking among those is something called fear!

Fear is insidious and is one of the most limiting emotions in life.

While most people harbor fear of some kind and are aware of that, many people are not aware of their fear until they're tested, at unexpected times and in different situations.

An insidious emotion, fear can affect many areas of a person's personal and business life. It can hold you back from doing what you really want to do, and if unresolved, fear can negatively affect others in your life as well.

Which is why fear can be so destructive and paralyzing. It was for me … way back.

However, if you are willing to grab your fears and deal with and resolve them as I did, you may be surprised by the results.

Why?

Fear is a gift in disguise and can become a positive opportunity.

I know from personal experience what it's like to grab fear by the feet, grab it by the head, grab the fear totally and do something about it, so in the future it doesn't affect you personally and in business. Only when you do that is it possible to live a better life and move forward with a stronger sense of confidence and mental freedom.

I did overcome my fears, but before doing that life wasn't easy.

As a child I was brought up in an extremely strict Victorian environment. For most of my childhood and teenage years I was not only painfully shy but I was forbidden to do anything I wanted to do. This became so destructive that fear just engulfed me.

I didn't want that strict life; it was limiting, confining, and it just seemed so "lacking" to me. I wanted more out of life than that. Somewhere deep down, I recall thinking "I'm in this life once, there has to be more to life than this."

Self-development theories were not widely known then, but I clearly recall saying this to myself: "if my life is to change, I had to change, and only I could change my life." So I did. I quietly made some plans, then left, much to the shock and horror of those around me, as I found out years later.

To this day, I have no idea where I gained the wisdom, confidence and strength to leave, even despite my fears. But I do recall that my burning desire to change my life and remove my fears was an overwhelmingly powerful emotion.

I started my quest for more of life by looking to do something that was different. Well, as the old story notes: "be careful what you wish for."

Perhaps I was rebellious—I'm not sure—but I chose to do rough, physically hard work for 14 hours a day: hand-picking tobacco and working in a sheep shearing gang. It was terrifying as all the workers were moved from farm to farm on the back of trucks on cold, rainy nights. Our quarters were invariably rough, tiny tin or wooden sheds, speckled with bird mess and bugs. Every rouseabout—or farm-worker—was allotted their own shed to wash and sleep in, with the bugs too. It was very rough, and all I could think of was "Di this is making you a better, stronger, more tolerant person."

Three years later, I returned to Australia then moved to the U.S. with my husband, only to be confronted with some frightening situations compounded by a severe Chicago winter.

For six months, our luggage with our clothes was stuck on a meat cargo ship in the Great Lakes. We had no winter clothes with us in Chicago, and just $1 a day to live on, which meant 33 cents a meal for both of us.

Since my visa didn't me permit to work at that time, I decided to address and overcome more of my fears. This kept me occupied and focused on doing something positive which didn't cost any money.

My first crack at dealing with those was when my husband was studying, and I found myself spending endless lonely hours in a tiny bedroom on the south side of Chicago, close to the University of Chicago. At the time it was a very frightening area.

I wrote a list of my fears then pondered, how could I overcome these fears? I harbored several, some more conspicuous than others. The first obvious one was lack of money, 33 cents for a meal. How could I produce a nutritious meal for 33 cents?

Searching for some no-cost advice, I rallied my nerves and went to a local library searching for information about cheap, nutritious foods, which I did find. I also read a little about fear and learned that fear isn't something you are born with, rather you gather it along the way and it does not magically disappear when you're an adult.

Yes, the library book on fear was a turning point for me.

It suggested a concept that seemed to me such a ridiculously simple solution: that fear could become a positive opportunity in one's life. I thought, "this is too simple; it could not be possible;" so I continued to let fear be a negative, paralyzing force in my life. Until it was apparent I needed to somehow make some changes, so I followed ideas from that book although some years later some tweaking was needed.

I looked at my main fears and why I felt so fearful, and considered when and where they first appeared. Once I'd done that, I took my three major fears and decided how efforts to overcome them could be broken down into baby steps. If a step seemed too big, I'd break that into smaller steps that I could practice each day or each week or month.

Until I did that exercise, I couldn't turn my fears into something positive. I spent hours planning my action list then decided to work through all the major ones no matter how long it took.

During those two years of struggle, I chose to focus on doing something that would benefit me in several areas—gaining the confidence to overcome the fear of speaking to people I didn't know.

With that goal in mind, I managed to find ways to learn classical guitar and singing. It was a lonely time then, so I studied and practiced for 14 hours a day. In time this increased my confidence, and I was asked to do some small performances.

But life has a funny way of interrupting the best-laid plans.

You can never tell what's around the corner!

Sometimes changes in your life can present a new set of challenges, fears, hurdles, possibilities … and opportunities.

Losing a job, a business, and investments, or losing a loved one, or experiencing divorce, all present new fears and hurdles. Experiencing some of these after moving to a new city or country certainly can present some very high hurdles to overcome.

But as I came to find out, unresolved fear can hold you back and negatively affect all areas of your life. It can play havoc with your health, general stability, confidence and interaction with others in work and your personal life.

The fear of being judged, of being embarrassed, of rejection, of being alone; the fear of failure, of being poor, of not being good enough, all these fears did affect my life because my life fell apart.

It seems that I had been studying voice and classical guitar so much my husband thought I was having an affair, which I wasn't, although perhaps I was with the guitar. He became violent and abusive and simply would not accept the truth, so he found another woman, and we divorced.

Suddenly my financial fears, fear of the unknown and of my future became a serious reality. Except for a few friends, I was alone now in Chicago, with little money to live on. For a long time before the break occurred, I had spent hours analyzing how I could deal with my fears and overcome them, but that was on paper.

Now I was forced to face and deal with my fears; it was all real. No one else could do it for me.

Then, something remarkable occurred; at least it was for me. My future looked brighter; it turned around in a surprising positive direction.

I was awarded three scholarships to go to Roosevelt University then De Paul University to study singing and classical guitar, all because of all my earlier dedication. As well, I was able to work teaching classical guitar and in so doing I set up my first small business.

Remarkably, I was asked to meet and interview one of the world's top classical guitarists, which was an exciting, unexpected opportunity. But one of my fears tried to take hold and stop me—lack of confidence. I could not let this opportunity slip by; it was too exciting.

Then another world classical guitarist visited Chicago and then another until I found myself face to face with the man credited with bringing the classical guitar to the concert stage, Andre Segovia. What an honor it was to speak with him for two hours! That was a high point of my life.

I wrote articles about each of the guitarists for a small American magazine.

Not long after, I was asked to promote some Australian wine; that seemed another good opportunity, which I took on, but with it came the need to do some public speaking about Australian wine. This progressed until I was engaged as director of a wine and cooking school. Some years later, I became Australia's first female wine importer in the U.S. In this role I did many television and radio interviews and was beginning to really enjoy it all.

Over the years I took on numerous different roles and challenges and in the process overcame those past fears.

I've moved nearly 50 times, packed up after five deaths, owned several companies in the U.S. and Australia. I learned—and to a degree mastered—the very difficult, yet soulfully nourishing Indian instrument, the sitar. Back in Australia I became an accredited event organizer and public relations practitioner; I taught PR to small-business owners at a well-known Australian education college, was a feature columnist in several daily newspapers, and regularly reviewed food books from many different major publishers. But then I suffered a major health setback. Toward the end of my recovery, I wrote my first book then became an accredited life change coach.

Yes, fear can present a positive opportunity—it is a gift in disguise, and I would never have achieved what I did had I not faced my fears and continued to move forward with a positive outlook. You just have to persist and find a way to unwrap those hidden gifts of yours ... because you never know where they will take you!

TOP 12 TIPS FOR TURNING YOUR FEAR INTO A POSITIVE OPPORTUNITY

Over the years in life and business, this is what I've learned to apply in many situations when turning fear into a positive opportunity. This is what you can do to help turn around this insidious emotion. It may take a while, but do be persistent.

1. First, accept that most people harbor fear of some kind even though many won't admit it to themselves. Fear can hold you back from doing things you really want to do, hold you back and prevent you from moving forward with any degree of confidence, to go after whatever it is you want to do and achieve.

   Why let that happen? Why, let this insidious emotion be a destructive force in your personal and business life?

2. Have you ever said to yourself or to others, "I really want to overcome my fear of ..., *but* I can't *because* ...," or you might have said, "I really want to do ..., *but* I can't *because* ..."

3. Ask yourself: "what does that "but" and "because" represent?

   What are you frightened of; what is holding you back?

   As an example, are you frightened of public speaking yet deep down you'd love to be a public speaker, because you like the thought of being in that industry? For now, do these next steps using public speaking as an example.

   The more you think about your fear and bring it into the open, to the forefront of your thinking, the easier it is to deal with this limiting emotion.

4. Break each fear down; define it in as few words as possible.

5. Then address the three "Ws": "When / Why / What." Look back at when that fear first became an issue; why does it exist in your life and what caused it?

6. Once you can clearly define your fear(s)—preferably in one or two words —and have answered the three "Ws," ask yourself, what is the positive opposite of your clearly defined fear?

7. Looking at that positive opposite and ask yourself: what actions and steps could be taken toward that? Don't put any limits on this list. Record all your answers.

8. Break down those actions into smaller baby steps and record all of them.

9. Again using the example of public speaking, if this was a fear of yours yet you wanted to be in that industry, identify one step you could take toward that today, a step which is positive, workable and achievable.

10. Each day select another step that is comfortable and achievable for you. Adopt the same approach for the next 30 and 60 days, by which time your fear may no longer be a fear but the opposite—a positive opportunity for your future.

    I still do that. And it works. You can too.

    However over the years, one overriding thought has kept me going and still does today.

11. It is this: constantly remind yourself, "Only I can make changes in my life." This premise applies to each of us, as does this thought:

12. "We are in this physical world once; make the most of it; don't let opportunities slip by."

    Most of all don't let fear hold you back from taking action in your professional and personal life.

You can never tell what's around the corner. If necessary, take a step into the unknown because it could change your life. It did mine.

Grab fear by the feet, grab it by the head, grab the fear totally as I did and do something about it. Because only then can you begin to live the life you want, live it with a high degree of mental freedom and confidence and in doing so achieve whatever goals you set for yourself.

Since the world is constantly evolving, and we need to evolve with it, life is one of constant change, transition, reinvention and new directions.

Whether we welcome it or not, create it or not, change will occur and present new challenges and fears. This is why these need to dealt with when they emerge, because only then can you find the gift that has been in disguise … up to now.

About Diana

Diana Todd-Banks is a woman who has had an incredibly varied life and conquered very high hurdles to make things happen and overcome many deep lows. Picking herself up and dusting herself off from these lows, she has moved forward with a positive outlook on life, which ultimately has opened up many new doors and opportunities.

Combining her vast wealth of experiences and insight with practical coaching strategies, Diana works with clients to help them achieve a new beginning following the loss of a loved one, a job or financial loss, divorce, retirement, or health or relocation setback. She also works with clients who have other specific goals they want to achieve.

A very down-to-earth woman, Diana has received extensive print media coverage and appeared on television and radio in both Australia and the United States. For 20 years she lived, worked and owned businesses in the U.S. She was a U.S. wine and food importer and an international marketing consultant for Australian businesses seeking new niche opportunities in the U.S. Prior to that, she gained a degree in classic guitar in Chicago.

In Australia her groundbreaking book has drawn significant media attention, because it was a world-first on the subject: *Wrapping It Up—Packing Up Possessions & Other End of Life Matters*. This was followed by *Estate Organizer—The Ultimate Guide to Recording Your Life Matters*.

This year, In addition to *Cracking the Success Code*, Diana's work was also included in another recent book alongside other top inspirational, self-development speakers and best selling authors: *In The Spirit of Success* with Deepak Chopra, Dr. Wayne Dyer, Esther & Jerry Hicks, Mark Victor Hansen, Neale Donald Walsch, and Sandy Forster.

To learn more about Diana, visit http://dianatoddbanks.com/lifecoach. If you register on the site, you can receive a free ebook, *15 Steps To Embrace Change*. Also visit www.wrappingitup.com.au to learn more about the book "nobody wants but everyone needs."

You can email Diana at dianatodd-banks@bigpond.com.

CHAPTER 31

How to Achieve Success in Retirement

By Radon Stancil

What does "financial success" mean to you? Ask 100 people, and you won't get the same answer twice. Some say it means no longer having to work. Others might say it has to do with how much money you have.

Regardless of the answer, each person has a definition in mind. Most people have no problem defining financial success. However, not everyone knows how to get there. With that in mind, many people search for the perfect financial vehicle to help them achieve success. Often they are disappointed because what they buy or invest in turns out to be much different than what they thought it would be. Not only did it not help them reach their goal, but many times they lost large sums of money because of poor performance or high fees.

IT'S NOT THE CLUB CHOICE!

If you are a golfer and strive to get better, you may have fallen into the false hope of getting the perfect club that fixes every problem you're having with your golf game. Your new club arrives and you head out to the course, line up to the ball and swing. To your dismay, you watch the ball go deep into the woods because of that same slice you have always had. What have you learned from those expensive lessons? Very little of the golf game is about your club. It is mostly about your swing. Once your swing is right, then you can then enhance it with good clubs.

This example also applies to financial planning. Many people look high and low for the perfect financial product or the secret investment strategy. Even if they find this "perfect" tool, they still have financial anxiety in their life. Financial success has much more to do with the "swing" or process we use to get the best results. It is important to get to a place where, no matter what the stock market or economy does, you can still have peace of mind.

In 2008, I saw many people terrified by the dramatic drop of the stock market and the U.S. economic bubble bursting. The ones that were calm were the ones that I had worked with to create a clear strategy to deal with uncertain times. These individuals had the right financial swing. We also made sure they enhanced their "swing" with sound investment strategies.

THE EASY WAY TO IMPROVE YOUR SWING

When I took golf lessons, the first thing that the instructor did was videotape me swinging the club. As I watched the video, the instructor showed me areas I needed to correct. It was so clear once I could see myself on the screen and was made clearer by the instructor telling me what to correct. I have created a similar approach for your financial swing. I call it the Peace of Mind Retirement Map™. Whenever I meet with someone new, I will show them this map and explain how we can build one for them. It is a one-page view of your complete financial situation. It is something we will review together and update regularly. By using this tool, you will improve in the areas needed and see the areas where you are doing really well.

Using the Peace of Mind Retirement Map™ will empower you to prepare for and live through retirement. It will relieve you of the worry about running out of money and at the same time get the income needed to do what you want to do.

PEACE OF MIND IN RETIREMENT

I strongly believe that if your financial assets are positioned correctly then you don't have to worry about market drops. If you have your money positioned correctly, your income will come from places that are not affected by market swings.

If you worry every time the market falls, then you need to re-evaluate your financial swing. Just a few adjustments can mean the difference between being financially depressed or having peace of mind.

FOUR THINGS YOU SHOULD KNOW BEFORE HIRING A FINANCIAL ADVISER

I feel you should know more than just the basics about your financial adviser. For instance, do you know exactly how your adviser gets paid and what their responsibility is to you? Is your adviser held to a fiduciary standard? Do they have a system in place to communicate with you regularly? Do you have a written document called an Investment Policy Statement? Here are four things you should know about before hiring your adviser.

Commissions and Fees

Understanding exactly how your adviser is compensated is very important. Consider this: If your adviser only receives a commission when they sell you something or change your mutual funds, how much can you trust their recommendations? If they are paid by fee only, that makes it important to understand what the fee is and how they charge it.

If you are interviewing a new adviser, make sure you ask about compensation up front. If the adviser is trying to sell you a product that is on a commission basis, you should know. By no means am I saying that commissions are wrong. What I am saying is that you should understand how your adviser gets paid. If you know how they are getting paid you can then ask why a particular product or service is being recommended. You could also ask if the adviser shopped around for the best, lowest cost product or if they chose a product that pays the highest commission.

Knowing how your adviser gets paid will help you tremendously. If your current adviser or an adviser you are considering hiring does not want to clearly answer questions about their compensation, that could be a sign they are trying to hide something. It may be an indication that they are not thinking of your best interest, but possibly of their own best interest. I encourage you to consider a different adviser if this is the case.

Is your Adviser Held to a Fiduciary Standard?

In the financial services industry, there are brokers and there are advisers. There are people who sell products and people who sell knowledge. There are people who look out for their commissions and people who look out for you. The difference is a fiduciary standard. *Merriam-Webster's* defines *fiduciary* as "held or founded in trust or confidence." A fiduciary standard is about your interests, goals and well-being. Do you know if your financial adviser is held to a fiduciary standard? I think they should be, to protect you and your financial livelihood. Do you expect your doctor or lawyer to put your interests first? Of course you do; doctors and lawyers are held to a fiduciary standard. As for financial advisers, the fact is many are not held to this high standard. Do you want your adviser to be required to put your interests first? If you currently have an adviser, ask them if they are required by law to put your interests first. If you are interviewing an adviser, make sure they are held to a fiduciary standard before you do business with them.

A Registered Investment Adviser (RIA) is a person or company that has registered with the U.S. Securities and Exchange Commission (SEC) or with a state securities division. This registration does not mean the SEC approves, sanctions, or attests to the merits of the person or company. It simply indicates the person or entity is registered and has agreed to abide by certain fiduciary standards. An RIA may be registered with a state securities division as well as with the SEC. The RIA and Investment Adviser (IA) designations came about from the Investment Advisers Act of 1940. The fiduciary standard is based on the laws that put this act put in place. The fiduciary standard means that an adviser is required to act only in the best interest of his or her client. This is true even if the interest conflicts with the adviser's financial interests. An adviser held to this standard is required to report any conflicts or potential conflicts of interest before and during the time the adviser is engaged by the client. Additionally, RIAs and IAs must disclose how they are compensated and agree to abide by a code of ethics.

Very few who claim to be financial advisers are actually federally- or state-registered. Most are considered to be broker-dealers, which are held to lower and nonregulated standards. Federal law requires broker-dealers to act in the best interest of their employer—not their clients. This does not mean they are unethical or plan to harm their clients. In fact, I feel confident most are ethical and do not intend harm to their clients. The scary thing is that they are not required by law to act in their client's best interest. If your adviser is not required to act in your best interest, then this limits your recourse if you feel you have been taken advantage of.

To guard against unethical violations, the SEC requires broker-dealers to include the following disclosure in their client agreements. Read this disclosure. Is this the type of relationship you want with your adviser?

> Your account is a brokerage account and not an advisory account. Our interests may not always be the same as yours. Please ask us questions to make sure you understand your rights and our obligations to you, including the extent of our obligations to disclose conflicts of interest and to act in your best interest. We are paid both by you and, sometimes, by people who compensate us based on what you buy. Therefore, our profits, and our salespersons' compensation, may vary by product and over time.

If you have signed an agreement with an adviser, go look at it. Is this disclaimer in there? If so, ask your adviser for more details. Decide if the relationship is in your best interest.

Get An Investment Policy Statement?

Do you have an Investment Policy Statement (IPS)? What is it? An IPS is a written statement that details the policies, procedures and goals that you and your adviser have agreed to in regards to managing your investments. This type of document is required when a fiduciary relationship exists. An IPS outlines a systematic approach for making decisions. It establishes a way to tackle difficult issues related to your investment choices. Having a plan provides clarity as you work with your adviser to meet certain expectations and goals. A well-thought-out statement helps your adviser understand what you expect. It also demonstrates your adviser's willingness to meet your investment needs and help you meet your goals.

Act in Your Own Best Interest

There are other things to consider when choosing an adviser, but looking at the topics detailed in this chapter can be a great start. Choosing a competent financial adviser whom you trust may be one of the most important decisions you make. Not only can your choice impact you, it can also impact your loved ones. Choose your adviser wisely. The right adviser can be a guide to you and your family throughout your life as you address specific financial concerns. They can help you find financial peace of mind and assist you in achieving your life goals. Never let an adviser scare you into becoming a client or make you feel guilty in order to keep you as a client. Take the time to get complete answers to all of your questions. Above all, act in your own best interest.

About Radon

Radon Stancil is a Certified Financial Planner™ in Raleigh, N.C. His specialty is working with individuals who are close to or already in retirement, as well as high-income business owners. His goal is to make sure his clients have the best understanding of their financial situation. He created the Peace of Mind Retirement Process™ to help his clients develop a systematic approach to retirement planning. He then created the Peace of Mind Retirement Map™ to help his clients track their progress. This unique approach removes the stress from retirement planning and gives an increased level of financial security.

Radon is the author of *Take Control Of Your Retirement Plan* and is regularly sought out by the media for his opinions and expertise. Radon has been seen on CBS, NBC, ABC and FOX affiliates and has been quoted in the *Wall Street Journal, USA Today and Newsweek.* He says, "I love helping my clients with their most pressing concerns. I like taking complicated topics and breaking them down in an easy to understand way. It brings me great satisfaction when a client says, 'OK, now I get it.'"

To learn more about Radon and his Peace of Mind Retirement Strategies™ visit www.FinancialPlanStrategies.com or call 919-787-8866.

CHAPTER 32

Where's Your Head At? The Awakening

By Elizabeth Potter

Ever wonder why things happen the way they do? Why is it so easy for some people but not so easy for others?

My favorite saying is from Henry Ford: "Whether you think *that you can or whether you think you can't … you are right!*"

I have always been high energy. Once I accomplished something, I had to move on. Some called me Sybil, others irresponsible; some even told me I would not amount to anything. Every time I felt good about myself, someone would come along and burst my bubble and I would fall back into my "poor me" puddle.

At the start 2007, I resolved to stop listening to people tell me that my glass was half empty. Instead, I decided I was going to focus on what *was working*. I was excited and optimistic. Life was good! I had a steady job; I had an ideal relationship with a man; and my kids, who were 9 and 7 at the time, were healthy and happy. I had always gone for my physical at the start of every year ever since my kids were born, and so on January 5, I went for my mammogram just like I had done the year before.

But this time, the medical staff said, "Mrs. Potter there seems to be something in your left breast, and we'd like to take a closer look by doing an ultrasound and possibly a biopsy." I had needed an ultrasound previously, so I thought nothing of this news. Little did I know that my life would change forever three weeks later.

On the day of January 19, the news came: "Mrs. Potter, you have cancer and we have arranged a date to see the surgeon, it's on ..." I stopped listening. My whole world came crashing down. My head started spinning, I couldn't breathe, and I started running around like a chicken with its head cut off. All the "if only I ..." scenarios were flooding my brain, and then the tears came and would not stop. I felt like I was being carried out to sea on the waves and there was nothing to grab onto. I was talking to everyone I knew looking for answers but few of them had any experience with cancer. Those that did saw death as the end result. I could sense their compassion but also realized they were thinking: "I'm glad it's not me!" Who was going to save me? I even asked the man I was dating to marry me ... like that was going to help!

All I could think about were my children. What would happen to them if I was to pass? Who would look after them? I wondered what they must be feeling. ... First, not much contact with their father and now they could lose their mother. I fell into a world of devastation and hopelessness. My mindset door was slammed, sealed, and delivered. ... I was going to die! I was in shock, a state of nothingness.

Contrary to my mood, the medical staff was very optimistic based on my health and age; chances were very good for my survival. Their optimism allowed hope to be born in me. In my first surgery, surgeons took five lymph nodes and a piece of my left breast. Thank goodness for pain killers. My spirits were lifted a notch because I had made it through the surgery. I rested at home, not complaining, and just thankful that I was going to be all right. My physical appearance was hardly impacted at all!

MORE BAD NEWS

However, 10 days later the news came. "Sorry Mrs. Potter. It seems we did not get all of it. We will need to do a complete removal of your breast." Now I was filled with fear like I had never felt before. Not only did I have to endure more pain from surgery, but the possibility of having chemo and radiation were there front and center, and I was about to be disfigured.

Quaking in my boots, I went into the next surgery. It was by far the most physically painful experience of my life. At the conclusion, I had 21 staples across my chest. It took many, many tries of counting before I could do it without wanting to vomit. To make matters worse, the call came again. ..."Mrs Potter, we seemed to have gotten all of it but would like to start chemo right away based on the cells found just in case. You have your consultation with the oncologist on. ..." I had stopped listening again. I was angry it wasn't over yet! There was still more to come.

At the consultation, the oncologists told me they were going to send me through various tests to see what my body could withstand and install a picc (peripherally inserted central catheter) in my arm because of the intensity of the treatment. They wanted to be very aggressive to ensure any micro cells that might have been left after the surgery would not survive. Again I went thru the motions; I felt numb but my mind was screaming, "This can't be happening!" The medical staff installed a tube in the vein on my right arm that went through to my heart. I lived with this invasion for the next six months. That was not very comfortable!

THE RED BAG

A week later, I found myself at the cancer center, wondering how this was all going to go. I heard my name called; scared out of my wits, I entered the chemo treatment room. This was going to be the first out of six chemo treatments, all four hours in duration. The chemo treatment room was in a large hospital ward with lots of windows overlooking a river and hills. As I entered the room, I became aware of the other people there. Some were lying in beds, and some were sitting up in reclining chairs, all hooked up to various colored IV bags. It occurred to me that they were all being poisoned! Some had hair, and some didn't. Some still had color in their faces, and some looked all gray. Some looked optimistic, while others looked like they had given up hope. All were in various stages of treatment. I felt like I was walking in a nightmare.

After I was seated in my recliner, my first treatment started. Four bags of varying sizes and colors were placed on my tray. The largest bag was red, and the nurses told me that was the last bag of the treatment and also the most powerful.

Embarking on a journey that I had never experienced before, I tried to keep an open mind and focused on my breathing. As I was being injected with each drug, I could feel my conscious mind becoming thinner and my guts feeling worse than with any flu I'd ever experienced. All I could taste and smell was metal. I was very afraid!

Then the red bag came. As it entered my body, a curtain seemed to rise with every beat of my heart. I could almost feel the splashing of the drug as it was being dispersed from my heart throughout my body. I felt like I was riding a big red wave into nothingness. I could not hold a single thought. It was like ... when you want to say something and the word is on the tip of your tongue but, for the life of you ... you can't vocalize it!

When I left the hospital that first day, walking beside my man, I was in a world of my own—seeing and hearing but not comprehending anything. When I got home, I was secluded from the others as I was very toxic and hazardous to their health.

As all this was proceeding for me, other events were occurring in my family. The children were still going about their lives, and my man was becoming more distant. It occurred to me that they were preparing for my departure on a subconscious level. I had never felt more alone in my entire life. I became angry. I didn't quite know what I wanted from my family, but I obviously needed something. I remember looking at myself in the mirror: disfigured and no hair. I looked like some kind of alien. I would ask myself, "where are you?" My eyes looked familiar, but they seemed hollow and lifeless. Giving up, I became very withdrawn to everything.

I went through the next couple of treatments like a drone—not caring about anything or anyone. I despised myself in my world of "poor me" and was angry with those around me for being healthy and going about their everyday lives. I was angry at the world. I was not getting along with anyone.

After my third treatment, I had a very big argument with my man. I was so angry and frustrated at everything: people staring at me like I was some kind of freak, the I'm sorry for you but I'm glad it's not me feelings I was sensing, but most of all I hated the fact that the life I had known was gone while others were still moving forward.

TRANSFORMATION BEGINS

Then something very amazing happened! It was like a transformation. My body and mind exploded. I was not going to take it anymore. It was like a cellular explosion. My body shook violently, and my vision shut off to the outside world. All I could see were stars, and a sound came from deep within, taking with it all that was bad. It was a cleansing of sorts, for when it was all over, a peace came over me like I've never felt before. It was an inner knowing that great changes were coming, and I was getting a second chance so I should make it count.

My last three chemo treatments were a completely different experience. Yes, the curtain went up every time—taking a piece of my brain with it—but it felt like I was on auto pilot. My mind was made up. I was going to live and make it count. I had no idea how it was all going to happen, but each day I was being driven from within to keep moving forward. I decided to walk away from everything that I knew with my kids in tow. Somehow I was provided with the right people and resources to assist in my transition; some of those people I never knew or saw again. Looking back, I am truly grateful for all the love and support I received!

In the fall of 2007, I was sitting in my new home, alone in an empty room with no job, no man, and two kids in tow. I was scared out of my wits, but I was so happy that I had made it this far and was still breathing. A friend of mine gave me a picture with a single man in a row boat in the middle of a lake with the word "Perseverance" at the bottom. As I looked at the picture everyday, it finally occurred to me that there was only one person in the boat.

For the next 18 months, I lived in a state of unconscious incompetence that some people call chemo brain. It's a quiet place; a place where no mind friction exists. While I was within this state, my other senses would come forward to guide me through my daily existence. Thinking hurt my head, watching TV overwhelmed me, and when my kids spoke to me I had to ask them to slow down so I could understand. I practiced memory skills every day, ate nutritious foods and went for walks. I was truly happy to be alive! And then one day, the fog lifted. I was able to remember little things like a phrase.

Little by little, I improved. Today I own my own businesses and live better than I ever thought possible!

LIFE LESSONS LEARNED

I learned many lessons from this experience. ... I remind myself every day of a few.

- Your mind is very powerful ... what are you feeding it?

- Happiness comes first ... be grateful for what you have right now.

- Your mind is your greatest asset ... investment pays you back ten-fold.

- Be kind to yourself ... you were only in a state of unconscious incompetence ... you can't know what you didn't know.

- Keep moving one small step at a time regardless of anything.

- There are opposites to everything ... thru your greatest adversities comes the greatest gifts.

- Life is a ride ... keep looking through your windshield—not the rear-view mirror.

- Everything is a progression ... be patient! Thoughts, feelings, actions, results.

- Random acts of kindness can create big changes for others ... make a difference!

- Who cares what others think about you. Are YOU OK with YOU?

About Elizabeth

Elizabeth Potter brings more than 25 years of experience with logistics, production, customer service and financing. Utilizing these skills, she opened her first company in 2007. As a professional organizer specializing in small business, she has built a reputation as a reliable, effective and proactive consultant. Elizabeth has worked with many small-business owners to create systems that help them understand and achieve greater efficiency and profitability.

Feedback from clients and realizing a niche for other services led Elizabeth to form a new company, Systemized For Play Ltd (www.systemizedforplay.com), in July 2010. The market for the services offered by Systemized For Play Ltd is not unusual; however, new thinking and up-to-date economic research offered by the company has proven to be very successful with various clients.

Her largest project started in 2009 where she started LP Credit Resolution LLC (www.LPcreditresolution.com), a debt-buying company committed to helping at least 10,000 people with their debt. She has trained in the areas of computer science, economics, accounting software, business management, sales and marketing and is a proud member of the American Credit Association, Professional Organizers of Canada as well as a member of the Progressive Group For Independent Business.

CHAPTER 33

The Factors Governing Success

By Siou-Foon Lee

According to the ancient wise masters, if we do the right thing (correct actions) at the right time and in the right place, we will be fortunate. If we do the wrong thing we get into strife. When I first learned of this advice I was fascinated with the mindset behind Chinese metaphysics, which has thousands of years of history. I had come to a point where I found myself at a fork in my path of life. It was at this time that I chose to delve deeper into my cultural heritage. I had grown up knowing more about Shakespeare and A. J. Cronin than Fu Xi and Chinese astrology.

I began my journey of learning traditions as practiced by masters in Asia. When I started to pursue this new passion, there was already an emergence of ancient knowledge from Asia. Earlier, many had been introduced to martial arts made popular by Chinese Kung Fu star Bruce Lee. But acupressure and Chinese medicines had not been widely accepted yet, and not many had heard of Sun Tzu's earliest known Chinese military classic, which has been introduced to the West shortly before the French Revolution. His famous line—"Know the enemy and know yourself; in a hundred battles you will never be in peril"—is ideally suited to today's needs. Countless Chinese generations have followed the most treasured Chinese wisdom found in *I Ching,* originally a book of divination.

The timing was right for me to gain mastery as many masters were keen to share the secrets embedded in theories, concepts and principles behind Chinese metaphysics which includes Fengshui and Chinese astrology. According to the teachings, the trinity of heaven, earth and human are factors that govern our success. In our path through life, we are also influenced by good deeds/virtues, knowledge and hard work. They are all pieces of the picture called life. It is good to know what the wise men of ancient times teach.

HEAVEN, EARTH AND HUMAN LUCK

Between heaven above and earth below, humans stand. In the traditional sense, destiny is heaven luck. The destiny analysis gives us information that allows us to know what direction to focus on and what decisions to make to get good outcomes. Homes and offices which tap into good energy are activating earth luck which is the analysis of the Fengshui of the land—finding the right place that can harness qi/energy to benefit us. Human luck translates into the action taken after receiving the information, making decisions to change and improve. It all starts in the mind that desires a change—humans do, earth heeds, heaven answers.

Heaven Luck

For centuries, the Chinese have been fascinated with the mystery of Chinese metaphysics allowing us to delve into the great mysteries of life, interpreting the destiny code written in the eight characters of our birth data.

Destiny analysis uses Chinese astrology—or BaZi—to decode our personal destiny defining our core values, personality and characteristics. These insights reveal our hidden potential to be maximized and also tell us about accepting our limitations. Knowing that time and tide wait for no man in good luck cycles and understanding it is not time to rest on our laurels but to prepare for good times ahead is crucial for our success.

The BaZi reading clarifies our purpose, direction, vision, fulfillment and focus. We see its relevance as an inner compass when seeking to align our life with our values. It is a way of life that young and old seek yearly updates for guidance for the duration of that year. Choosing the right employer is just as crucial—and as much a leap of faith—as picking the best career path.

It is customary for couples wishing to tie the knot to submit their birth details to choose an auspicious date for marriage. Even new entrepreneurs use their birth dates to select auspicious dates to have an official opening for their business to ensure optimal business success.

Human Luck

Asians generally believe in the trilogy as a tool to transform life and business. Some of them define success as monetary wealth, power and social status, while others value inner peace and life fulfillment. Successful people are clear on their core values by understanding their destiny.

Knowledge of any kind is good, but it has no impact on life if it is not used to extend ourselves to our highest good. Knowledge in the Chinese context is about knowing the right thing to do. It is not just about education. The gained insights can be the catalyst for maximizing potentials and seeking competence in the chosen field of expertise. The factor governing our success lies in our action. To take quick action, a person also needs skills to do the right thing. With skills gained from experiences, we are able to make quick, informed decisions. Inaction and procrastination can eventually lead us to mar our own luck. So it is important to know what kind of human luck we have.

Many have investigated this alternative life management system that appears on the face of it to have a tenuous link to life consultation, yet has actually been used successfully in very practical environments. If we could be advised about imminent negativity, would we appreciate tips to mitigate the risk of bad events occurring? If we knew about an incoming positive spell, we would seek to be bolder and maximize the opportunity to succeed. Chinese astrology has helped with personal and business goals. This practice does not seek to tell us what to do. Instead, it enables us to know when to walk and when to run. Delve a little deeper, and we are pleasantly surprised at how practical the system actually is. By using the knowledge of what is to come in terms of fortune, we can still thrive during challenging times, thus giving us the opportunity to control our destiny.

Life's journey is full of choices, and we cannot always see where they will lead us. However, it is worthwhile to find the path to our own personal success in order to enjoy vibrant health, joyous relationships, abundant wealth, self-empowerment and life fulfillment.

It is not unusual to be at a fork in the road unable to read the road signs. We must choose between two paths. We can be overwhelmed. It becomes a dilemma. In such difficult times, BaZi can be of immense help. The clarity gained will allow us to take the right road. Our path in life suddenly has road signs that we can read.

Earth Luck

Fengshui is an ancient art of harnessing vital earth qi by interacting with the environment. Qi can be defined as the breath of life flowing in us as well as circulating in our environment. This tradition uses natural laws to explain the life force energy of the planet operating in the physical environment in relation to living spaces and individuals. It is working in harmony with a given space through balancing the yin-yang, enhancing the capacity of the land for residence or business for creating wealth, health and happiness.

Buildings are like containers. It is important to place the door in the building to harness the positive qi. Placed correctly, there are good outcomes but when wrongly placed, there are poor outcomes. It is the harmonious interaction that gives us comfort and a sense of security necessary to lead balanced lives. Just like in any key relationship, it is important to be in balanced interaction with loved ones; even more so with spaces we occupy. Homes that can tap into positive qi have added advantages.

The added benefit of pursuing earth luck is the accumulating positive cosmic energy for us. It is of paramount importance that we lead lives in a deliberate way with determination and willingness to put concrete plans into action to get to the next level of success. These actions, skills displayed and decisions made are seen as part of the factors that the ancient sages teach that govern success.

We live in a constantly evolving world, and applying solutions derived from classical texts does not mean that ancient skills are inapplicable to modern situations. This art is just as relevant in contemporary living. We still desire fulfillment of personal goals, good relationships, retaining good staff, profitability and personal/business success. We are still filled with fear, frustration, challenges and anxiety over profit loss, poor cash flow and bankruptcy. Times may have changed, but nothing has changed.

The Chinese accept it as a science and art form as a result of direct empirical experience. Over centuries peoples' success from direct experience is enough although they cannot prove it objectively. The solution-based and result-driven approach to challenges faced by businesses has been embraced as a way of thinking for corporate and commercial enterprises. Its design solutions and its flow in commercial spaces are created to address a high level of employee stress. With balanced and aesthetic working environments, the corporate staff can progress ultimately to achieve corporate results that every employer desires.

Earth luck is regularly integrated into most Asian daily life, with entrepreneurs using preventive measures for the sake of productivity. Corporations see it as an investment—not an expense. Unfortunately, nonbelievers think it belongs to the realm of mystical traditions. But Fengshui is not a mystical discipline—there is no enlightenment involved when it is applied correctly. It deals with life-force energy, a concept often considered strange in the Western world. The practice lies in assessing outcomes based on influence of qi upon a living environment. It advocates the harmonious interaction within working spaces. Good outcomes occur when environmental qi is tapped harmoniously.

Traditional Fengshui uses ancient techniques focusing on problem-solving for modern day challenges. Like any science, there are principles underlying these systems. Its holistic approach looks beyond furniture placement, symbolic objects and popular folklore. Its authenticity is rooted in a systematic methodology which can enable end users to achieve optimal success. However its practice is generally perceived with skepticism. Instead of respect for an ancient tradition that has lasted 3,500 years, it is put in the same basket as hocus-pocus. Many would be surprised to learn that a set of systems and underlying concepts stand behind this age-old philosophy but definitely no requirement of any belief system.

This ancient art is an important and necessary aid to personal and business success. Entrepreneurs starting a new business can be categorized into three groups.

Group 1 believes risk is the biggest threat so it is either make or break.

Group 2 believes in determination and perseverance, working the hardest and getting paid the least—a job he can't quit.

Group 3 believes that beyond motivation and positive thinking, premises do play a significant role in shaping destiny. They employ Fengshui systems to run profitable ventures and avoid running business in a struggle mode.

This third group sees the ancient art as a business solution—from shop selection to opening dates. The new entrepreneurs want to see effective profits within six months of operations, and their official opening for business serves to entice customers.

CONCLUSION

Human luck is the element of action. Actions, skills and decisions are inter-related. Selecting a good home to live according to Fengshui principles is using the right place. In the trilogy governing success, our destiny cannot be rewritten, but the quality of earth luck can be improved. Earth luck has the ability and energy to restore balance and harmony when our current luck cycle in our destiny charts is full of setbacks and obstacles.

David Starr Jordan described simply the factors for success when he said that wisdom is knowing what to do next, skill is knowing how to do it, and virtue is doing it. Very simply put. And it all starts in the mind that desires a change: Humans do, Earth heeds, Heaven answers.

Here are 15 tips and tricks to ensure your destiny, luck and action are properly connected.

1. Do you know who you really are? If you do not know, do whatever it takes to get this essential knowledge. If you do not know yourself, how can you understand others?

2. Knowing what lies ahead is essentially helpful for crucial decisions taken in challenging times. What is stopping you from achieving your potential? If you are at a turning point—move away from it. Ultimately you control your own destiny.

3. When you want to be the most successful person, you need to align your talents, passion and values that you have identified. Timing is of the essence. Know yourself. Know your environment.

4. The more specifics you know about where your talents lie, the better you can connect with them, and the more successful you can become. Doing the right thing at the right time brings good fortune.

5. When a window of opportunity opens, study the landscape but also look far into the horizon. Grab the opportunity and success is yours; procrastinate and the ship has left the harbor.

6. You need opportunities. When correctly applied, Fengshui opens the door to luck, and luck brings opportunities. Be in the right place at the right time.

7. You want more money, more meaning in life and more free time—choose the path of least resistance. Look back to the past so as to move forward. Study the obstacles that held you back from achieving the lifestyle you want to taste.

8. To achieve breakthrough results and create success, put your plan into action. Goals need clarity, purpose and direction. The factor governing your success lies in your action.

9. It is not good enough to want to create massive wealth if you are not prepared to do the hard work. Know how to work smart but don't work so hard just to survive.

10. Commit wholeheartedly to your goal. Stay on this specific plan of action. There are no shortcuts for success outside of your commitment to this specific path.

11. If you are still feeling fear, then you are not feeling confident. Cross the threshold of fear. Put systems into place. Now is the time to grow your confidence. Your fate lies in your hands.

12. There is no time for hesitation if you decide you want to change. Train yourself to make decisions and commitments when you need to. You now have the insights into your destiny.

13. To reach your potential faster, do not be sidetracked or distracted with too much multitasking. Learn about priority. The inability to focus can be a detriment to achieving success.

14. Authentic Fengshui is a crucial tool for success. The best line of defense is applying it at the outset of a new project.

15. A good date selection ensures a good harvest when a project or milestone event is started on the right date, time and the right footing.

About Siou-Foon

Since founding Fengshui Innovations, Master Siou-Foon Lee has risen to become an expert of authentic, classical Fengshui and Chinese astrology. A seminar leader, she is also a public speaker having spoken in Germany, Australia, India and Malaysia. Leaving her education profession behind, Siou Foon first chose to train with Master Zheng Hao of Chi Healing College and went on to teach Chinese acupressure at the Australian College of Natural Therapies, Broadway. She also appeared on SBS as a Chinese massage therapist. Siou Foon first studied traditional Chinese Fengshui and continued extensive studies, training with traditional masters.

She completed her mastery training, where she was named best student. Siou Foon also won another prestigious honor that boosted her respected international reputation when her peers selected her as the most helpful student. As she began to practice Fengshui, she saw remarkable results in her clients' lives. Her own Fengshui business grew so rapidly that she was forced to make a choice between lecturing and consulting. She followed her passion for Chinese metaphysics dedicating her time to her passion for an ancient art form. Her choice of a career in Chinese metaphysics paid off when she subsequently became a professional trainer.

She has hosted numerous seminars for the principals, Grand Master Yap Cheng Hai and Joey Yap, contributing further to the spread of classical Fengshui. She was chosen to speak in Germany at the First World Classical Fengshui Conference. She is recognized for pioneering classical Fengshui and Chinese astrology in Australia. Siou Foon introduced the subject to TV viewers and has actively participated in festivals and shows popularizing the ancient tradition. She has gained extensive exposure in the media over the years.

Siou Foon travels in Australia, the U.S., India, England, Singapore and Malaysia both as a consultant and a trainer. This is where Siou Foon shares her values, integrity and dedication to the ancient art as practiced by traditional masters. A firm believer that "learning is a lifelong journey," she travels and continues her passion for Chinese metaphysics, seeking out highly qualified but low-profile masters from a long impressive lineage. She has been very fortunate to be able to advance and seek more truths in such a complex environment. The first step taken on this journey of attaining mastery has never stopped.

CHAPTER 34

Action Living

By Ethan Hale

December 31, 1993. I got out of bed, had breakfast, then moved to the living room and took out the implements of my death. I had a pistol, and I had a syringe with all the drugs I would need to kill myself. I wasn't in the depths of depression, nor did I have a terminal illness. But I had promised myself on January 1 of 1993 that if I had not quit drugs by the end of the year I would kill myself. It was the last day of the year, and I was still using drugs. I was 16 days past my 29th birthday, and I had been an intravenous crystal meth user since I was 16 years old. I had "quit" for up to a year a couple of times but that hadn't stuck.

I had made a conscious decision to return to the drug lifestyle. When I said made a conscious decision I mean literally. In 1988, I was living in Louisiana and had been drug-free for a little over a year. The company I had been working for had failed due to circumstances outside of our control, and the owners had returned to their home in Paris. After help-ing them load up or sell off all their stuff, I was blessed to receive a bonus car and a good severance check. I told my wife at the time that I was moving back to Oklahoma to be a drug dealer. Then I asked if she wanted to come with me. I had been driving the Sunday school bus at my local Pentecostal church, preaching at the nursing home and teach-ing 12-year-old Sunday school students. Life was going pretty well, but for some reason I had been formulating and planning to leave Louisiana because of the lack of work there, and I knew I could make a living deal-ing drugs back in Oklahoma.

And I did exactly that. When I arrived in Oklahoma, I drove immediately to my drug dealer's house. He wouldn't sell me drugs because I had been clean and living right, but his friend there did sell me drugs. Once I was involved in drugs again, my dealer took me back as a client. We all have ways of justifying our behavior. Funny.

Anyway, as I sat on the couch thinking about killing myself, I decided that I wouldn't shoot myself because I didn't want my girlfriend to have to clean up the mess. I decided I was going to overdose on drugs, so I mixed up enough crystal meth to certainly do the job and then I set the syringe down, sat back and thought about what had brought me to this point in my life.

I thought about my abusive childhood, my wild teen years, my time in the Army and my outlaw years. I noted that in the last year I had separated from my wife, lost my job, got hurt while working a manual labor job, lost my apartment and lost a home I was buying in the country. You would think a drug dealer would have money saved, but I spent it as if it was free money because it's hard to explain where material goods come from if you don't have a job. I lost respect for myself and hated almost everyone else. Not to mention the fact that my personal drug use costs had risen to several hundred dollars per day. It didn't take that much; I just thought I wanted that much.

There were some good things also. I did have some good friends, and my mother still loved me. I had a drug-free girlfriend who was supportive of my desire to be a better human. I decided that since I was blessed with intelligence, I would make a list of reasons to live and reasons to kill myself.

Maybe it was a self-fulfilling task, but the reasons-to-live side of the list was about four lines longer than the reasons-to-die side. In order to live, I needed to do so more fully. I knew I would need to quit drugs because that was the reason I was here now. So, how could I make a life change that would work? I needed to take action.

On the paper where I had made my list, I wrote the word ACTION. Then for some reason I decided to write it vertically.

A
C
T
I
O
N

When I saw the word written that way, I had an epiphany. The word would be the acronym for the steps to achieve success. They were the same steps I had just engaged in while reviewing my life. Well, the first two were, and the rest came as I looked at them—although I must admit it took a while to associate Orientation with the "O."

A = Assess

C = Choose

T = Tools

I = Itinerary

O = Orientation

N = Now

Assess my situation. Look at what choices, circumstances and decisions had brought me to this point.

Choose what I want out of life.

Tools. What tools—both mental and physical—will I use to get the things I want out of life?

Itinerary is the plan or the roadmap to follow to get me to the place/person I want to be.

Orientation is the compass or the way to ensure I am travelling the right path in the right direction. Everything matters.

Now is the time to begin.

Using that plan, I quit drugs on the spot. I had opportunity to test my resolve not long after that. A few weeks after I made up my mind to quit, my dealer came by my house and wanted to use my scales to weigh product. Of course, I let him; there was no reason he couldn't—I wasn't using them. He used them at my home, and when he was done there was a mess to clean up and a big crystal meth rock on the scale. I picked it up and put it in my mouth out of habit and without thinking. However, the moment the meth hit my tongue, I spit it out and wiped my tongue off. My "friend" said, "what are you doing?" I looked at him calmly and said, "That's not quitting." I knew then that I was drug-free! Nineteen years later, that is still true.

Having just acquired a life-changing tool that worked for me, I did what anyone would do, of course. I began to tell my story of achievement through ACTION. Depending on the group or organization, I would either tell the back-story or share only the six-step process needed to reach one's goals, desires and dreams. I have included the story here because it is important to show what can be accomplished even for people starting from at or near the bottom.

Let me elaborate on these six steps because they work individually, in careers, companies and organizations of all sizes. I know. I have taught them. I even teamed up with a corporate trainer, Garland McWatters, and we wrote an award-winning training program based on these steps. We have received rave reviews from satisfied participants ranging from alternative school kids to small and large corporations; from groups as small as seven to crowds as large as several hundred at a time. The steps work.

ASSESS

Assess: to estimate or judge the value, character, etc., of; evaluate. (All definitions are taken from *dictionary.com*.)

"Crude men who feel themselves insulted tend to assess the degree of insult as high as possible, and talk about the offense in greatly exaggerated language, only so they can revel to their heart's content in the aroused feelings of hatred and revenge" ~ Friedrich Nietzsche.

Nietzsche assumed that men who feel this way have been insulted by an external source. But I had brought myself to a place where I was ready to exact revenge on myself because I hated who I was. Through assessing my life, I was able to identify areas where I could make choices and decisions that would lead to better circumstances.

By engaging in this technique, you and/or your organization can identify areas for improvement and potential areas for expansion and growth. Key areas to note are sales, payment, procurement, budgeting, problem solving—or the term I prefer, solution seeking—and manufacturing or delivery. Ask why, and does this add value? Utilize process mapping here. It is important to understand how work gets done.

CHOOSE

Choose: to select from a number of possibilities; pick by preference.

To make life more bearable and pleasant for everybody, choose the issues that are significant enough to fight over and ignore or distract yourself away from those you can let slide that day. Picking your battles will eliminate a number of conflicts and yet will still leave you feeling in control.

Brian Tracy says, "When you choose to do any one thing you choose not to do everything else." I chose to start with identifying what I didn't like about my life and then what I did like. From there I chose how I would go about getting more of what I liked and less of what I didn't. Starting with not killing myself!

In your company, choose the things that will have the biggest impact on your bottom line in the short term and plan to implement an itinerary that will lead to the path of performance, productivity and honorable profitability.

TOOLS

Tools: anything used as a means of accomplishing a task or purpose.

"To do good work, one must first have good tools"
~ unknown author.

I needed to identify what tools would work to get the life I wanted. Organizations also need to identify the tools available to allow them to effectively and efficiently accomplish the goals they have set. In this day of digital availability you most likely are using some form of CRM, ERP or Lean Process of some kind. If not should you? If so, is it doing what it should?

Is it about skills or training or failure in the system? Do your tools work? Are your people and their skills sharpened? Don't forget that staff can make or break an organization, and that tool needs to be well maintained. Individuals reading this, are you keeping yourself valuable to the marketplace?

ITINERARY

Itinerary: a detailed plan for a journey, especially a list of places to visit; plan of travel.

It is true that movement and momentum count and even more true that being on the right path matters. Anything worth doing in business must have a deadline attached. The late and great Jim Rohn used the analogy of school chairs and them becoming smaller as people got bigger to represent this concept. If you're too big for the chair, you should have moved on already. Things happen. They should happen on time or sooner. Trust but verify that deadlines are being met. Coach and encourage as needed.

ORIENTATION

Orientation: the ability to locate oneself in one's environment with reference to time, place and people.

"Every orientation presupposes a disorientation"
~ Hans Magnus Enzensberger.

For an organization, this has to do with character and transparency as well as the guiding direction provided by leadership. Every great company has great leaders. Great leaders recognize the greatness of the members and position them accordingly.

Being a leader is not about being a cheerleader; it is about ensuring that the people trusted to do the work have the tools and resources needed to do them better than adequately and the right focus to deliver quality work. Are you headed in the right direction? With all the negative publicity out there about individual and corporate greed and scams, are you monitoring your direction?

NOW

Now: without further delay; immediately; at once.

"Do it now and do it again!" ~ Ethan Hale.

Take ACTION on yourself, your career, your company or your organization. Do it NOW. Then do it again because as new heights are achieved, new heights are revealed. There are abundant resources available to help guide, grow and inspire you to identify possibilities and improve performance and productivity while increasing profitability and allowing you to implement philanthropy.

Finally, here's a quick recap of the six-step process to success. It has made the difference in my life and the life of countless others. I have heard stories of other people choosing to redirect their lives, of companies refocusing their direction and of individuals signing contracts with major labels based on using the ACTION Living strategies. I hope you find them useful, dear reader.

Assess your situation. Look at what choices, circumstances and decisions brought you to this point.

Choose what you want out of life or for the organization.

Tools. What mental and physical tools will get those things for you?

Itinerary is the plan or the roadmap to follow to get you to the place/person/organization you want to be.

Orientation is the compass or the way to ensure you are traveling the right path in the right direction. Everything matters. Focus on success.

Now is when to begin.

About Ethan

Ethan Hale, founder of E. F. Hale Enterprises, LLC, has been select-ed as an expert blogger for FastCompany.com. Ethan's blog series, "3rd Millennium Thinking Skills," will appear regularly on Fast Com-pany's Leadership page. The blog features cool brain/mind related topics relevant to business in the third millennium.

Hale said he started life from a broken home, had an extremely physically abusive stepfather and overcame drug addiction and divorce. In the years since he first be-gan using the six-step process, he earned his G.E.D. and went to college, where he earned an A.A. and B.S. in psychology and a Master's degree in counseling. He says, "I have three beautiful daughters who never knew me as that person I was and have no fear that I will ever harm them. Life is trying at times for all of us but by choosing life and taking ACTION, you can achieve anything you work towards in life."

Ethan has been an entrepreneur most of his life, and all things related to how people learn fascinate him. He has an M.Sc. in psychology and a Master's level certificate as a certified vocational evaluator; he is a Licensed Professional Counselor, NLP trainer, hypnotherapist, author, trainer, life and business coach, martial arts instructor and motorcycle instructor. He puts 50,000 miles a year on his Harley and loves every one. Ethan shares his insights with hundreds of people every year in trainings, articles, books and videos.

"I have always been fascinated by choices and decision-making in our lives. My mother had brain cancer twice and I became even more amazed at the way our choices affect our health, healing and growth. This has led me to seek out knowl-edge in a wide array of topics and synergistically merge them into useful formats," remarked Ethan.

Hale is also the author of the books *3rd Millennium Marketing Musts* and *3rd Mil-lennium Thinking Skills,* due out in 2012, and editor of *3rd Millennium Marketing Mag.* Ethan is now returning his attention to some of his first business loves: train-ing, seminars and Internet marketing. To learn more about Ethan Hale, please visit www.efhale.com.

CHAPTER 35

Success: Reality or Delusion? You Must Choose

By Dr. John Moranville

In Steven Spielberg's movie, "Indiana Jones and the Last Crusade," Harrison Ford in his role as Indiana Jones is searching for the Holy Grail, which is believed to be the cup used by Jesus during the Last Supper. After a series of challenges, Indy reaches the cave or "temple" and finds a knight: "the last of three brothers who were chosen to guard the Grail."

The knight attempts to attack Indy with his sword, but then falls to his knees in reverence assuming that Indy has been sent to take his place and relieve him of his hundreds of years of service in protecting the Grail. Then suddenly, Elsa, the evil Nazi doctor, and the equally sinister and opportunistic archaeologist, Donovan, make their entrance and everyone notices that there is not just one, but many cups or "chalices."

Elsa asks, "which one is it?" The knight responds, "You must choose, but choose wisely, for whereas the true grail will bring you eternal life, the false grail will take it away." Elsa's choice is a jewel-studded, solid gold cup. Donovan grabs the cup from her hand, scoops some water from the fountain, and drinks. Initially he appears fine, but then a macabre scene unfolds where Donovan's age is vastly accelerated, and then his body begins to disintegrate, eventually crumbling into a blowing pile of dust.

Indiana Jones, motivated by love for his dying father, begins to feverishly sort through the cups to find "the cup of a carpenter." He finds a small, simple, nondescript cup made out of wood. He goes to the same fountain, scoops up some water, drinks from the true Grail and nothing happens. He then takes the water to his father, who is dying from a gunshot wound. After drinking from the Grail, Indy's father, Henry, is miraculously healed. Later, Elsa falls to her death when she reaches for the grail instead of Indy's outstretched hand. In contrast, Indy chooses his father's outstretched hand and lets go of the Grail. At the end of the movie, Indy's father says about Elsa, "she thought she found the prize." Indiana, who we learn took the name of his boyhood dog in lieu of being called Henry Jones Junior, asks his father, "What did you find, Dad?" Henry replies, "Illumination. Illumination." Then they ride off into the sunset with their two friends.

Illumination means to shed light on. The story in this movie sheds light on how the choices we make determine our reality and ultimately determine whether we live or die. The ironies of this story are humorous. Indiana Jones has become one of the most revered heroes of all time, yet we find he chose to use the name of his dog over his given name of Junior. We also learn that the choice of a cup which is shiny and expensive over a handmade cup that is simple and plain means the difference between life and death. Further, we learn that choosing the "prize" may lead us on a deadly pursuit.

A deeper interpretation of these movie events helps illuminate how every choice we make has far-reaching consequences for ourselves and those around us. We make choices based on the way we interpret the world around us, what we call "reality." But your reality is not my reality, which is not anyone else's reality.

Reality, as defined by *Merriam Webster*'s dictionary, is the state of being real. Real is defined as of or relating to fixed, permanent, or immovable things. Delusion, on the other hand, is defined as a state of being deluded or a false sense of reality that is held to be true despite overwhelming evidence to the contrary. Success is defined as a favorable or desired outcome.

Given these three definitions, how do we know if we are or if we can be successful in our lives? You probably bought this book because you want to be successful, or you already are and want to be more successful. So how do you know if you are successful?

First of all, you need to determine what you consider a favorable outcome for your life and then strive to get there. You must be able to clearly identify and visualize your ultimate view of success in every aspect of your life. You may find you are very successful in your family life, yet your career and income are not what you want them to be. Or you may find that you have a successful career and are financially independent, yet your spiritual life is a mess. Everyone else in the world may see you as the most successful person who ever lived, yet you may not believe that to be true.

The bottom line is the difference between reality and delusion is only a matter of semantics. Everything we see, hear, smell, feel or taste is processed in our brain in the context of our previous experiences and through the genetic code that makes our brain unique. Every aspect of our perception is a series of messages relayed from one brain cell to another through a complex network using a variety of chemicals called neurotransmitters as messengers.

Our very thoughts are merely the translation of everything and everyone that has been and is currently around us. In my role as a psychiatrist, I often tell patients who have experienced extreme delusions that there is no such thing as reality. To help them understand this, I will give an example of five separate eyewitness accounts of a car accident. In such an example, each story would vary somewhat in the details of exactly what happened. Each witness would choose certain aspects of the accident to focus on at the expense of noticing other aspects, which may be perceived as extremely important to another observer.

The brain of each observer "interprets" the series of events through a series of censoring and filtering. This process of censoring and filtering leads to thoughts about the accident, and then further censoring and filtering determines which thoughts about the accident are considered valid.

Cognitive theory states that thoughts lead to feelings, which lead to actions. Nobody knows exactly how thoughts are generated, but we do have a choice of which thoughts we believe to be true and which thoughts we believe to be false. Most, if not all, thoughts, however, are partially true and partially false.

You MUST choose! Choose wisely! Choose success and you shall have success. Success will become **your** reality!

About John

Dr. John Moranville is a psychiatrist and addiction medicine specialist with more than 25 years of professional experience. Recently he was recognized as VIP of the year for Cambridge Who's Who and as one of America's Top Psychiatrists.

After graduating medical school at the University of Iowa, John spent three years at the University of California, San Diego, as the diagnostician for a large multidisciplinary study of schizophrenia and helped author 13 scientific publications. He then moved to the San Francisco area, where he spent 12 years treating veterans who suffered from both mental illness and substance abuse. Since 2002, he has been somewhat of a free agent—working part-time in a variety of settings, including geriatric facilities, community clinics and psychiatric emergency rooms. He even spent a little time at San Quentin (with a key fortunately).

John has also experienced severe manic and depressive episodes over the past 25 years, which have given him a unique insight into mental health because he has been on both sides of a locked psychiatric facility. He says he still doesn't quite know what kept him from jumping off a bridge 25 years ago when he heard the voice of Jesus telling him to jump. Ten years later, John was caught in the middle of the Battle of Armageddon, faced with a decision about whether he was Jesus Christ or the Antichrist. For the past 20 years, he has been relatively stable. He continues to take medication and has personally experienced many debilitating side effects. John has his own psychiatrist, who helps him to carefully monitor his mood, sleep patterns, and thought processes as well as prescribe medications.

John has learned the hard way that self-treatment is not a wise option. This chapter, "Success: Reality or Delusion," is about his outlook on life in general and about how John has successfully chosen the reality that has led him to become one of the world's experts on bipolar disorder, other severe mental illnesses and addiction medicine.

CHAPTER 36

Financial Advisers: Oh, What an Interesting Group We Are!

By Philip M. Cioppa

The biggest question any of us faces is "what am I going to do with the rest of my life?" According to statistics, we ask that question more than once. In fact, on average, the typical American, for one reason or another, changes occupations three to four times in a lifetime. I am no exception. My journey led me through years of Roman Catholic priesthood, banking, marketing, until finally I found myself in the world of financial services. Today I am the managing principal and chief investment officer for Arbol Financial Strategies, LLC. Did I ever think I would get here? Never! However, as the song goes … "it's a long, long road, with many a winding turn"!

What do you really need to be an effective financial adviser? Time and time again, I hear that question. I have spent countless hours speaking with both men and women interested in this profession. Some chose the path and burnt out, some chose the path and succeeded, and some, after discussion, took another route along the highway of employment. There really is no "magic" formula to cracking open the success code for financial advising, but there are certain things that should be known if you decide to take this path.

A financial adviser may feel like he or she has to be all things to all people. Although the adviser sees the wealthy for the sustenance of a practice, what about the middle-class—or that which is a remnant of a socioeconomic swath that was referred to decades ago as the middle class? Many people who are considered neither wealthy nor poor, but fall in the cracks in between, tend to feel they don't deserve or need an adviser. The mentality is that an adviser is over-priced and will only push products to make a living. After all, what is a day without a bit of insurance, annuity and some assets under management, if but not a perfect storm for the adviser?

Out of this conundrum comes the adviser of the second decade of the 21st century. A little bit battered, a little bit living without respect, but still hanging in there hoping to make a difference for the client. In reality, the adviser today is a hybrid of many things: stocks and bonds, mutual funds, ETFs, fee-based accounts, planning, life, health and disability insurance, annuities and banking. Out of all this, some specialize while others choose to be a general practitioner. One of my colleagues is a group retirement planner, while another chooses to specialize in asset management. Although I tend to be a general practitioner, I admittedly side in the area of insurance planning. It was not by choice per se, but from my employment experience with companies and the perceived needs of individuals. The sum total of this description is that a financial adviser has a wide open field to choose a position to pursue.

So, you want to be a financial adviser? The biggest choice is which avenue to pursue. There are hybrid models, but the three main avenues that one may pursue as a financial adviser are working as an employee for a large "warehouse" firm (named because they have everything under one roof and tend to be very large), a "captive" firm (where you sell one company's product exclusively), or as an independent where you can clear your business through a broker/dealer who provides your compliance oversight, but is your company where you own your book of business. Let's break each one out, as I have been a part of all three models.

I began my career at Smith Barney when it was totally owned and operated by Citicorp. I was hired with a decent salary in hand for 18 months, which decreased after that time to straight commission over six months more. If I had not passed the FINRA Series 7 exam first time out, however, my contract would have ended. Luckily, I handily passed it. During that time, not only did I study for exams, but I was constantly being trained in the acquisition of business and how to run a successful practice. The training was outstanding, and my local branch manager was excellent. I did notice a disconnect among the brokers, but soon realized it was every person for him/herself, so it did not leave much time for socialization or "water cooler" Olympics. I was very happy there, until my salary days were coming to an end, and I found that commissions paid by the firm were constantly shifting due to volatility in the parent organization. The payout was extremely low, although the company did provide for all my expenses, but in return, I did not own exclusive rights over my book of business. This is typical warehouse practice, neither good nor bad, just the way it is. I loved my time there, and only speak well of the training and support I received. I just was not sure I could survive on the payout that it provided.

My next journey was to a "captive" firm; in reality, a fraternal benefit society. A fraternal benefit society is established to provide benefits for a particular group of individuals and/or families who claim a common purpose, i.e., the Knights of Columbus, the Woodsmen Association, etc. I chose a religiously-affiliated captive firm that had a long history of service to its members. The prospecting was easy—just being in the right place at the right time. I did exceedingly well, rising over 2½ years to the top 1 percent of the firm, and raking in a whole lot of money. However, I made some poor business decisions and ended up pouring that money back into an infrastructure that was an uneven distribution of my profits and expenditures. Therefore, the more I made, the more I shared with my "partners," and the more I paid to keep our little business alive. Although not recognized as an incorporated entity, as not permitted by the fraternal benefit society, we acted in such manner at their encouragement. As I reflect back, I loved every minute of what I was doing, except for some of the overly wrought compliance measures that were employed due to their positioning in the market and fear of the regulatory environment. However, I realized after a while that what I could offer clients was very limited as only proprietary to that particular firm. Therefore, with the encouragement of my current business partner, I made the decision to transition to independence.

Now, this is easier said than done. Every broker/dealer will ask you how many assets can you bring with you to your own company? Yet, at the same time, every firm has a restrictive covenant when you leave them. Due to my NOT reading the fine print, I invited 13 of my 280 clients to move with me. That was enough to create a stir. Most, if not all advisers, face this at one time or another should they choose to move firms. In the end, I was sued for a phenomenally ridiculous amount of money but settled for a small sum, which was a pittance next to what they paid to sue me. Yes, that is an idiosyncrasy of the financial world! But, beware and, unlike me, read the fine print, and realize the "hero" of today can easily become the "enemy" of tomorrow in this realm. Unfortunately, on a personal level, that which had been so wonderful is now a rather ugly memory.

Ah, but independence! I could say that it was easier, but I would be lying. It requires capital, stamina, an unbelievable amount of risk, and most of all, a sense of humor! Come to think of it, sense of humor should be listed first. My partner and I started pretty much from scratch. The name "Arbol" means tree in Spanish and was not our first choice. Our first, second and third choices were taken. In retrospect, however, the name means a lot now. We started as a seedling, not sure where we would go, and little by little, we have nourished the firm into the entity it is today. We choose not to be large, but shy away from the description of "boutique." In this business, you do not want to be trapped by the "catch words" of the moment. In addition, it has allowed me to venture into new territory via writing, syndicated radio and cable TV. I have been forced to stay educated on the facts and to be renewed in my think-ing at every turn. My partner, Dan Fahringer, is the business manager for us, as my acumen (if you remember from my previous experience) in that area is apparently not very high. He keeps us grounded, while I keep trying to fly every which way. I often think that a successful business venture needs to have divergence of personality and approach. We are still finding our way, and open to that which may come along, but the great thing is that it is ours, and no one else's. I learned quickly that in this venture money is not everything, which is a good thing, as we did not have much of it. We have been fortunate to find ourselves a grand partner with The MacNamee Group in West Chester, PA, a life and health insurance firm with a guru, Steve MacNamee, at the helm. We have joined ourselves together as a "seamless garment" as described by the late Roman Catholic Cardinal Joseph Bernadin of Chicago. In the end, all good things come to those who watch and wait.

Now comes the hard part. It seems like thus far all that I have written tends to be somewhat discouraging. Not only do you have the public perception of what a financial adviser is all about, but also the quandary one faces when entering this field. Which avenue should you choose?

Are you too young or too old? Do you have resources to keep you going in case things do not go the way you like? Do you have any natural prospects already around you for cultivation of business? Should you join a large firm, a "captive" firm or attempt to go the independent route? Is there really a correct answer to any of these questions?

First and foremost, you must decide on dedicating yourself to this profession. With the drop-out rate so staggeringly high, it requires a firm resolve that nothing will knock you off your commitment. Others will try to discourage you. There are many naysayers out there who will attempt to discourage you at every step of the way. The tough part is that their reasoning is often correct. There has to be a fire inside of you that really compels you to succeed. You will meet people who liken what you do to a door-to-door salesman of old. Personally, I like that analogy, as some of the greatest business practices came from that generation. No one can give you the desire to succeed. That is something that you have or do not have deep inside of you. This one factor is more important than all the capital markets, insurance, annuities and banking information you can display to your clients. If you have passion, that is what will shine through the most and begin to set you apart from the mediocre in our field who measure themselves by their paycheck, and not their commitment or service. I have been there, and almost got sucked in to that mentality. Keep people around you who will remind you why you do what you do. Planes, trains and automobiles do not make a practice—what you bring to the table with integrity and honesty does.

Second, remember that the financial world lives in a frightened box. The SEC and FINRA are omnipresent, and one might often think omniscient. New regulations are put into practice, and those who monitor compliance in this field do so at their own risk. Some days, you might think you need a hard hat to go to the office, as a new policy has come down the pike that affects you either blatantly or inadvertently. In lieu of compliance officers, many companies call these "keepers of the gate," "field supervisors." No matter what they are called, they are charged with a daunting task, and some days will stifle the very life out of you. But, as the old adage goes, better safe than sorry. You will always have to go through the muck and mire of compliance, but just swallow it as a part of the profession.

Third, you have to stay up on what is happening in the economy and in the world of financial services. You quickly learn that what happens in Beijing has an effect on what is happening to your clients. Due to the media, even the most unknowing of clients can easily draw the dots today. Yet, do not think you have all the answers. No matter how many letters demonstrating your credentials that you are entitled to after your name, there is no guarantee that you know everything. Collaborate with others and maintain an open line of communication with various professionals who make up your community. Find a couple of attorneys, accountants, property and casualty insurance providers, bankers and others who can benefit your clients and who share the same ethic of service you do. This will take trial and error. Eventually, you will find those folks who share what you need and benefit from what you have. Mutuality is a key word in this field for successful entrepreneurship.

Fourth, blaze your own trail. You do not have to run your business like anyone else. Within the confines of our regulatory environment, find the way that is your way. It does not have to be like anyone else's way. Be unique—find out what that is for you and employ those talents for the benefit of your clients.

Fifth, do not let client complaints distract you. You cannot control the capital markets, the economy, insurance premium rates or annuity performance. You can only control your response to those around you who are unhappy with performance. Some may come after you, right or wrong, via complaints and even litigation. Yet do not be deterred. If you did what was right in your mind, mitigate your personal and professional hurt, and move on.

Sixth, know when to turn your financial light off. Often, I hear advisers say that they work 18-20 hours per day, and seem to measure themselves by that barometer. Remember, that your family and friends come first. You have a right and license to a private life—take the wheel and steer correctly.

Seventh, be proactive and not reactive. If there is something that needs to be dealt with, do not put it off until tomorrow. Take care of it today, as tomorrow will have its own challenge. Procrastination is not a character trait that leads you to success as a financial adviser.

When all is said and done, only you can decide if this career track will crack open your internal success code. I chose it and continue to choose it. Oh, not every day is a happy one, but it is my day, and my way, and most of all, my career. If you choose to come into the water, welcome and swim wisely!

About Philip

Philip M. Cioppa is the managing principal and chief investment officer of Arbol Financial Strategies, LLC (www.arbolfinancialstrategies.com), located in Norwalk, CT, and Harrisburg, PA. With over 10 years in financial service experience, he has served as a Certified Trust and Financial Adviser and has distinguished himself among his peers as a top adviser at Thrivent Financial for Lutherans prior to co-founding Arbol Financial Strategies. Phil brings a proprietary and unique client-centered approach and a sense of humor to his work as a financial adviser. He is very passionate about his work with clients, and as chief investment officer, he specializes in asset management strategies, insurance planning and taxation issues.

Prior to starting his journey in financial services, Phil pursued his passion for religious studies with a Bachelor of Arts from State University of New York at Albany, Masters of Divinity at St. Bernard's Institute in Rochester and his Doctor of Ministry from Graduate Theological Foundation in Mishawaka, Indiana. Phil served as a Roman Catholic priest for 18 ½ years, leaving active ministry in excellent standing to pursue his new passage.

Phil has been featured on NBC, CBS, ABC and Fox affiliates, FOXNews.com/Live, FOX BUSINESS as well as local and national radio talk shows. He is a recurring guest on The Lars Larson Show and the Bill Martinez Show, and he hosts his own weekly financial radio show on WGCH, Greenwich, Conn., now being nationally syndicated.

Phil is married to a wonderful wife, Janie, and lives in Danbury, Conn., with Janie; his niece Amanda and great-nephew Edrien. Securities offered through LPL Finacial, member FINRA/SIPC.

CHAPTER 37

Vision, Passion, Excellence: The Three Most Essential Ingredients to the Recipe of Success

By Simone Hoa

Have you heard, seen or met anybody who has achieved success in their life without having a vision, without living their passion—meaning they absolutely love what they do every day—and above all, not having an attitude for excellence in what they do? For me, having followed, watched and learned from all the top achievers in the world, I have observed they all have these three vital components in order to "crack the success code" in their personal and professional life.

So let's first analyze these three words: *vision, passion* and *excellence* individually, and then we will look at why and how these three ingredients are so essential to the success recipe.

VISION GIVES DIRECTION TO OUR LIFE

What is vision, you might ask? My definition of vision is the ability to think and see not with our eyes but with our mind, soul and heart where our future lies, and plan it to fit into our personal as well as professional life. Vision gives us a direction and makes us see a destination for ourselves to strive for personally and professionally. Personal vision gives

331

us the picture of our dream; professional vision helps us to envision our professional success to achieve our personal vision and our dream.

As a fast-growth business strategist, the first thing I look at before starting a project with a client is his or her vision; the same approach applies to my marketing workshops: we start with vision, vision, vision, similarly to the word location, location, location in real estate investments. As we look at the future and plan for the future, time frames such as short-, medium- and long-term planning have to be considered in the setting of specific goals to achieve.

Another strong point I like to make: this vision is YOUR vision, not a vision seen or planned by somebody else for you. People without a vision are easily influenced by their environment, in particular by their close one, more often than not by their own parents. As a result, they take on something which is not theirs, which does not come from their heart and soul. Consequently, they will feel unhappy and unfulfilled until they realize they have lost time, energy and even money and decide to get back to the real and true track of their own life vision.

OUR VISION MUST BE CLEAR

Realizing the importance of having a vision, the next vital characteristic to determine the potential success of our vision is CLARITY. Clarity provides the ROADMAP to our vision; clarity is the EYE to help us see the road we will walk toward our goals and dreams. If you don't know where you are going, how can you create a plan or a roadmap to get there? You can't: without clarity, you cannot devise a strategic plan of action to reach your objectives or achieve your goals.

I find this quotation from Alfred Montapert so relevant to this point: "To accomplish great things, we must first dream, then visualize, and then plan."

Without a clear vision, you get inconsistent results that lead nowhere and consequently cause a complete loss of time which cannot be retrieved. Maybe we can remake the money we lost with a better and clearer vision after we learned from our mistake, but we can never regain the time we lost. Hence, the big emphasis here is to have a vision with complete clarity. When you understand you need to clarify what you want your personal life to look like first, then you can shape your professional life to turn that vision into reality.

TIPS FOR CLARITY IN VISION

The Four Ps forming the foundation of a clear vision:

- Passion
- Personal values
- Personal life experiences
- Professional experiences, including talent/s and skills.

Personal Vision
Here are some questions to ask regarding your future life.

What does my life look like in 20 years, 15 years, 10 years, five years, two years, one year from now? With the accomplishment of my vision, where do I see myself? What would my lifestyle look like? Where will I be? What kind of a life companion would I have?

Here are some questions to ask regarding your present life.

Where am I right now in my life? How is my health situation? Am I single or married? With children or without children? Am I happy or unhappy with my family situation? How is my financial situation? My social environment? What are my present values and priorities? What do I like or don't like in my life right now? What are the changes I need to make to improve my personal life?

Professional vision
What is my present career situation? Am I happy or unhappy with my job or business situation? Am I passionate about what I do every day to earn my living? Do I have the necessary talent or skills to perform at my best? Am I an expert in my field? If not, what do I need to do to become one? How do I envision my future professional life with the success I aim for? What steps do I have to take to achieve my goals?

As your personal vision is woven into your professional vision, it is crucial to have and create a SUPER CLEAR vision for the latter based on doing what you LOVE every day. It will help prioritize various aspects of your life and direct your activities and thoughts to the most important goals.

A successful business or career always requires the help of a team to realize its vision. Few people become successful without the help and support of others. As a leader of a team, you must have a very clear understanding of the direction of your organization to be able to articulate a clear plan of action to get people behind you who believe and share your vision to get inspired to work beside you to achieve it with you.

As John Patterson, one of the most successful Canadian businessmen said: "To succeed in business, it is necessary to make others see things as you see them."

Even with all this clarity, we still need the PASSION behind our vision to provide the necessary ENERGY that drives us to take action, to weather the storms along the way, to persevere, to never give up and just keep going until we achieve our goals and fulfill our ultimate dreams. I love this quote from Joel Barker: "Vision without action is merely a dream. Action without vision just passes the time. Vision with action can change the world."

PASSION GIVES ENERGY TO OUR LIFE

So what is passion, that powerful force, that extraordinary drive that keeps pushing and moving us toward our dream? Let's look at some definitions of passion and I think it would be appropriate to start with mine.

"It is a BURNING DESIRE inside all of us, waiting anxiously to be liberated to live its own life outside of us, to express itself through the activities we do, and to guide us to do what we LOVE to get the MAXIMUM enjoyment, fulfilment and happiness from what we do and from life."

Now I would like to quote some definitions from authors whose books I love.

Let's start with Gary Vaynerchuk , a social entrepreneur and bestselling author of a book I enjoy so much I cannot help quoting his definition. On page 1 of *Crush It: Why Now Is the Time To Cash in Your Passion,* he wrote: "Passion is an all-consuming feeling that keeps you awake at night with your brain swimming with ideas and dreams" (New York: Harper Collins, 2009). I identify my passion and myself so well with this definition that I laughed out loud reading his book one morning while eating breakfast by myself. I make it a routine to read at least half an hour every morning no matter what. I encourage you to do the same if you like to succeed.

How about another more expanded definition from an international speaker and bestselling author I absolutely admire and respect, John C.

Maxwell, who defines passion as follows in his book, *Put Your Dream to the Test*: "It's an enthusiasm that not only gives you energy and focus in the present, but also gives you power to keep moving towards the future. It gives you fuel to pursue your dream." Then he paraphrased columnist Will Hobbs: "Passion makes possible waking in the morning, whoever you are, wherever you are, however old or young, and bounding out of bed because there is something out there that you love to do, that you believe in, that you're good at, something bigger than you are, and you can hardly wait to get at it again today" (Nashville: Thomas Nelson, 2009, p. 73). I have emphasized the important words in this beautiful and powerful quote as I agree wholeheartedly with Will Hobbs. Passion makes me feel ALIVE. I wake up in the morning and feel I can shake the world with my passion. For me, there are not enough hours in the day to do what I love to do; I sleep and eat with my passion, I breathe it like breathing air. I don't feel I actually work; as the wise Chinese philosopher Lao Tzu put it so rightly: "Love what you do every day and you don't have to work a day in your life."

Reading through the above definitions of passion, I can say without hesitation the nonnegotiable ingredient to the success recipe is PASSION: it is the ROOT of all success and fulfilled dreams. A vision without passion will not lead to real success. If we look at the lives of successful people throughout history in any context, their success was and has been attributed to their passion, the passion for what they did and how they lived their lives. I cannot imagine that legends such as Michelangelo with his art masterpieces, Monet and Picasso with their world renowned paintings, Mozart and Beethoven with their magical music, and all the inventors with their extraordinary inventions could have left their undeniable heritage for us to enjoy without a huge passion driving their lives.

Being conscious of the vital role of passion in success, I would like to emphasize another aspect of passion in the realization of success: we have to live our TRUE passion for our TRUE potential to be released from our deep fertile mind to achieve truly significant success. So the question you might ask is "am I pursuing my true passion?" My reply is a resounding "Yes I am: I am passionate about inspirational speaking and spreading my message in order to help people discovering and living their true passion to achieve success as early as possible in their life, and moreover, how to make money doing what they love."

This true passion discovery was the result of a five-year process through painful detours and reconnections to redefine my true identity after a disastrous huge loss of money caused by a dishonest partner in my last business that put me in a hole. I lived through a lengthy, miserable process to get out of the hole. I then realized I can help people who are serious about discovering their passion and making changes in their life to pursue their dream with this process. From this realization, my 5A-Process to passion discovery was born; and thereafter, I discovered my life purpose and mission at the same time. This process is described in more detail in my chapter titled "The Power of Passion" in the book *Mastering the Art of Success* that I co-authored with Jack Canfield, Mark Victor Hansen and Les Brown, as well as in another book, *Woman Entrepreneur Extraordinaire* that I co-authored with 20 women entrepreneurs giving our readers secrets on how to make money doing what we love. This process shortens the passion discovery journey drastically to only weeks or months, not the years it took me.

EXCELLENCE BRINGS SUCCESS TO OUR LIFE

The next most important ingredient is EXCELLENCE. Even with a clear vision and a true passion, without excellence, we are not going very far. Excellence is one of the success principles essential to all successful achievers. Adopt an attitude for excellence and surround yourself with excellence. Did you notice millionaires hanging around millionaires? You can only learn from people who share the same values and beliefs as you do. Learn from people who have walked the success path before you, who "have been there and done it." I just love this Chinese proverb: "An intelligent person learns from his own mistakes; a wise person learns from other people's mistakes." How about this quote from Sir Isaac Newton: "If I have seen further, it is by standing upon the shoulders of giants." You can achieve success faster this way.

So what is excellence? To me, it is a state of mind, an *attitude* to excel: to excel is to do something very ordinary but to do it well, to turn something ordinary into something extraordinary, to do something very common in an uncommon manner. Either you have this attitude or you don't, there is no halfway feeling for excellence. How does one acquire this attitude?

With *passion*: without passion, the pursuit of excellence won't be there as you can only strive for excellence if you love what you do.

With *experience*: as you achieve excellent results, you feel encouraged to achieve even better results.

With continuous *self-education*: by learning from books and other educational materials available to you, and by learning from others. Jim Rohn, one of my mentors who unfortunately passed away in early December 2009, has said: "Standard education earns you a living; self-education earns you a fortune."

With *consistence* and *discipline*: these two qualities reinforce the attitude for excellence.

In summary, how do vision, passion, and excellence contribute so significantly to the recipe of success? I suggest we look first at the definition of success: is it measured in terms of money or material wealth? Or rather by the way we live our life doing what we love, and more importantly, sharing our success and wisdom with the rest of the world to make a difference in people's lives. As Zig Ziglar said so well—you can get everything in life if you just help enough other people get what they want.

However, we cannot help other people if we are not well-equipped ourselves, but equipped with what? With the achievement of our dreams, the creation of our own success to live a fulfilled life built on our initial vision, our true passion and our attitude for excellence.

I would like to end this chapter with a quote from Napoleon Hill: "Cherish your visions and your dreams, as they are the children of your soul, the blueprints of your ultimate achievements." This beautiful quote has always been my fundamental belief that has helped me to achieve the success I am proud of and deserve today and will continue to do so for me to realize my ultimate dream, the creation of the Passion 2 Success Academy as my heritage.

About Simone

Simone Hoa is a well-known inspirational speaker, a fast-growth business strategist, trainer and coach in business and personal development producing rapid, concrete results with her company Passion 2 Success Inc. How she became an inspirational speaker at the sunset of her life is a dramatic and compelling story worth telling.

Simone is Vietnamese and has a long career track behind her. Even though she lost her father when she was only 5, Simone is a world-wise businesswoman who has traveled the world, experienced four cultures and lived in three countries: Vietnam until the age of 19 where she completed her Baccalaureate in French; Australia where she won a scholarship to complete her university studies with three degrees in economics, education and library sciences and lived there for 18 years; and Canada where she migrated to join her mother and two sisters in 1985. In Montreal, she was an entrepreneur in the fashion industry (her passion at the time) but suffered a huge financial loss instigated by a deceptive partner who caused the demise of her business in 2004, resulting in the closing of her company. After five years of painful reconnecting and searching for her real identity through intense self-education in personal development, a course with Dale Carnegie and a strong involvement with Toastmasters International, she discovered her new passion in the art of public speaking. She then decided to take on a new, most challenging career at the age of 63 to become an inspirational speaker to use her voice to inspire and help people across the world to discover and have the courage to live their true passion and potential to achieve success and live the life of their dream.

Realizing also the power of written words, Simone envisions leaving a heritage behind with her books: she is proud to be a contributing author to four books to be published in the U.S. with celebrities such as Jack Canfield, Deepak Chopra, Ken Blanchard, Dr. Warren Bennis, former U.S. Senator George Mitchell and this future bestseller with Brian Tracy.

Simone is also the author of her own book to be published in 2012 titled "Success Has No Age: You Are Never too Young or too Old to Live your Passion."

Her fast success earned her the 2010 BEST GROWTH Trophy from The Montreal Leaders Boomers Entrepreneurs within her first year being a speaker, and her workshops at Toastmasters International Regional Conferences and Toastmasters International Leadership Institute are very well-loved. She is also a lifetime member of Worldwide Who's Who and was just named its 2012 Executive, Professional and Entrepreneur of the Year in Motivational Speaking.

To learn more about Simone Hoa, the services offered by Passion 2 Success Inc., and how to get your free MP3 audio and chapter from her book, "*Passion to Success: Secrets for Making Money Doing What You Love*," visit www.passion2success.com or call 514-777-9785.

CHAPTER 38

12 Simple Steps To Win the Fight on Behavioral Issues and Be a Champion for Your Kids

By Troy Price

As a kid growing up, my favorite arcade game was Punch-Out!! I loved it for two reasons: One, I enjoy boxing, and two; I could never beat Bald Bull (the Mr. T look alike from Istanbul, Turkey). No matter how hard I tried, it seemed Bald Bull had me figured out and knew exactly how to beat me. And to add insult to injury, he would laugh in a sadistic, digital voice after each victory, which made me hate him even more.

One day after school, I decided that I had enough. I wasn't going to allow some stupid animated figure get the better of me. Nope, on this day, Bald Bull was mine! However, as I approached the game, to my surprise someone else was playing it. It just so happened that this person was fighting Bald Bull! This I had to see. I had never seen anyone beat Bald Bull before, and I quickly concluded that this poor sap was just another notch on Bull's belt. But wait, what was this? The kid actually won and beat the life out of Bald Bull! I couldn't believe it! This guy suddenly became my new best friend.

I asked the kid afterward, "How did you do it?"

"Do what?" he said.

"How did you know how to beat Bald Bull?"

The kid laughed and said, "Who doesn't know how to beat Bald Bull?" He continued by saying, "Every player in the game is easy to beat once you know their weakness and how to counterattack. For Bald Bull, he loves to back up and do his signature "bull charge"; when he gets to you, he will throw a vicious uppercut, and if he lands it, it's lights out for his opponent. However, if you hit him in the stomach at the right moment while he is charging in, it will instantly knock him down. You can always tell when he will throw the uppercut because his eyes get bigger. The eyes never lie. Look for the sign by looking at his eyes and you will win every time."

I took this kid's advice to heart and on the very next quarter, I played Bald Bull and destroyed him! I can't describe how exhilarating it was to finally knock out Bald Bull for the first time! It was an accomplishment that I am still proud of to this day.

I played Punch- Out!! a dozen times thereafter and never again did Bald Bull beat me. Once I learned how to counterattack and "Look for the eyes," I never lost. For me, that was a defining moment in my young life. Not because I had beaten an arch nemeses in Bald Bull (although that was cool) but because of the lesson I had learned. All I needed was someone who knew **how** to win to **teach** me how to win; that made all the difference in the world.

I could have saved about $200 worth of quarters and not been late for class so much, but that's life. Sometimes you get knocked down and knocked out but, you always get up off the canvas and try again.

Since that day so many years ago, I have never forgotten those words, "Know your opponent's weakness"; "look for the eyes'" and "counterattack." I realized at that time the reason I had been losing and learned how not to make those same mistakes in life.

I want to share with you 12 valuable lessons that I learned from an arcade game and how it made me a smarter parent.

LESSON 1: DRUNK WITH EMOTION

It didn't take much to get me riled up, especially when the thought of Bald Bull entered my mind. I couldn't stand the guy. I wanted so badly to pummel him and send him back to Turkey in a body bag, but of course I couldn't. The constant thought of wanting to destroy Bald Bull become an everyday obsession for me. This obsession became so bad that it literally ruled my other thoughts and emotions, which made it difficult to concentrate on school work and sleep at night.

In my naïve 12-year-old mind, I thought that being all jacked up with emotion and adrenalin would be the key to my success. Envisioning Bald Bull's rearranged face was motivation enough for me.

However, as I would painfully learn, emotion got the better of me, which lead to my downfall. Whenever I found myself in a quandary, instead of easing off the emotion accelerator, I pushed harder—hoping it would bail me out, but each time it failed me. What I should have done is remain calm and relaxed, but in the heat of battle, emotions trump everything else. When this happens, reasoning and logic disappear, and the outcome always results in a loss.

It's difficult to think and act with reason when emotion is involved. The best method to remove emotion from the equation is by removing yourself or the other person. This may include a timeout for your child, yourself, or both. Once cooler heads prevail, then is the time to sit and talk things over.

LESSON 2: NO ACTION PLAN

I had one thought going into the fight with Bald Bull—to beat him. I was consumed by the idea. The problem? I forget to figure out *how* I was going to beat him. I entered the ring completely unprepared—without a game plan or strategy. I figured I would rely on my past failures and quickly remember not to make those same mistakes. I also thought that somehow "lady luck" would prevail and be on my side for once. Well, neither happened. You see, those mistakes I made in my previous losses, they unconsciously resurfaced and repeated themselves over and over again, and I didn't even realize what I was doing until it was too late. As for luck, there is no such thing. Luck only comes to those who have prepared well, which I had not done.

Always have a plan of action for when things go well and not so well. Never be caught off guard and left dazed and confused when conflict arises. Be calm, keep your composure, and implement your plan of action with confidence.

LESSON 3: FALSE SENSE OF SECURITY

What I thought were my strengths became my weaknesses. I had success with earlier fighters prior to Bald Bull with the jab. And when you have success, you stick with that technique because it works, right? So I kept doing the same things over and over expecting success with Bald Bull, but it never happened because my jabs were not only predictable but played right into Bald Bull's strengths. That is a sure formula for disaster. I underestimated my opponent; and worse, I overestimated what I thought were my strengths.

Just because you've had success raising one child does not guarantee that you will have the same success with other children you raise. You will learn something new from each child and learn to do things differently.

LESSON 4: KNOW YOUR OPPONENT

Every opponent is different. Therefore, what works on Glass Joe will not work on Bald Bull, Mr. Sandman, or anyone else. Styles make fighters, and so I needed to have a different strategy in place for each fighter to counterattack their styles and be successful.

No two people are alike. Therefore, when it comes to disciplining your children, what works for one will not necessarily work for the other. Be selective when it comes to imposing punishment and privileges and keep in mind the different learning styles of each child.

LESSON 5: SELF-SABOTAGE

In my heart, I knew I could beat Bald Bull, but in the back of my mind, there was always this sliver of self-doubt saying I was going to lose. This reoccurring negative voice subconsciously kept saying, "You'll never win!" and guess what? That is exactly what happened. It was almost like a self-fulfilled prophesy that came true 100 percent of the time. I was dead before I even started. I doubted myself and my abilities, which was natural since I hadn't prepared nor did I have a strategy in place.

It is natural to feel doubt and lose hope, but don't succumb to those negative feelings because they will control you. Instead, train yourself to turn those ill feelings off and replace them with positive words and thoughts. You'll be amazed at how easy it is to do once you get into the habit of doing so.

LESSON 6: NO BACK-UP PLAN

I had no backup plan in the heat of the battle to counterattack Bald Bull's barrage. Instead, I panicked and resorted to the only thing I knew and that was jabs—even though I knew jabs didn't work on Bald Bull.

Once panic set in, I lost control of my thoughts and acted on emotion— hitting every button hoping something would work. The harder I tried, the worse things got, and Bald Bull knew that. He remained calm and composed while I was coming apart at the seams.

As a parent, you must have a back-up plan when things go awry. If you don't, your child will run all over you and leave you exhausted. Have a contingency plan in place and be prepared to use it.

LESSON 7: FOCUS ON THE SOLUTION

Because I had acted on emotion, I focused solely on the problem (not to get knocked out). Instead, I should have been proactive and focused on the solution (how to beat Bald Bull). In other words, I played not to lose instead of playing to win.

When your child misbehaves, focus on the solution of how you can properly teach correct behavior instead of dwelling on the punishment and who wins or gains control in the end.

LESSON 8: LEARN FROM OTHERS

It wasn't until I watched and learned from someone who knew how to win that I found success. I had to swallow my pride and allow someone else to teach me before I could overcome the major obstacle (Bald Bull) that was standing in my way of winning.

You can learn a lot simply by studying others and incorporating their strengths into your own. Also, most people are willing to help and offer advice if you are sincere and appreciative.

Being a parent isn't easy, and so any help and advice you can get is always good. I find that joining parenting groups or participating in parenting forums is therapeutic as well as rewarding. You can learn new ideas and gain a better perspective simply by reaching out to others and imitating the best practices of others.

LESSON 9: DON'T COMPARE YOURSELF TO OTHERS

I assumed that everyone must have been like me and struggled to beat Bald Bull. After all, I spent on average two hours a day trying to figure him out with no success. Then one day, out of nowhere, a stranger shows up and completely schools Bald Bull and thinks nothing of it.

I learned that what comes naturally and easily for some is difficult for others. For me, I struggled with keeping my emotions in check and not being able to see the tree for the forest. I kept making the same mistakes instead of taking a step back, reevaluating why I lost and devising a different strategy.

This stranger had only played Punch Out!! a few times and already knew what it took to win. For him, it was easy because of his previous experiences and quick recognition to be able to see how the pieces fit together.

Don't compare one child with another. Every child is unique, and when you compare, it sends the wrong message to your child—saying you don't love or appreciate him/her as much as so and so. Not only is that unfair but it also puts a lot of pressure on the one child trying to live up to your unreasonable expectations.

Embrace each child and her or his uniqueness and love that child for what and who she or he is.

LESSON 10: WINNING BREEDS CONFIDENCE

When you taste victory for the first time, it's a sweet feeling that you hope will never end. It is a feeling that fills you with immediate energy and exuberance so addicting that it leaves you wanting more.

When I finally beat Bald Bull, I had the feeling that I could beat anyone. My confidence went from 0 to 100 in just one fight; and with that, I was able to go on and beat much tougher opponents. It wasn't until I was able to physically and mentally beat Bald Bull that I could enjoy success at a higher level.

Celebrate and enjoy the small victories that come. When you see your children progress and change their negative behavior, recognize and reward them through praise and love. This will boost their self-esteem and give them the confidence they need to succeed in other areas in life.

LESSON 11: CLIMB A NEW MOUNTAIN

Once I knew how to beat Bald Bull and did so consistently, it was no longer a challenge for me. In fact, it was boring and no fun. It was as though my purpose in playing Punch Out!! was over, and I had accomplished my goal. I knew that it was time for me to move on to another game and tackle a new nemesis.

For you, once your child has replaced a positive behavior with a negative behavior, it is important to immediately work on changing other behaviors. Don't become complacent with just one small victory. Remember, discipline takes time and consistency, so keep at it.

LESSON 12: LEARN THE LESSON IN LOSING

Losing is never fun or easy, but it is a necessary step to victory. I learned more in losing than I did in beating Bald Bull.

I learned that the value of accomplishing a goal is not what I achieved but what I gained in the journey it took to get there. I learned a lot about patience and persistence and that sometimes being stubborn can be a good thing.

As a parent, learn from your mistakes and let go of the past. Be forgiving of yourself and move forward with renewed hope and optimism.

Who said videogames were bad for you? I learned a lot from being punched out both in the videogame and in real life. Yes, there will always be the Bald Bulls standing in your way, but no matter how difficult it may be, you must overcome and endure if you want to be successful.

Apply these strategies in your life, and you will be a smarter parent and have a stronger relationship with your children now and in the future.

About Troy

Troy Price is an accomplished author, speaker and trainer on the subject of child discipline. As parent of three and a former school-teacher, Troy has worked with children of all ages over the past 12 years. He knows from first-hand experience the difficult challenges that professional educators and parents deal with on a daily basis when it comes to unruly children.

His unique approach and design to eliminate negative behavior is garnering much attention, and he is in constant demand speaking and training teachers and parents throughout North America.

As the creator of Parenting with Results, Troy has developed innovative programs such as Dynamite Discipline™ and The Hidden Success Model of Parenting.™ His unique style of teaching and humor are not only engaging but also enlightening and fun.

To learn more about Troy Price and how you can receive your free special report on "10 Ways To Be a Terrific Parent!" please visit www.parentingwithresults.com or call 1-403-892-1050.

CHAPTER 39

Rejuvenation: Look Better, Feel Better and Build Your Business!

By Luba Winter

The focus of *Cracking The Success Code* is algorithm, coding how to rejuvenate, design and transform your life.

Why? I truly believe that self-love and right skin care is where the transforming begins. With positive and profound change rejuvenating your toughs, and the right skin care steps, you will learn how to love, accept and respect your image.

Have you tried everything but still feel inadequate, miserable and not completely satisfied by how you look? Are you on the brink of having great skin?

Do you have an intuitive sense that there is an even easier and better way for you to have healthy, beautiful skin that feels just beyond your reach? Do you want to know the feeling of deep personal treatment with a sample strategy that steps toward your skin-care regime?

Making a profound change in your life requires burning desire, the willingness to do what it takes and the courage to act.

Are you ready?

In this chapter, we will briefly touch on some of these questions, but I have chosen to allocate space where there is more to learn.

MY PASSION

Inspiring others is my passion. I love helping people understand new concepts, making them feel pretty and beautiful and giving them tools so that they can excel in their life and their passions.

My first "official" experience inspiring others came at the University of Ukraine when I became a student and started researching and studying the technology concept. From there, I traveled to Sweden and Italy and then continued my work with a top beauty specialist in the U.S.

THE ULTIMATE BEAUTY START

I was 30 years old, living in Portland, Oregon, and one evening I was painting and decorating a beauty salon that we were opening with my friend in Vancouver.

One of our clients came over and she said that her mother always says, "You're only as old as you feel." I don't mean to dampen anyone's spirits, but wouldn't it be a lot easier to believe in that sentiment if you didn't discover a new wrinkle or fine line every time you looked into the mirror? Our conversation moved to the struggle my friend had experienced with her skin, how painful and expensive her skin-care regime was. And she said the words that I had heard so many times in my life—how bad she wanted a device that would deliver a real result in her home skin care.

When I went home, I started checking out my journal where I collected pieces of wisdom from various self-help books. I flipped throughout the pages of my journal, and started at a blank, new page; as usual, my inner nerd needed to find an answer. I had an idea of creating one easy and safe device to deliver remarkable skin-care results for people who could benefit from it. My search led me to begin writing down what I needed to do to make that idea happen, who I needed to talk with to be able to bring it to life.

My research and ability to work with top engineers and partner with leading dermatologists and cosmetic surgeons from Sweden, Italy and the U.S. truly turned skincare into a science.

My dream had begun much earlier, when I was a child.

In a small, beautiful town in Ukraine, I spent amazing summers with my grandmother. I remember the beautiful scenery there and walking barefoot slowly on silky grass with the evening dew droplets sparkling. The air was fresh and captivating.

One time I remember my grandmother was looking at me, then she took my hand, took a deep breath and said, "Oh, how bad I want to get rid of these wrinkles and have beautiful soft skin!" I wish that someone would invent a machine that would be able to do that, she said.

And right then, at that moment, I was inspired!

THE SCIENCE OF SKIN CARE

After many years of testing and researching, the Rejuvenation G4 was born. The dream of my beautiful grandmother had become a reality. Rejuvenation G4 has changed many lives by helping people look younger and feel better. It is celebrated by hundreds of men and women who get amazing results from their daily skin-care routine, and now have reclaimed self-esteem and started bold, happy lives.

Present-day skin care has become both an art and a science. Gone are the days when it was a simple, superficial procedure of washing the face with soap and water. Today, it encompasses an educated understanding of the skin's many functions and how lifestyle habits (both internal and external) affect it. Our skin covers an average of 19 square feet and weighs about seven pounds.

A cross-section reveals three defined layers. The epidermis is the outermost layer known as the cuticle or protective layer and is made of tightly packed, scale-like cells, which are continually being shed. An entirely new cuticle layer of skin forms every 28 days.

The next layer is the dermis. It is also called the "true skin" because most of the vital functions of the skin are performed or housed here. It contains the glands that secrete perspiration and sebum (oil), the papilla (hair manufacturing plant), nerve fibers, blood vessels, lymph glands and sense receptors. The dermis has an elastic quality that is due to the protein connective tissues called elastin and collagen. They allow for strength as well as flexibility.

Below the dermis is the third layer called the subcutaneous layer. It is made of a fatter tissue that gives the body smoothness and contour and serves as a shock absorber for the vital organs. In addition, it stores energy and is an effective insulator.

Together, these three layers form the miraculous "living fabric" known as skin. The skin serves to maintain our health and well-being in an amazing variety of ways. In one square centimeter there are 100 sweat glands, 12 feet of nerves, hundreds of nerve endings, 10 hair follicles, 20 sebaceous glands, six feet of blood vessels, 16 heat sensors, four cold sensors and thousands of cells. Unbroken, the skin is our first line of defense against disease and bacterial invasion. It regulates body temperatures, sends neurological messages to the brain, detoxifies by excreting wastes from the body, respirates (absorbs oxygen and releases carbon dioxide), absorbs nutrients, manufactures vitamin D and protects the body from ultra violet damage from the sun. Fundamental skin care recognizes that the skin is our largest vital organ, and it requires care and attention to look its best and to maintain peak performance.

TRANSFORM YOUR LOOKS AND YOUR LIFE FROM THE INSIDE OUT.

Imagine how your life would BE TRANSFORMED if you could:

- Eliminate the anxiety and stress.
- Feel a sense of control over the impulse to impose our own vision and ideas on our physical selves.
- Put an end to the striving for ideas dictated by culture.
- Feel a positive, balanced and consistent level of energy throughout the day.
- Naturally support your ability to create something even more stunning.

ARE YOU READY TO BE TRANSFORMED?

Beauty is not about hard work after all—if you have the right tools. This revolutionary guide peels away the layers of conventional body and beauty wisdom to uncover for real transformation. Uncover that physical potential and avoid the extreme, tedious—even dangerous measures we've been programmed to believe are necessary. Where to start?

So, now that you know a little bit more about anti-aging, where de you start? There are a huge number of products out there. Do you need 10 treatment products?

Working with top beauty-care strategists, I discovered that my goal is to help bring cohesion, relevance and simplicity to the role of beauty care for people the world over. I help men and women understand that youthful beauty has only one role ... to prevent the aging process.

By focusing on efforts to support the role of beauty care (and not simply its function), I'm able to help them realize a measurable impact of taking care that is in alignment with the skin-care process and larger vision of how they may look if they don't take care of it.

I focus exclusively on the three areas of skin care strategy where the process can be exceptional so that users won't waste time (or try their patience) trying to do all things. By playing to my strengths, the Rejuvenation G4 is able to deliver exceptional results in the areas of skin care that impact value and prevent aging. Its purpose is to fight the war against aging.

Minimally invasive procedures will significantly outperform surgical options and will continue to secure the majority of the aesthetic medical procedures market over more invasive, expensive surgical offerings.

The public will choose these less expensive and less risky procedures over surgeries. People generally desire to look 10 years younger, and minimally invasive procedures can achieve this desired outcome.

"During hard economic times, men and women look to non-invasive treatment such as Rejuvenation G4 galvanic, ultrasound, and phototherapy treatment as a means to feel and look better about themselves physically and emotionally," says Dr. Max Grishkevich from vipmedispa in Clackams, Oregon. Now you have the power to change the past, present and future of your skin with Rejuvenation G4, The Transformation Power of Touch!

LOOK GREAT, FEEL GREAT.

Male beauty: one of the most pervasive—and dangerous—rumors is that men don't need skin care: that's not even close to true.

With changing standards of aesthetics of the male face, and more liberal attitudes concerning facial rejuvenation treatment, many men are now seeking the benefits of facial procedure. The concept of facelift and neck lift in men is basically the same as in women, but the approach is tailored to highlight and sharpen the angular structures of the jaw, neck and chin, with less emphasis on crow's feet, cheekbones and naso-labial (fold from nose to corners of the mouth) regions. The facelift and neck lift treatment will restore the major facial contours, especially the jaw-line, finer wrinkles.

I hope that men will become more confident about cosmetic anti-aging products. It will deliver the energy to the level of muscles where the face lift normally would be done. It's a two to three times a week treatment, which can deliver professional results from the comfort of your home, or when you travel, and after you see the tithing of the connective tissue.

I truly believe that these steps will help you to move to a different path in your life, and help others see potential in theirs. To feel wonderful and love the life you are living.

If you've ever written a book, created a product, or put your heart and soul into something, you know all too well how easy it can be to get emotionally involved in the value associated with that amazing thing you've just created.

This I know all too well since I have invested the better part of my life creating the Rejuvenation G4. When you eat, drink and sleep a project over such a focused period of time, you get emotionally invested. I put my best offer into this system with goal of empowering men and women the world over to enhance and rejuvenate their skin.

Finally, because of how much searching it took for me to finally find a best way how to make a revolution for skin-care regime, the information sources that met my own informed criterion, and because I don't believe in putting up with low-end products in order to live well and stay beautiful, I couldn't have created this device and program without an extensive, descriptive and personally tested resources collection.

Thanks in advance for spreading the word to people you know who can benefit. With your support and some thoughtful and deliberate action on the parts of those who are ready to shine with the right tools and without painful effort, dried wrinkled skin can soon be a thing of the past. Soon we'll all have a whole lot more to celebrate with you, who can look years younger, with a natural, refreshed appearance.

I just want to wrap up our conversation about beauty and how important it is to have that balance in your life with important aspects of taking good care of one of the most important and largest organs in your body. By having healthy, fresh skin you will feel more confident, beautiful and happy.

I truly believe that everyone should understand how important and how different it could be if they used the right tools for their skin care regime. It is like a toothbrush, which you have to use at least twice a day in order to have healthy, beautiful teeth.

When you look good, you feel good; it's more than just helping you stay away from stress and anxiety, it's helping you to be confident and succeed in your personal and business life!

As Pablo Picasso said, "youth has no age."

About Luba

Rejuvenation G4 from Nu Way Beauty developed by Luba Winter is on a mission to guide men and women around the world to love what they see in the mirror. Three "ABC-Skin Care" steps help them unlock the secret to a healthy skin and start loving their lives as soon as possible.

Her popular Rejuvenation G4 is an FDA-cleared, patent pending device safe and easy to use, celebrated by hundreds of men and women who have seen amazing results from their daily skin-care routine, reclaimed self-esteem, and started bold, happy lives with Luba and her proven Rejuvenation program.

Being inspired by her grandmother 27 years ego, Luba along with top worldwide engineers and cosmetologists, developed a very unique device where she put all amazing beauty technology of "Galvanic, Ultrasound and Photo Therapy" in one convenient unit to begin a journey to guide others to live more joyous, balanced lives. Luba believes that self love and right skin care is where the transformation begins.

Cracking The Success Code, Rejuvenation G4, NuWayBeauty.com and aGeniusVision. com reflect Luba's passion for inspiring. Even now, you can often find her "handing out" at aGeniusVision.com, helping users who stop by for assistance.

Luba's Rejuvenation G4 device and "ABC-Skin Care" is a life-changing program for men and women who struggle with skin-care routine and want to prevent themselves from the aging process. Learn more about Rejuvenation G4 at www.nuwaybeauty.com

Nataliya Okynskaya, national success life coach, says, "The Luba Winter approach challenges several basic notions that many in my field rely on when they run out of answers. She provides a much-needed wake-up call for the millions of people who could benefit from her message."

ACKNOWLEDGEMENTS FROM LUBA WINTER

There are many people without whom this chapter would not have been "born" and to whom I wish to extend my deepest gratitude:

To Brian Tracy, who was the first person who touched my heart with his message and wisdom to make a difference in this world, who sent me the invitation to write my chapter in this book.

To the managing editor for guiding and delivering my "baby" true to form. To Nick Nanton, JW Dicks and Mike Raines for letting me do the book I was born to do. And to Kelsey Bealert as well as Jess Todtfeld, for their hours of work and expertise. A very special thanks to the amazing Diana, Nataly and Phillip who have been such an inspiration in my life.